Online Public Access Catalogs:
The User Interface

OCLC Library, Information, and Computer Science Series

Online Public Access Catalogs:
The User Interface

Charles R. Hildreth

6565 Frantz Road
Dublin, Ohio 43017

ISBN: 0-933418-35-3 (Series)
      0-933418-34-5

        3   4   5   6 | 85   84   83

Library of Congress Catalog Card Number 82-8224

Library of Congress Cataloging in Publication Data

Hildreth, Charles R., 1938-
    Online public access catalogs: the user interface.

    (OCLC library, information, and computer science series)
    Bibliography: p.
    Includes index.
    1. On-line bibliographic searching. 2. Information storage and retrieval systems.
3. Library catalogs--Automation. I. OCLC.
II. Title. III. Series.
Z699.22.H54 1982   025.5'24   82-8224
ISBN 0-933418-34-5

Contents

List of Figures

List of Tables

Foreword

Libraries of all descriptions, sizes and types have taken advantage of computer services offered by a variety of institutions to record in machine-readable form bibliographic information about their collections. As these databases have grown, usually in response to the need to produce catalog cards, it has become obvious that the databases can be used for other purposes. In the aggregate, they can be used as union catalogs as OCLC has done from the beginning. But, single institutions, or smaller clusters of institutions, have been developing the database to support machine-readable alternatives to the printed card catalog.

Early in 1980, the Council on Library Resources received several unsolicited proposals dealing with one or another aspect of online public access catalogs. The proposals were individual, unrelated efforts to deal with a complex entity, the online catalog and its development. It was apparent that the level of expertise reflected in the proposals was uneven and that none had been prepared with the benefit of a comprehensive overview of the then present state-of-development of this potentially powerful tool.

OCLC Online Computer Library Center, Inc. and the Research Libraries Group, Inc. (RLG) agreed to work together with the Council to organize a meeting of representatives of those institutions that already had some experience with online public access catalogs or were in the final stages of developing such a service. That meeting, having been convened at the Dartmouth Minary Conference Center, became known among the twenty-six participants as the Dartmouth Conference. A summary of those proceedings was jointly produced by OCLC and RLG.

Four recommendations for action relative to online public access catalogs flowed from that conference:

       1.   Analyze user requirements and behavior

       2.   Monitor existing online catalog systems

       3.   Develop methods of cost management

       4.   Develop distributed computing and system links

A few weeks after the Dartmouth Conference, OCLC and RLG were joined by Joe Matthews & Associates, and the University of California Systemwide Administration, Division of Library Automation, in a Council-funded effort to develop a way to gather data to address the first two recommendations. As part of this joint effort, OCLC undertook the task of establishing some basic understanding of ten operating online public access catalog systems. The result of this task, one that turned into a mammoth undertaking, is this report.

Aside from difficulties in obtaining information on the various systems in a timely manner, a frustrating aspect of the task was the fact that each of the systems was a moving target. As weaknesses were identified by users, and in at least one system this information was collected online, system managers made appropriate adjustments. Little attention could be paid to the desirability, from a research standpoint, of maintaining the status quo throughout a study period.

As this report is read, the reader must understand that the data is not presented for purposes of evaluation. It is hard not to make some comparisons between systems. Remember though, that they are not comparable systems. They use different equipment and software, and all were developed under different conditions.

Though the actual data presented may already have changed since it was collected (through the fall of 1981), the literature review, definitions, and the discussions of system facets are extremely valuable additions to the literature of online catalogs. The issues identified must be dealt with by any online catalog system designer or, for that matter, anyone designing database access systems for the general public.

As the first step in understanding online catalogs, this work is a significant contribution. It can also serve as a model for future work designed to evaluate and document the online public access catalogs of the future. The Council on Library Resources extends its thanks to the ten institutions that took the time and effort to cooperate in this study. Finally, the Council is pleased to have been associated with this effort and commend the OCLC staff, particularly Charles Hildreth, for a job well done. No subsequent effort in this field can escape being affected by this work.

                                        C. Lee Jones
                                        Program Officer
                                        Council on Library Resources, Inc.

Preface

An earlier form of this monograph comprised a major part of OCLC's April 1982
Final Report to the Council on Library Resources, "Online Public Access
Systems: Data Collection Instruments for Patron and System Evaluation," by
Neal K. Kaske and Charles R. Hildreth. With encouragement from the Council on
Library Resources and from those who reviewed early drafts of the Final
Report, OCLC made the decision to separately publish that part of the Final
Report which reviewed the state-of-the-art in user-system interface design for
online public access catalogs and compared the features of ten operational
online catalogs. The part of the Final Report entitled "Online Public Access
Catalogs: The User Interface" has been revised for this monograph and the
discussions and accompanying tables have been updated to include recent
additions and enhancements to several of the online catalogs included in this
study.

From an initial desire to present the features and command languages of ten
online public access catalogs (OPACs) in an easy-to-identify, easy-to-compare
format, the study grew in breadth to cover the fundamental components of the
user-system interface in interactive systems. Understanding the wide
diversity of features and command-entry techniques discovered in OPACs (and
conveying that understanding) required extensive conceptual elucidation of
descriptive terms and the creation of new modes of analysis. Little research
and analysis has been undertaken on the characteristics and performance of
online library catalogs, most of which are currently prototypes or have been
operational, on the average, for only two or three years. "Older" systems
like LCS at Ohio State University, and LUIS at Northwestern are currently
undergoing modifications which impact on the user-system interface in each
system.

An extensive review of the literature was conducted and several online catalog
design teams were consulted to gain an understanding of the state-of-the-art
in online retrieval system research and development. The literature review
included what has become known as the "human factors" literature and spanned
the published findings of research on the user-system interface in interactive
systems, whatever the specific application. The Project Bibliography
represents a modest sample of the many publications in these growing areas of
research and development.

Several approaches may be taken in reading this lengthy report with its eleven chapters and three appendices. A reading of chapters 1-3 will suffice for a brief overview of the project's background, methodology, and the original presentation of OPAC features (Tables 2-6) required as part of this CLR-funded project. Chapters 4 and 5 represent a review of the state-of-the-art in research and development efforts directed toward understanding and improving the user-system interface in interactive systems.

Chapters 7, 8, 9, and 10 each discuss separate, major components of the user-system interface in online catalogs (dialogue techniques, command languages, access points and search mechanics, output features and display formats, and online user assistance features). Reviews of the related characteristics of the ten OPACs are included in each of these chapters. For example, if the reader wishes to learn of the output features and formats of one or more of the ten OPACs, he may go directly to chapter 9.

Chapter 11 includes a detailed overview of the hardware and software architectures and file structures of the OPACs at Ohio State University, Mankato State University, and University of California/Division of Library Automation.

The tables distributed throughout the monograph generally permit easy identification and comparison of the presence or absence of features in the ten OPACs. The reader is directed to the List of Tables for the locations of these tables.

Numerous illustrations of OPAC screen displays are included in chapters 7-10. Because character sets differ on the various printer terminals used to obtain printed copy of displays, the text in these illustrations may not precisely match the text displayed on a particular system's visual display terminals.

Because no uniform terminology exists for describing and analyzing the properties and behavior of online catalogs, the development of a glossary became an indispensable part of this study. As a working document, the Glossary went through many editions right up to the time the report was being finished. Because the conceptual and operational ground is shifting constantly at this early period of online catalog development, the version of the Glossary presented here should not be viewed as the final, authoritative set of terms and their definitions. However, browsing through the Glossary can provide many insights into the problems and promises of this exciting new bibliographic retrieval instrument we call the online public access catalog.

Acknowledgments

The author gratefully acknowledges the financial support for this study provided by the Council on Library Resources, and specifically acknowledges the patience and steadfast encouragement during this extended effort supplied by C. Lee Jones, Council Program Officer for the project. This project could not have succeeded without the generous cooperation of the ten participating organizations that provided documentation and access to their online public access catalog (OPAC) systems. The author and members of the OCLC Online Public Access Catalog Project Team express their appreciation to those on the staff of these organizations who made significant contributions throughout the duration of the project.

The author would like to thank Dr. W. David Penniman, Vice President, OCLC Office of Planning and Research, and Dr. Neal K. Kaske, Director, Office of Research for their administrative support of the project. Dr. Kaske also served as Principal Investigator for this project.

Many individuals have made substantial contributions to this final report. Special thanks must be given to Trong Do and Brian Raynor, Research Assistants in the OCLC Office of Research, for their tireless, determined efforts to thoroughly document the interface properties and behavior of the ten OPACs during the first stage of this study. Do and Raynor also carried out the initial lexicographical research for the Project Glossary. Trong Do undertook the investigation of system architecture and files presented in chapter 11, and wrote the first draft of that chapter. It was a special pleasure to work with these aggressive intellects.

The author is grateful for the extensive editorial assistance of Larry Morwick and the assistance of Carol Lauber and other staff of the Documentation Department in preparing the manuscript.

Among the individuals who have read all or part of this report and have offered sympathetic criticism and significant suggestions, the author expresses special thanks to Pauline Atherton Cochrane, Denise P. Kaplan, Frederick G. Kilgour, Karen Markey, and William H. Mischo.

Introduction

1.1 Project Background

As more and more libraries plan for and offer online public access to library catalogs, there is a need to ascertain the state-of-the-art of online catalog design as reflected in operational systems and those currently under development. In addition to system-specific features (e.g., hardware, software, database maintenance, etc.), there is a special need to examine the user-system interfaces being implemented and to compare their functional features and command structures which are responses to the user's functional needs as perceived by system designers. To collect and disseminate information on existing online public access catalogs (OPACs), the Council on Library Resources has sponsored several projects being conducted by OCLC Online Computer Library Center, Inc., The Research Libraries Group, Inc. (RLG), the Library of Congress, the University of Toronto Library Automation System (UTLAS), the University of California Division of Library Automation, Joseph R. Matthews and Associates, and several other institutions. At a working session* at the Dartmouth College Conference Center, July 20-22, 1980, representatives of twenty-five organizations involved in the planning, development, or maintenance of OPACs identified the following four areas as having the highest priority for study and action:

1. Analyzing user behavior and requirements

2. Examining existing online public access systems

3. Developing methods for cost analysis and management

4. Developing distributed computing techniques and system-to-system links.

Scarcely six months after the Dartmouth session, the Council awarded OCLC a grant to study the first two priority areas, specifically, user and use characteristics, interface characteristics, and computing environments. This report addresses the second of the four priority areas, including an analysis of the user-system interface and representative computing environments. The need to study interface characteristics and the functional features of existing OPACs was underlined by the Dartmouth participants. Many of those

---

*Online Public Access to Library Bibliographic Data Bases: Development, Issues and Priorities. OCLC, Inc. and The Research Libraries Group, Inc; Sept. 1980. ED 195275.

present are currently involved in the planning, procurement, or development of future systems, and seek to learn both from the experiences of others and through a discussion of the actual performance capabilities of existing online systems.

1.2 Institutions Participating in the OPAC Study

OCLC's Office of Research contacted and obtained the support of ten institutions to participate in this study of OPACs. The author managed the study's project team and coordinated the data collection and analysis activities from both online and offline sources of documentation. The ten participating institutions are listed and briefly described in Table 1. The participants were:

1. Two bibliographic networks: OCLC and RLG/RLIN

2. Three large university libraries: The University of California, The Ohio State University, and Northwestern University

3. Four small academic libraries: The Claremont Colleges, Dartmouth College, Mankato State University, and Mission College

4. One public library system: Pikes Peak Library District

Rather than being representative of institutions offering online public access systems, the participants in this study are marked by their interest and commitment to the research project. They were the first within a limited time period to respond to the call for participation, yet the OPACs studied represent a fascinating variety of design philosophies. To qualify for participation the system had to be operational, available to patrons for searching the library catalog, and available to OCLC project staff for comprehensive online use. In addition, the institution had to supply user and system documentation capable of supporting the project's objectives, designate a design team member to answer questions from the OCLC project team, and otherwise assist with access to the system.

Table 1. Institutions Participating in the Online
Public Access Catalog Research Project

	System Name	Date First Available for Public Use	No. of Public Access Terminals*	Approximate Size of Database (Records)*
California, University of	MELVYL	August, 1981	100	733,000
Claremont Colleges	Total Library System (TLS)	December, 1979	12	55,000
Dartmouth College	"User Cordial Interface" and BRS/SEARCH	July, 1980	4 with "Interface" 300 Dial access	400,000
Mankato State University	Minnesota State University System: Project for Automated Library Systems (MSUS/PALS)	September, 1980	105	1,760,000
Mission College	Universal Library Systems (ULISYS)	April, 1980	10	70,000
Northwestern University	Northwestern Online Total Integrated System/ Library User Information Service (NOTIS/LUIS)	May, 1980 (LUIS)	12	480,000
OCLC	Online Computer Library Center	January, 1974	84	7,500,000
Ohio State University	Library Control System (LCS)	January, 1975	115	1,700,000
Pikes Peak Library District	Maggie's Place	June, 1980 (dial access); May, 1981 (dedicated in-house)	101	400,000
RLG/RLIN	Research Libraries Group/ Research Libraries Information Network	December, 1974	45	765,000

* July, 1981

1.3 Study Objectives

A user-oriented perspective was adopted throughout all phases of the study. This perspective focuses on the functional, environmental, and psychological needs of an online library catalog user. Of the specific research objectives listed below, 3, 4, and 5 were identified in the Project Proposal, while 1 and 2 were implicit in the sense that they represent groundwork required to satisfy the stated objectives. The remaining objectives were adopted by the study team to describe and illustrate the broader context of user-system interface design practices and issues.

1. To review and evaluate offline and online documentation, and other evidence bearing on OPAC functional features and command languages

2. To provide uniform terminology and working definitions for command-based capabilities and related system features, capable of denoting the many varieties found in existing systems and often described with conflicting or vague terminology

3. To document in a uniform format the functions and commands of the OPACs

4. To provide a common, systematic framework and format for comparing OPAC system functional capabilities and command languages

5. To review and describe how three OPAC systems support and implement these user-perceived functional features at the file access and retrieval level, given their particular hardware/software configurations

6. To identify and illustrate all interface characteristics and components that may have an impact on the effective use of the system's functional capabilities

7. To review the recent literature on interface design and experimentation

8. To identify crucial (from the user's point of view) interface design alternatives.

This final report is the first effort to systematically document the state-of-the-art in the development of user interfaces in online public access catalogs. Although important, the issues of system cost, reliability, efficiency, and search performance were not addressed in this study. The intended audience for this comparative analysis includes present and future system designers, those responsible for planning online catalogs, whether to be developed "in-house" or purchased, and all persons committed to effective access to bibliographic information through automated systems. The findings of this study will aid decision-makers and system designers planning to develop or acquire online public access catalogs.

Our sentiments are best expressed by introductory comments in a report on the first features study of this kind:

> *Hopefully, the report will ease the transition to a common*
> *vocabulary for talking about searching, and perhaps facilitate*
> *the development of a common interface for invoking different*
> *systems. At the very least, it should reduce chances that*
> *future designers build new systems in ignorance of experience*
> *acquired by their predecessors.**

---

*Thomas H. Martin, A Feature Analysis of Interactive Retrieval Systems. Prepared for The National Science Foundation; Institute for Communication Research: NTIS PB-235 952; 1974 September.

Project Study Methods

2.1 Documents and Documentation

Each institution participating in this study of online public access catalogs
was required to provide written documentation bearing on the system's
functional features, commands, and any other user-confronted factors.
Documentation describing system "internals," such as hardware architecture,
system control software, and database maintenance procedures, was not
requested initially from the ten participants. Once three OPAC systems were
selected for an in-depth review of system support and implementation of the
functional features, system documentation was requested from each of the three
institutions agreeing to participate in this phase of the study.

As the received materials were logged-in, an attempt to classify them
according to content or purpose seemed desirable. Such classification would
facilitate later reference to the OPAC files by members of the project team,
and identify gaps where additional information regarding the OPAC systems
would be needed. The documents received had little in common. This was
surprising since these online catalogs were designed, presumably, to be used
by end users having varying degrees of experience or training. We assumed
that user manuals or pamphlets and training materials would be forthcoming
from all participants. This was not the case.

The study team chose five categories to characterize the vast array of
documents received. This classification was roughly based on content,
intended audience/reader, and format. Among the materials received were (1)
comprehensive, detailed user manuals or guides, (2) systems operations
manuals, (3) informational/promotional brochures or flyers, (4) written
correspondence and other unpublished ephemera, and (5) miscellaneous "other"
materials such as system overviews, "working papers," vendor literature, and
technical reports. Much of the documentation was not written for the user,
but rather for designers, librarians, or library administrators. Five of the
participating institutions submitted comprehensive, detailed user
documentation that could be used for general reference or instruction in the
use of the system. All but three submitted some form of booklet, brochure, or
leaflet intended for the user of the online catalog. However, not all of
these contained an explanation of the system's commands, or a simple guide to
system use, unaided by a staff member or prior training.

The project team found no common format or degree of coverage among the
documents most descriptive of each system's functions and commands. It became

apparent from the beginning that a uniform format for listing and describing
these features would have to be designed. Later online experience and
discussions with system design staff revealed that much of the written
documentation was incomplete, out-of-date, or, in some cases, incorrect. The
state-of-the-art of online catalog documentation leaves a great deal to be
desired, whatever the user's need. There are at least three explanations for
this: (1) limited funds, staff, or both cause a low priority to be placed on
the creation and maintenance of either user or system documentation, (2) some
of the OPAC systems are in a prototype or early stage of development,
undergoing rapid development such that documentation efforts lag behind, and
(3) some administrators or designers have chosen not to provide printed user
documentation in any form, preferring to supply all the information and
assistance a user needs online, during the use of the system itself.

Detailed worksheets were designed to enable members of the study team to
describe in uniform language and format the various systems under examination
(see Figure 1). Each worksheet required the statement of the function
provided by the system, the precise command language associated with that
function, a depiction of the syntactical properties of the language, examples
of the command in use (with sample arguments or keywords), and special notes
on command language semantics and syntax. A meta-notation was created to
describe the syntax of the commands, permitting analysis not dependent on
remembering system-specific names or codes. This approach enabled us to
identify rules for such things as command abbreviation and mutually exclusive
alternatives or options for command parameters or augmentation.

As the detailed function/command worksheets were being completed, the study
team encountered additional information needs and problems. The systems not
only differed in the range and complexity of their functional features, they
used different terms to describe them and different commands for invoking
them. Thus, certain "meta"-level tasks had to be undertaken before the
analysis could proceed. We began to develop a list of functions and command
capabilities available to the user, and assigned general names to these
functional capabilities. We soon discovered that these names (or their
synonyms) possessed varying shades or levels of meaning from system to system,
and that the same function or command was given many different names. We
could not speak to each other, much less present a comparative analysis to
others, until we developed a common descriptive language. A glossary (see
Appendix A) was developed and maintained online, passing through more than
twenty editions. It represented at any given time our working understanding
of the terms and concepts under analysis.

As the pages of detailed documentation grew and grew, we recognized the need
for capturing the systems' features and commands in a more condensed and
convenient form, as well as providing ready access to selected items of
interest. For each OPAC system a notebook was maintained, containing sections
for logon procedures, brief summary command reference guides, display formats,
"help" screens, and the set of detailed worksheets previously described. As
data became available, we added a section on indexing methods to some of the
notebooks. After extensive online experience was gained with each system, a
demonstration script was written for each and included in the notebooks.
Practicing these demonstrations ensured that we would maintain a synthetic,
"as-used" perspective on each system while proceeding with the detailed
analysis of its functional features. These notebooks, with their uniform
modes of documentation, became invaluable sources of data that later would be
required for constructing the many comparative tables.

FUNCTIONAL DESCRIPTION OF COMMAND LANGUAGE   OCLC - R8Ø9

WORKSHEET (A)   Page 37

III. OUTPUT CONTROL   SYSTEM: University of California

FUNCTION/OPERATION	COMMAND/SYMBOL	STRUCTURE/SYNTAX	SYNTAX NOTES
Display Selected Fields	DISPLAY	(see structure below)	(see notes below)

STRUCTURE/SYNTAX:

```
DISPLAY¹ { record number [-record number]² }
         {            ALL⁴             }
         [,record number]³

         { search field⁵ [ᵇsearch field]⁶                  }
         { TAG marc field⁷ [ {-marc field⁸}¹⁰ ]            }
         {                  { ᵇmarc field⁹ }               }

Examples:

DISPLAY 2 TITLE

DIS 1-3,5 AUT SUB

D 4,7 TAG 245 650

DI 1 TAG 300-500

DIS ALL TAG 6XX
```

SYNTAX NOTES:

1. Command word may be abbreviated down to 1 letter.

2. Blanks can be placed between record numbers in addition to the comma or hyphen if so desired.

3. A comma between record numbers allows entering a string of individual record numbers; a hyphen between record numbers indicates a range of record numbers.

4. If all records retrieved are desired then the word "ALL" is entered.

Continued on page 38

COMMENTS

Allows display of range of fields for one or more records.

Figure 1.   Function/Command Worksheet

2.2 Online Confirmation

Through existing or special arrangements, dial access to each of the OPAC systems (except OCLC) was provided for the study team. This access was generally unlimited and team members spent hundreds of hours learning and using each system's features, from logon to online assistance and logoff. The majority of these sessions were captured in hard copy by using printer terminals. This enabled us to review actual sessions and provided sample screen displays for the system notebooks. Some system features that are terminal-specific (e.g., prompt cues, cursor placement and control) could not be replicated precisely on our output devices, but these are largely incidental to the use of the system for search and retrieval.

Our online use of the OPAC systems enabled us to both confirm and complete the documentation described in section 2.1. We discovered things online for which we had no written documentation. In a few cases, online experience conflicted with the written accounts. In some cases, online documentation conflicted with actual online use; e.g., a feature explained on an introductory or "help" screen had not yet been implemented, or in another case, the instruction on how to enter a command was incorrect and would result in an error message. These unhappy discoveries were the exception however, primarily because little or no online documentation and assistance is provided in many of the systems.

Our online discoveries of functional features and options (as well as constraints and apparent problems) made it necessary to consult frequently with the designated system design team representatives. These individuals generously confirmed our discoveries or explained our problems and difficulties. In two cases, user-apparent interface features were changed or modified as a result of our discussions with members of the system design teams. The dozens of conversations with system designers proved to be the most educational part of this study effort. Systems cannot be fully understood by use alone. The motivations and perceptions of the designers (as well as the constraints placed upon them) often explain the unique "personality" and quirks observed by users at the user-system interface.

Our online use of the OPAC systems was not for performance testing purposes. Our aim was to experience what they (the OPACs) did, how they did it from the user's point of view, and how it "felt" to use the system. To "refresh our palates," we did not use more than one system on a given day until the documentation was completed. Our use was more akin to extensively test driving a new automobile on ordinary streets rather than running it through its paces on an experimental test track. We desired to discover everything about how the systems could be used, and made no attempt to rate them. Uniform searches and other operations were performed to obtain printouts of the various display formats and user assistance features. The system notebooks were updated or corrected progressively as a result of our online experience with the OPAC systems, and our consultations with design staff.

2.3 Comparative Analysis

As the documentation of each system's features and commands proceeded, a review of the literature was undertaken to discover previous attempts to describe and compare online retrieval system features and commands. Useful classifications of commands were discovered on the command comparison tables prepared as guides for searchers of various database search services (see CONGER, 1980, and LAWRENCE and PREWITT, 1977). Efforts to construct the Common Command Language for the EURONET user (see NEGUS, 1977) or the experimental CONIT virtual interface to heterogeneous systems (see MARCUS and REINTJES, 1976) provided useful insights about fundamental features independent of particular systems. A review of the work of the ANSI Z39-G Committee, charged with developing a standard command language for information retrieval systems, helped us complete our list of "command capabilities" by which the ten OPAC systems could be compared.

The project team's working list of command capabilities developed over a period of time as a result of reviewing related efforts reported in the literature, developing the Project Glossary (Appendix A), and cataloging the functions and commands discovered in each of the ten OPACs. If a feature was not found in any of the ten OPACs, it was dropped from the list. Definitions had to be revised or extended due to the discovery of unique variations in online use. What was gained in the generality of a concept was often lost in the variety of its implementations. Apparent conflicts in the meaning of a feature had to be resolved by distinguishing <u>levels</u> of meaning (the most general vs. specific cases) and identifying specific variations in practice. "Truncation" illustrates this problem excellently. Not only are there several forms or methods of truncation, the same method may be implemented at the command level in fundamentally different ways. One system requires the use of a special symbol following the character string entered as the search argument; another performs the same truncation operation only if no symbol is used at the end of the character string. No standard language of functional features and commands exists presently, so in many cases we had to stipulate the terms and the definitions for the purposes of this comparative analysis. (The classified list of command capabilities is represented in Figure 2 in the next chapter.)

Few system-by-system comparisons which include more than two or three online systems and adopt the perspective and aims of this study can be found in the literature. Systems have been previously compared on the basis of their hardware resources, software architecture, and database organization and management. This has often been done to compare costs, efficiency, capacity, or reliability. Three studies have been especially useful because they emphasize the user's functional needs and the online experience in several retrieval systems (BOYLE and MILLER, 1980, CONGER, 1980, and T. MARTIN, 1974).

We have generally followed the features analysis approach of MARTIN by constructing a classified set of command capabilities to form the framework for comparing the ten OPAC systems. The various groupings of command or command-related capabilities are used to form the several comparison matrices represented by Tables 2-6 in the following chapter. These tables permit comparison of the systems only at a high level of meaning. Individual system variations and extensions of these capabilities are indicated on Tables 7-13 and through the discussions accompanying them. In all, Tables 1-13, and Figures 9-11 (comparisons of input syntax) provide a convenient way to discover the common and not so common functional capabilities of the ten OPAC systems. A collection of bibliographic record display formats available in all the systems studied is included as Appendix C. Beginning with chapter 6, individual functional areas of the user-system interface are treated independently, as listed in the Contents.

Three OPAC systems were chosen for a system-level analysis and comparison (see chapter 11). The aim was to illustrate the hardware and software components which support the functional features of the three systems, and to indicate alternative approaches to file design and maintenance as represented in these systems. Collectively, these systems represent the state-of-the-art in online catalog system design. But this art is rapidly evolving and no single system can be viewed as the prototype of future systems. We hope we have provided a useful framework for the comparison of OPAC systems as they emerge, a framework that will cause the right questions to be asked of system designers and suppliers.

3

3.1 Classification of Command Capabilities: Four Functional Areas
3.2 System-by-System Checklists of Command Capabilities

Comparisons of OPAC Command Capabilities

3.1 Classification of Command Capabilities: Four Functional Areas

Our documentation and analysis of the ten OPAC systems revealed more differences than similarities among the systems. We discovered that a wide range of functions and search capabilities exists across the systems. In a relative sense, some of the OPACs are functionally simple, others are far more complex. The names (words, abbreviations, or symbols) for commands, as well as the total number of separate commands, varies considerably from system to system. The same command name may invoke entirely different functions in different systems. In addition, different command names often invoke the same function in different systems.

Since no standard command language exists, and it was not one of our tasks to propose such a standard, we chose to develop a list of "command capabilities" (see Figure 2). Functions are performed by the computer system as it executes certain operations invoked by user-entered commands. Command capabilities are the means available to the user to invoke these operations or functions. Not only do existing command languages (vocabulary, syntax) differ considerably, commands may be entered by the user in ways other than typing command words (e.g., menu selection, question-answer, function keys, etc.).

This list of command capabilities permits comparisons between systems which have different command languages or employ different command-entry techniques. Some capabilities have commonly understood meanings and the selection of a single word or phrase to describe each of these presented no problems. In other cases, no common understanding existed where it was expected (e.g., truncation, Boolean or free text searching, dialogue mode selection, help facilities, etc.). The development of the list of command capabilities was an iterative effort which included review of similar lists in the literature and post-review discussions with representatives of the ten OPAC systems. These discussions revealed not only the lack of a common interpretation in some cases, but also fundamental conflicts in preferred meanings. This situation led to the development of the Project Glossary (see Appendix A). This Glossary and the discussions which follow will aid in the understanding of these function-invoking capabilities available to the users of these ten OPACs.

As the features and commands of each system were documented, the command capabilities list was updated and used as a checklist. The length of the list alone (fifty-two command-related features) required some structure to permit

the development and easy review of comparison formats. Moreover, grouping
related capabilities together facilitates comparisons of systems on the basis
of kinds or categories of features. A system not having a particular feature
may have several related features, and such an approach readily indicates
this.

In developing a useful framework for comparison, we reviewed several related
efforts to list and classify online retrieval system commands and features.
These previous studies were undertaken to (1) provide command reference guides
for multiple system users, (2) facilitate comparative evaluation of the
features of different systems, or (3) provide the basis for command language
standardization efforts.

I. Operational Control

    1. Logon or other begin session protocol
    2. Select general function desired (e.g.,
            searching, circulation, ILL)
    3. System has default for function
    4. Select file desired (e.g., type of
            material or collection location)
    5. System has default for file
    6. Set default values for session
    7. Set system message length (e.g., terse or
            verbose)
    8. Select dialogue mode (e.g., prompt, menu,
            command language)
    9. Edit input (erase/modify)
    10. Interrupt online output
    11. Stack commands
    12. Save search statements
    13. Purge search statements
    14. Logoff or other end session protocol

II. Search Formulation Control

    1. Search is system default function
    2. General search command is used
    3. Derived search keys are required
    4. Controlled term searching
    5. Free-text search on entire record
    6. Free-text search on selected field
    7. Restrict/limit search results
    8. Boolean operators
    9. Relational operators, explicit use
    10. Proximity operators, explicit use
    11. Truncation, explicit use

Access Points

    1. Personal author
    2. Corporate author
    3. Author/title
    4. Title
    5. Subject
    6. Call number
    7. LC card number
    8. ISBN
    9. ISSN
    10. Government document number
    11. Other control number
    12. Additional access points

III. Output Control

    1. General command to display search results
    2. Select a predefined format for display
    3. Select specific record(s) for display
    4. Select specific field(s) for display
    5. Sort results for display
    6. Merge results for display
    7. Display forward (records or screens)
    8. Display backward (records or screens)
    9. Scroll display of results
    10. Interrupt scroll
    11. Request offline hardcopy print
    12. Produce online hardcopy print
    13. Cancel offline print request

IV. User Assistance: Information and Instruction

    1. List accessible files for review
    2. List searchable fields for review
    3. List commands for review
    4. Show related group of index or thesaurus
            terms
    5. Show search history
    6. Show session time elapsed or cost
    7. Show system/database news or other special
            messages
    8. Explain system messages (e.g., error
            messages)
    9. Identify offline assistance
    10. Indicate item "on shelf" location
    11. Indicate item availability status
    12. Procedural prompts or guiding comments
            routinely provided
    13. Help displays retrievable by command
    14. Online tutorial(s) available

Figure 2. System Command Capabilities by Functional Areas

The useful chart, "ON-LINE COMMANDS: A User's Quick Guide for Bibliographic Retrieval Systems" (compiled by LAWRENCE and PREWITT, revised by BEARMAN, 1977), groups twenty-four command capabilities into four functional areas:

1.   Housekeeping (including logon, logoff, request to list files, display time and cost, and purge unwanted search statements)

2.   Searching

3.   Output

4.   Support (including system news, explanations of commands and services, instruction in system use, search history, and offline assistance)

The "ON-LINE COMMAND CHART" prepared by CONGER (1980) lists thirty-nine "operations" and displays this implicit structure of four functional areas:

1.   Housekeeping (logon, logoff, setting default values, listing files, file selection, changing files, time and charges)

2.   Searching

3.   Output

4.   Miscellaneous online and offline support facilities

MARTIN's (1974) "A Feature Analysis of Interactive Retrieval Systems" divides the "functional needs of a searcher sitting at a terminal" into these three categories:

1.   Instructional, Diagnostic, and Control

2.   Query Formulation

3.   Result Manipulation

The actual analysis, as presented in the published report, does not include in category one: logon, file selection, setting defaults and other control features.

The features comparison approach of BOYLE and MILLER (1980) includes a classified arrangement of user-oriented features based on three broad categories:

1.   User interaction and control

2.   Search input and processing

3.   Manipulation and display of results

The first category includes features which "facilitate the use and understanding of the system" (e.g., online instruction, database descriptions, available search fields, clear prompting for user input).

The draft standard prepared by the ANSI Z39-G Committee (COCHRANE, 1981) to recommend terms and abbreviations for command language in online retrieval systems includes these four functional areas:

    1.   Operational Control

    2.   Output Control

    3.   Search Control

    4.   Support

As defined in the ANSI draft, operational control functions are those functions that are performed prior to, during, or after the actual search process to facilitate the searching and retrieval processes. These functions include logon, logoff, database selection, output interruption, error correction, and requests for news or explanations of databases or commands. Output control functions facilitate the display or printing of bibliographic references selected during the search process. Search control functions include logical or matching operations on specified search terms for identifying and isolating document descriptions (records) pertinent to the inquiry. The support functions relate to ordering documents and accounting facilities.

The project team worked closely with Pauline Cochrane, chairperson of ANSI Z39-G, and the work of that Standards Committee proved to be very helpful in our attempts to construct a useful, comprehensive, classified list of command capabilities. However, as Figure 2 illustrates, we have not used the ambiguous notion of "support" as a category, and we have created an independent category to cover user assistance features and capabilities.

In our review of the literature, "support" was found to be used to characterize "housekeeping" functions, offline support facilities, and even some search-related functions. We decided the term was both too general and ambiguous to be useful in our classification scheme. We accepted the other three category labels adopted by ANSI Z39-G as being sufficiently self-evident and distinct in their implied meanings. The emphasis on user "control" in the ANSI Z39-G classification of retrieval system functions was considered important and we incorporated it in our approach.

Another departure from the ANSI Z39-G structure of four functional areas is reflected in our decision to group user assistance features together in an independent category. (ANSI Z39-G included these features in the operational control category.) This departure may be explained by a difference in mission. One of our objectives was to provide a useful framework and format for comparing OPAC functions and command capabilities. Another objective was to identify and illustrate user interface features that impact on the effective use of online catalogs. These two objectives considered in conjunction with a sympathetic understanding of the wide variety of online catalog users (including those unskilled and untrained in the use of computer systems) make it something of an analytic requirement to invite comparisons of user assistance features in OPAC systems.

Our focus in this study is on the direct end user of OPACs, not the trained, professional search intermediary. The direct use of an OPAC by an end user is neither an issue to be resolved nor an assumption of this study. Such use is our empirically-grounded starting point. These OPAC systems are being used today by trained and untrained users in a variety of library settings. Some are being used via dial-access facilities in the home or office. Assistance in the form of training, library staff consultation, or even offline documentation cannot be provided uniformly for all members of this new community of online catalog users. For this reason, we have chosen to place equal importance on online user assistance features in our classification of functions and command capabilities. Included in this category are capabilities to request operational or search-related information, general system or session-related information, instructional facilities, and other guidance or user assistance features.

Each of the four functional categories of the command capabilities list, plus the group of access points, form the basis for a separate comparison matrix for the ten OPAC systems. A two-dimensional matrix format was chosen to (1) permit easy examination of the similarities and differences between OPACs and (2) serve as a features checklist for a particular system. These comparison matrices are represented by Tables 2, 3, 4, 5, and 6 which are presented and discussed in the following section.

3.2 System-by-System Checklists of Command Capabilities

The series of five tables which follows permits comparisons of many OPAC features only in a very general sense. Actual system performance of several of the functions listed varies in kind and degree from OPAC to OPAC. No judgment about the quality of system performance in any of the functional areas should be made solely on the basis of the number of positive marks ("X's") recorded for a particular system.

The manner in which a command capability is initiated by the user also differs from system to system. These differences include command entry technique, command vocabulary, and command syntax. Some of the variations discovered in actual system use will be discussed in this section. For more detailed discussions of OPAC functions and command capabilities, the reader is referred to later chapters which include analyses of command languages (7), access points and search capabilities (8), display/print capabilities (9), and user assistance features (10). Definitions of the command capabilities may be found in the Project Glossary.

Table 2.   System-by-System Checklist of Command Capabilities:
Functional Area I. Operational Control

COMMAND CAPABILITIES (available to, or under the control of the user)	California, University of	Claremont Colleges	Dartmouth College	Mankato State University	Mission College	Northwestern University	OCLC	Ohio State University	Pikes Peak Library District	RLG/RLIN
Logon (begin session protocol)	$X^{2,3}$	X	$X^{2,3}$	$X^{2,3}$	$X^{2,3}$		X	X^2	X	X
Select function desired		X	X		X	X			X	X
System has default for function	X		X	X	X		X	X^5		X
Select file desired	X		X	X			X		X	X
System has default for file	X	X		X	X	X	X	X	X	X
Set default values for session	X			X						X
Set system message length				X						
Select dialogue mode	X		X							
Edit input (erase/modify)	X	X	X	X	X	X	X	X	X	X
Interrupt online output	X	X	1		X	4	X^2		X	X
Stack commands			X					X		X
Save search statements	1		X	X						
Purge search statements	X		X	X	X					
Logoff (end session protocol)	X^2	X^2	X^2	X^2	X^2		X	X^2	X	X

X = Command capability available to, or under the control of the user

NOTES: 1. To be implemented
2. Dial access only
3. Onsite users are encouraged to enter a begin-session command such as "START", HI", "BEGIN".
4. Entering a command interrupts output in dial access only.
5. At some locations, terminals provide both search and copy "HOLD" functions.

3.2.1 Notes on Operational Control Capabilities

<u>Logon</u>

Remote users of time-sharing computer systems are familiar with the cumbersome
access protocols which include entry of passwords, account numbers, and file
or database selection. Fortunately, onsite users of OPACs are not required to
logon in this complex manner. Some systems do require library staff to ready
the OPAC for patron use at the start of each day. This was not considered a
"capability" available to the end user. However, OPAC users may be requested
or required to follow a "begin session" protocol. This could include the
entry of a special command or the patron's library identification number.
This protocol is often used for the purpose of logging a user's transaction
activity within a session.

<u>Select function desired</u>

The OPAC may be ready for the user to search the bibliographic database. In
other cases, in a multi-function system (interlibrary loan, circulation,
community information), the user may have to undertake some explicit action to
"set" the system for bibliographic searching.

<u>System has default for function</u>

A predetermined function is "assumed" by the system when none is explicitly
selected by the user. Not all systems reviewed default in function to
searching the bibliographic database.

<u>Select file desired</u>

Some systems offer both bibliographic and nonbibliographic files for
searching. Other file divisions may be made on the basis of type or format of
material. The user is given the capability to select the file or files to be
searched.

<u>Set default values for session</u>

This general capability to set implied or system default values (to be assumed
when no others are explicitly specified) at the beginning of a search session
may include the selection of a search type, field or fields to be searched,
display format, or dialogue mode. A system may also offer a "reset"
capability which may be used at any point in a session to change default
values.

<u>Set system message length</u>

System messages include error messages, guiding prompts, and retrievable
"help" displays. With this capability, the user may select, for example, a
terse or verbose mode for these messages.

<u>Select dialogue mode</u>

The user may choose between a computer-guided mode of interaction or a user-guided mode. Many varieties of these basic modes of interaction may be found in OPAC systems. Some systems employ an eclectic mix of dialogue techniques in one or the other of these basic dialogue modes.

<u>Interrupt online output</u>

The user may wish to stop the continuing display or print of output either to enter another command, or, in the case of scrolling, to view data before it leaves the screen. The user's implementation of this capability varies from system to system.

<u>Stack commands</u>

Single entry of multiple commands. The user may wish to combine commands in one input operation, for example, to indicate that the results of a specific search are to be displayed in a brief format, arranged alphabetically by title.

<u>Purge search statements</u>

In the process of refining a search through the use of search statements which qualify a previous query (such as requesting Boolean intersection or restricting a previous search to a specific type of material or range of years), the user may choose to "backup" to an earlier stage of the search, or to delete one of the intermittent search statements (and its results) previously entered.

3.2.2 Notes on Search Formulation Control Capabilities

<u>General search command is used</u>

Systems which require the use of a formal command language as the primary command entry technique may provide a specific command word for conducting searches (e.g., FIND, SELECT). This general command word is usually followed by a qualifier indicating search type or field, then the search term itself. In other systems this general search command is either implicit or indicated by the syntax of the search argument.

<u>Derived search keys are required</u>

Search arguments must be entered according to a predetermined format which abbreviates the components of a search term. Some systems permit the use of derived search keys as an optional entry technique.

Table 3. System-by-System Checklist of Command Capabilities: Functional Area II. Search Formulation Control

COMMAND CAPABILITIES (available to, or under the control of the user)	California, University of	Claremont Colleges	Dartmouth College	Mankato State University	Mission College	Northwestern University	OCLC	Ohio State University	Pikes Peak Library District	RLG/RLIN
Search is default function	X		X	X	X		X	X^2		X
General search command is used	X									X
Derived search keys are required							X	X		
Controlled term searching	X	X	X	X	X	X		X	X	X
Free-text term searching:										
entire record			X							
selected field(s)	X	X	X	X						X
Restrict/limit search results	X	X	X	X			X	X		
Boolean operators:										
on any searchable field	X		X	X						X
on selected fields	X	X	X	X	X					X
Relational operators, explicit use	X	X	X	X			X	X		
Truncation, explicit use	X	X	X	X	X	X	X^3	X	X	X
Proximity operators, explicit use	1		X							

X = Command capability available to, or under the control of the user

NOTES: 1. To be implemented
        2. At some locations, terminals default to both search and copy "HOLD" functions.
        3. Some components of a derived search key may be truncated or omitted.

Controlled term searching

Controlled term searching is limited here to the ability to search on Library of Congress Subject Headings. None of the OPACs assign controlled vocabulary terms from another subject thesaurus. In another sense, all exact-match word or phrase searching (e.g., author, title, subject) of a bibliographic record constitutes "controlled term searching" since the data entered in the fields is "controlled" by the rules and conventions of a cataloging code such as AACR2. Full call number searching is another kind of controlled term searching.

Free text term searching

This type of access is often referred to as "keyword" or "component word" searching. Natural language words or phrases which appear in one or more fields of a record may be entered as search terms. Usually the field to be searched for the occurrence of a word or phrase must be specified with the search command. Most common is title keyword searching where the entry of one or more words of a title may retrieve the desired record even if the exact title (as cataloged) is not known. The capability to search for component words in a multi-word controlled vocabulary phrase (e.g., subject heading, authoritative form of a name) may also be provided in some OPACs. Free text searching is sometimes understood as "full text" searching. This applies to the case where the component words from searchable fields are stored in the indexes and the search is not restricted to any specific field(s).

Restrict/limit search results

Search statements may be further qualified by parameters such as language of the desired bibliographic item, type of publication, or date(s) of publication. This is done to reduce and confine the results of a search to a desired domain.

Boolean operators

The standard Boolean logical operators (e.g., OR, AND, NOT) must be entered by the user when constructing a search argument. A variation on the use of a formal command language vocabulary and syntax to enter the commands is provided by the use of prompts or questions posed to the user. The user may be queried or prompted for the entry of terms (e.g., subject and author and/or title) to be "combined" by the system in the search process. Boolean capabilities are limited in some systems to (1) the processing of only one or two of the logical operations or (2) the processing of logical operations only on selected searchable fields. Some systems process certain searches using implicit Boolean logic even though the user has not chosen to use Boolean operators.

Relational operators, explicit use

Using some symbolic expression of "greater than," "less than," or "equal to," the user may choose to restrict or limit the results of a search to a specific range of dates.

Truncation, explicit use

Many varieties of truncation exist in the OPAC systems. All permit some form
of shortening a search term (word or phrase) for the purpose of broadening a
search. The system is instructed to search for all terms in the specified
index(es) which begin with the truncated character string entered by the user.
The method of indicating a truncated term varies from OPAC to OPAC. Some
require the use of a special symbol placed at the end of the truncated search
term, others carry out the desired search only when no special symbol is
entered (that the search term has been truncated is assumed). The method of
indicating a truncated term search is determined by the search and retrieval
software programs of a particular system.

Proximity operators, explicit use

Often referred to as "positional" operators, they are used in free text
searching to enable the user to specify the position in a field or fields of
search terms vis-a-vis one another. For example, the user may specify that
two search terms must appear immediately adjacent to one another in a
designated field of the record, or that the two terms appear in the same
field, or only that the two terms appear anywhere in the same record. The
capability to indicate precise positional relationships of words entered as
search terms requires the inclusion of positional data in the index record.

3.2.3 Notes on Access Points

Present database organization methods facilitate online access to
bibliographic records by indexing the information contained in the fields of
those records. The library catalog is an index to the library's collection of
bibliographic works, but for that catalog to be effectively searched online,
its records must be indexed as well. When the user enters a search term
(number, word, phrase, statement) at an online catalog terminal, the computer
attempts to find that term in a specified index. If the term has not been
entered in the index (or linked to one that has been entered), no retrieval of
the desired record is possible.

In the construction and maintenance of index files, the system's designers
decide which fields of a bibliographic record are to be indexed (i.e., made
searchable). Further decisions determine which components of the data
contained in a field (words, punctuation, entire subfields) are "significant"
and are to be included in an index record. Nonsignificant words form the
exclusion list commonly known as the "stoplist." A variety of indexing
policies, as reflected in these decisions, was discovered in our analysis of
these OPAC systems. Since the extent and quality of access to bibliographic
records depends largely on the number and kinds of indexes provided, access
varies considerably among these OPACs.

The "access points" listed in Table 4 serve only partially to indicate this
variety of access. Access points, as considered here, are the fields of a
record that are indexed. Some systems combine related fields in a single
index (e.g., personal, corporate, or conference name), others segment
searchable fields into separate indexes. In the latter case, the user may
have to explicitly identify the correct index (e.g., corporate author, uniform
title) to be searched.

Table 4. System-by-System Checklist of Command Capabilities:
Functional Area II. Access Points

COMMAND CAPABILITIES (available to, or under the control of the user)	California, University of	Claremont Colleges	Dartmouth College	Mankato State University	Mission College	Northwestern University	OCLC	Ohio State University	Pikes Peak Library District	RLG/RLIN
ACCESS POINTS*										
personal author	X	X	X	X	X	X	X	X	X	X
corporate author	X	X	X	X	X	X	X	X	X	X
author/title	X⁴		X⁴	X³	X³		X²	X²		X⁴
title	X	X	X	X	X	X	X	X	X	X
subject	X	X	X	X	X	X		X	X	X
call number		X	X		X			X	X	X
LC card number	X		X	X	X	X			X	X
ISBN	X		X	X	X	X				X
ISSN	X		X	X		X				X
government document number			X			X				X
other control number	X		X	X			X	X	X	X
additional access points		X	X		X		X			X

X = Command capability available to, or under the control of the user

NOTES: 1. To be implemented
2. An algorithmically derived search key is required.
3. Terms are entered in combination, but no explicit use of Boolean operators is required.
4. Explicit designation of indexes and use of Boolean operators is required.

* Some systems combine or further segment some of these access points in their indexes.

Conclusions about the quality of access in a particular OPAC should not be based on the total number of its access points. It would be unrealistic to compare these OPACs on that basis. Many other factors determine the quality of access in online retrieval systems. The entry of a search in any online catalog will include an instruction to the computer as to which index (or indexes) is to be searched. All the OPACs studied permit personal author, corporate author, and title searching, yet the indexes searched vary considerably in record content (fields) and structure. Added author and title entries are not indexed in some systems. The length of field-derived data (number of characters) varies from system to system. Once beyond initial articles, stopword lists are not uniform. Rules for the exclusion of punctuation when creating an index record from one or more fields differ from system to system.

Online catalogs add new dimensions to the traditional problems of access to bibliographic records. In existing OPACs, the user encounters command entry difficulties presented by unfriendly interfaces and a bewildering variety of display formats for a given record. In addition, different indexing policies for the same machine-readable (MARC) bibliographic record are reflected in the indexes of these OPAC systems. Efforts expended for bibliographic control need to be augmented by an equal concern for index control. Indexing for online access is not governed by rules and conventions such as those contained in AACR2. Rather, locally adopted or assumed indexing policies determine the number of indexes, as well as the content and structure of their records.

Searching the various OPACs, the user cannot be assured of finding equal access to the same bibliographic record via joint authors, for example, or by entering a name or subject heading exactly as cataloged in the LC MARC record. To compound the problem, needed information regarding these local indexing practices (e.g., the exclusion of added entries, indexing only a limited number of characters from a field, including locally added punctuation in the index record which must be entered with the search term to produce a match) is usually not provided in a form useful to the new or occasional user of the online catalog.

More powerful, flexible, and convenient access is possible through the use of sophisticated online capabilities such as searching on truncated terms, keyword searching aided by the use of Boolean or word proximity operators, and limiting search results by language, format, or date(s) of publication. Being able to select the formats and arrangement of results to be displayed or printed also advances the user beyond other forms of the catalog in terms of flexibility and convenience of use. However, these special features provided with some online catalogs cannot alleviate the problems caused by inconsistencies or omissions of useful data in constructing and maintaining indexes.

Table 5. System-by-System Checklist of Command Capabilities:
Functional Area III. Output Control

COMMAND CAPABILITIES (available to, or under the control of the user)	California, University of	Claremont Colleges	Dartmouth College	Mankato State University	Mission College	Northwestern University	OCLC	Ohio State University	Pikes Peak Library District	RLG/RLIN
General command to display results	X	X	X	X	X	X	X	X	X	X
Select display from predefined formats	X	X	X	X	X	X	X	X	X	X
Select specific record(s) for display	X	X	X	X	X	X	X	X		X
Select specific field(s) for display	X		X							X
Sort results for display	1		X[4]							
Merge results for display			X							
Display forward (records or screens)	X	X	X	X	X	X	X	X	X	X
Display backward (records or screens)	X	X	X	X	X	X	X	X		X
Scroll		X	X	X						X[3]
Interrupt scroll		X	1							X[3]
Request offline hardcopy print	1		X	X	X					
Produce online hardcopy print	X[2]		X	X[2]	X		X[2]	X	X	X[2]
Cancel offline print request	1		X							

X = Command capability available to, or under the control of the user

NOTES: 1. To be implemented
        2. Some member institutions provide hardcopy terminals or attached printers.
        3. Dial access only
        4. Available only for offline print

3.2.4 Notes on Output Control Capabilities

General command to display results

Systems using a formal command language as the primary command entry technique
provide a command word or symbol (e.g., DISPLAY, PRINT, DI, P) for requesting
the display of a retrieved record. If multiple records are retrieved and/or
more than one display format is available, the user may have to qualify the
display command with a record number or range qualifier, and a format
qualifier (e.g., DI 2-4 BRIEF). Some OPACs provide a default value for these
parameters. Other OPACs do not require the use of a general display command
(results display automatically or require only the entry of a line or record
number from a menu of abbreviated listings), but provide special purpose
display commands for results manipulation. These special commands may be used
to retrieve a previously displayed record, or to select a standard display
such as one containing circulation data or the "full" bibliographic record.

Select display from predefined formats

All of the OPACs examined offer the user more than one format for the display
of a retrieved record. In the simplest case, the user is given the capability
to select the "standard" (only within a particular OPAC) format after viewing
a brief, truncated version of the record, either displayed by itself or among
a listing of other abbreviated records. The latter is sometimes called an
"index listing" but includes enough components of the record (author, title,
date) to permit initial identification. If more than two display formats are
available, the user must specify the desired format or accept the default
format.

Select specific record(s) for display

When multiple records are retrieved in a single search, the user is given the
capability to choose one or more from among them for display (e.g., DISPLAY 1,
4-6).

Select specific fields for display

The capability permits the user to select one or more fields of the retrieved
record(s) for display. The user may desire to browse only the titles, or the
subject headings, of those records retrieved. Call number and title only may
be selected as a prelude for browsing the stacks.

Sort results for display

For either display or print (hardcopy) purposes, the user may wish to have the
results of a search or searches arranged sequentially by a particular field or
subfield value, for example, alphabetically by title, or in chronological
order by date of publication.

Merge results for display

The capability to combine the results of more than one search in a single
output is often used in conjunction with a sort command to bring like records
from different searches together.

Display forward (records or screens)

Many "local" (nonstandard, often terminal dependent) commands exist for what
is really a set of result manipulation capabilities. Multiple records and/or
screens of data may result from a retrieval or request. The user must be able
to move forward to the next record or screen (or jump several) in the browsing
or preselection decision process.

Display backward (records or screens)

(See above). Not all OPACs which provide a display forward command enable the
user to select a previously displayed record or screen from a retrieved set.
Some permit browsing forward through a file (e.g., shelf list) but not
backward. Once the record has been viewed, the search must be reinitiated if
the record is to be displayed again.

Scroll

Scrolling is a terminal display capability which permits the continuous
display of information line by line, successively, until the end of the
information. Contrast with discrete page by page displays. The lines appear
to roll up or down the Visual Display Unit (VDU) screen. The "leading" line
disappears off the screen to make room for a new line.

Interrupt scroll

The user may wish to stop a scrolling display either to enter another command
or to view carefully a record or other information being displayed. In
computer-guided dialogue, the user may have no choice but to view (with
occasional pauses) all the information being displayed by the scrolling method
before being permitted to enter another command. This is accomplished by
locking the keyboard during the scrolling process.

Request offline hardcopy print

A user may wish to obtain a printed list of search results previously
displayed at the terminal. If no hardcopy printer terminal or VDU with an
attached printer is available to the user, this request may be satisfied by
offline batch processing. This hardcopy of selected search results is made
available to the user at a later time.

Produce online hardcopy print

This capability is supported by either a printer terminal (without a VDU) or a
VDU terminal with an attached printer. In either case, the results are
printed on paper while the user is online. When using an attached printer,
the user must pause and enter a command to have the VDU's screen contents
printed on paper.

Table 6. System-by-System Checklist of Command Capabilities:
Functional Area IV. User Assistance: Information
and Instruction

COMMAND CAPABILITIES (available to, or under the control of the user)	California, University of	Claremont Colleges	Dartmouth College	Mankato State University	Mission College	Northwestern University	OCLC	Ohio State University	Pikes Peak Library District	RLG/RLIN
List files for review	X		X	X					X	X
List searchable fields for review	X	X	X	X	X	X			X	X
List commands for review	X	X	X	X	X	X			X	X
Show index or thesaurus terms	X		X		X	X[2]	X			
Show search history	X		X	X						X
Show time elapsed or cost			X						X	X
Show news or special messages	X		X	X			X		X	X
Explain system messages	X					X				
Identify offline assistance			X			X	X			X
Indicate item location	X	X		X	X	X	X	X	X	X
Indicate item availability		X			X	X		X	X	
Prompts or guidance comments	X	X	X	X	X	X	X	X		X
Help displays retrievable	X	X	X	X	X	X			X	X
Online tutorial(s)[3]	[1]									

X = Command capability available to, or under the control of the user

NOTES: 1. To be implemented
2. Index display results from author and title searches
3. A structured series of interactive lessons or instructional modules

3.2.5 Notes on User Assistance Features

Operational control features facilitate the basic use of a search and
retrieval system, but additional user assistance may be needed for a fuller
understanding of the system to facilitate its most effective use. This need
is a function both of the complexity of the system and the ability of the user
to use it for his needs. Even the experienced online searcher needs to know
what files or records (by format and date, i.e., database contents and
coverage) are available for searching on a particular OPAC. A display of
searchable fields is essential when not all are indexed (e.g., added entries,
uniform titles, series, subject headings). All users forget from time to time
a command word or symbol, or the proper syntax for using them.

User assistance may be analyzed under three categories:

1. General operational, search-related information (e.g., a display of
    searchable files or fields, or a display of system commands)

2. Specific search or session-related information (e.g., a display of
    index terms related to a search term, a display of search history, or
    clear, informative system messages)

3. Instructional facilities including guiding prompts embedded in the
    user-system dialogue, retrievable and automatic "help" displays, and
    online tutorial packages.

A review of Table 6 reveals the wide range of user assistance features offered
by these OPACs. A more detailed discussion of the degree and levels of user
assistance available in each OPAC is contained in chapter 10 of this book.
The amount, complexity, and format of information provided under any of these
headings varies considerably from OPAC to OPAC. For example, one OPAC
provides a single "help" screen, another provides more than 150. Most OPACs
list "searchable fields" only generically (e.g., "author", "title"), leaving
the user to guess whether or not all related fields (e.g., corporate author,
uniform title, series title) are searchable. Online prompts may range from a
simple "Page 1 of 2" to a suggestion for another term selection or a warning
not to enter words contained in a "stoplist." One OPAC informs the user that
Library of Congress Subject Headings must be used for subject searching, and
prompts the user to try a keyword search on another field if the subject
search is not successful.

The world of OPACs is an exciting, if sometimes confusing and frustrating,
world to experience at this early period of development. The reader is warned
not to make final comparative judgements on the basis of these tables alone.
They are offered as a preliminary indication of the state-of-the-art in online
catalog design, and can in no way demonstrate the quality of bibliographic
access provided by the OPACs included in this study. Most of the OPACs
analyzed are still undergoing development at this time, adding, deleting, or
modifying features. It is hoped that this report will bring the reader,
better informed, into this new arena of debate, discussion, and design of
online public access catalog systems.

The User-System Interface:
A State-of-the-Art Review

4.1 Online Catalogs: A Radical Departure for the Catalog User

Witnessing the growing momentum toward online catalogs, BAUSSER (1981b) reports:

> *What was once an almost utopian ideal has become an acknowledged necessity for some. The desire to provide faster and more flexible access to the library's collection, the enticement of Boolean searching, the ease of changing and updating access points, the integration with other library functions such as acquisitions and circulation, and the capability of linking with other libraries for resource sharing make the online catalog especially attractive for libraries that manage large, complex, bibliographic files and for all libraries that want to provide the utmost in bibliographic access and service.*

A review of the classified list of command capabilities and the tables which serve to illustrate the varying implementations of these capabilities in the ten online catalogs presented in the previous chapter should suffice to indicate that the replacement of a manual catalog with an online catalog involves much more than simply "plugging the card catalog into the wall," or exchanging the card drawer for a VDU (Visual Display Unit) terminal as a medium for record storage and display.

The online catalog is not merely a flashy electronic card or book catalog, fashioned in someone's Rube Goldberg-like fantasy, having the same access and display capabilities for unit records that just happen to be stored in a highly reduced form in a foreign, coded, machine-readable language. Nor is the transition to an online catalog from a manual catalog analogous to, or an inevitable "natural" continuation of, the conversion to a COM (Computer Output Microform) catalog from a card catalog. These confused notions need to be dispelled. In addition to its functions or "objects" (in Cutter's sense), its principles of organization, and all the wisdom, folly, and folklore expressed by the Platonic Idea of Bibliographic Control (AACR2), a library catalog may be viewed as an entity along two dimensions as:

1. a <u>store</u> or repository of information about the library's collection, "the main bibliographic record of library stock" (WILLERS, 1981), or

2. a <u>functional</u> communications system or tool providing direction and access to bibliographic information.

The catalog may be stored on a variety of media: 3x5 cards, pages in a book, microfilm or microfiche, or in machine-readable form on magnetic tape or disk. Converting the catalog to machine-readable form does not constitute, in itself, having a computer catalog, for it may simply be used as a reprographic device to produce human-readable cards or microfilm.

As a store of bibliographic information, the card catalog and the COM catalog are not essentially dissimilar. A COM catalog is an electro-mechanical device capable of displaying miniaturized bibliographic unit records that happen to be recorded on microfilm or microfiche rather than on 3x5 cards. Each entry in both a card and COM catalog is represented by a single physical record. (Physically speaking, a COM catalog can be updated and replicated relatively inexpensively for distribution to many sites.) While a microform catalog can be produced (inefficiently) using pre-automated technology, a machine-readable store is a prerequisite for either a COM catalog or an online catalog. This commonality at the machine-readable level may explain the not uncommon belief that both COM and online catalogs are "computer catalogs" (often used as synonymous with "machine-readable catalog"). A library may choose to convert its catalog to a machine-readable database, however, without making a commitment to a particular form of catalog. Any of the common forms of the catalog, from card to online, can be computer-produced.

When the catalog is approached as a functional, guiding and access-providing tool, the card and COM catalogs are essentially the same kind of catalog from the user's point of view. (We have seen cards as difficult to read as poorly focused screen displays on a COM viewer.) The access points are the same, and the filing arrangement or mode of organization (divided, dictionary) may be the same in both the card and COM catalogs. Whether one is viewing the catalog along either the storage dimension or the functional dimension, the card and COM catalogs have more in common with each other than either has with the online catalog. As a diverse and powerful functional instrument capable of providing "the utmost in bibliographic access and service," comparing an online computer catalog to a manual or mechanized catalog is akin to comparing a bicycle, albeit motorized, to a manned space vehicle. Both facilitate the transporting of humans from place to place, but there the similarity ends.

The online catalog offers the user both expanded and more convenient access to bibliographic records, and provides functional capabilities, even in the simpler implementations, far more diverse and powerful than those of any previous form of catalog. (We are aware of course, that some view the online catalog as a new tool which performs the same functions, through the same access points, as the card catalog; but for reasons of efficient file maintenance and storage economy, it operates on records converted to a machine-readable format.) Expanded access and increased functionality alone cannot convey an understanding of the quantum, discontinuous leap to a new world of information retrieval undertaken when one replaces a card catalog with an online, interactive retrieval system.

Online catalogs represent a special application of interactive computer systems, and the searching of an online catalog is a subset of human interaction with computers. Choosing an online catalog is choosing to enter the world of "human-computer interaction," with all that world's new opportunities, challenges, and alas, problems. As an interactive computer system, the online catalog is a fundamentally different kind of problem-solving tool, the problem in this case being, simply put, the retrieval of desired or needed bibliographic information (whether the aim is to find a known item or to gather materials on a topic or work of interest).

Like the manned space vehicle, the online catalog creates a new problem-solving environment in which the problem-solving activities themselves undergo transformation. How we go about solving the problem, that is, the logic of the solution (search formulation and strategy), as well as the techniques we use in this process, are new and will not be found in the experience of most catalog users. Although models of the process of library catalog searching have been constructed (MARKEY, 1980), it will not do to constrain our thinking about and planning for catalog use to those models of information retrieval or manual catalog use, simply because the expanding experience of end users with interactive systems will outstrip such models. Limiting design to previous models of catalog use would be like designing an automobile to be ridden like a horse.

The new functional capabilities of an online catalog will both support and encourage new methods of carrying out the tasks necessary to achieve one's information retrieval goals. Both the structural components of the retrieval system and the available processes of information retrieval are fundamentally different in the case of an online catalog. The telling difference between an online catalog and a card catalog does not lie in the area of bibliographic description, control, or record storage, but rather in the way the user interacts with and is assisted by the online catalog.

4.2 What is the User Interface?

As interactive computer systems, online catalogs add an entirely new dimension to catalog use not present or encountered in noninteractive catalog systems. In terms of process, this new dimension is referred to as human-computer interaction or man-machine communication. In structural terms it is known as the user-system interface or man-machine interface component of the computer system or environment.

To understand the uniqueness of online catalogs, it is necessary to achieve a fuller understanding of the promises and problems of human-computer interaction as it is manifested in current state-of-the-art applications. The user-system interface, or simply, user interface, is the locus of that interaction undertaken in the use of interactive computer systems, such as online catalogs and other information retrieval systems. A review of the characteristic properties of the user interface in interactive retrieval systems will provide a deeper understanding of the diverse and powerful functional capabilities of online catalogs, and such a review will also make it clear why users are frequently unable or unwilling to take advantage of these powerful retrieval systems.

In the Project Glossary (Appendix A) we define "interface," in part, as "the point or process which joins two or more system components." With regard to the user-system interface in interactive systems, the components to be "joined" are the user and the system. This may seem self-evident and trivially true, but not until recently has this overwhelmingly important user/system dynamic come to be of any interest to system designers. Implicit in our general definition of "interface" is the notion that the user, whether an intermediary or a direct user, is an integral component of the system. This view of the user as an active, creative and productive participant within the system itself, rather than just being an external recipient of its products or services, has major consequences for the design of interactive systems, as well as for our evaluation of systems currently in use.

The user interface is largely uncharted territory which we must traverse in our efforts to achieve effective information retrieval from online bibliographic databases. The territory varies from system to system, and the signposts are few, and scarcely discoverable, in most systems. Yet the features of the system are encountered by the user at the interface; the system's functions must be directly invoked at the interface. This is the domain in which requests are formulated and conveyed to the system and a variety of messages is returned to the user, but it is a dynamic domain which requires communication techniques and skills on the part of the user never required in the use of a nonautomated catalog.

4.3 Absence of a User-Oriented Model for Interface Design

Unfortunately, until very recently, designers of interactive retrieval systems have extended little effort to understand the nature and needs of the user-system interface, or to include in their designs features that would provide for these needs while improving the convenience and effectiveness of the information retrieval process. System designers have not had the users, especially direct end users, in mind when undertaking the design and implementation of their systems. Design usually proceeds from some model or conceptualization of the problem-solving process domain in the real world. The relationships between the participants in that process should be an integral part of that conceptualization and accounted for in the model. At worst, the model will be divorced from the real problem-solving domain and be constructed on the basis of the most elegant (efficient?) combinations of state-of-the-art hardware and system software (i.e., computer architecture).

We are using "model" to mean "a description of interacting variables." In a sense, no model will ever be descriptively complete, but may be judged on its adequacy or relevancy. The variables chosen and their defined associations reflect an implicit statement regarding the factors considered to be relevant to the design situation. However, we can ask, "Has it captured the determining variables and adequately described their interaction, that is, their role in affecting the results of the problem solving activity being modelled?"

The process of information retrieval in today's world is both complex and changing. But we agree with COCHRANE (1981) in our belief that "we should try to agree on a model of that process and then explain how our work or focus fits it." Mere common sense would seem to dictate that any model of information retrieval should incorporate both the actions of the user and the various components of the system as variables whose interaction affects both the process itself as well as possible outcomes of that process. Yet this "sensible" approach to, and basis for, the design of interactive retrieval systems has not been the common ground on which most existing systems have been built.

One explanation for this lack of user orientation in design points us to the prevailing interests of computer scientists and design teams.

> *Computer science's main interest lies in the core of computer systems, in such topics as architecture and software. Interest wanes, however, as we move outward through the computer system from its core to the periphery--the 'terminal' seeming to indicate that we have reached the boundary of the system. A system does not, alas, terminate at its terminals--users are attached (MORAN, 1981a).*

This system orientation is captured graphically by MARCUS (1977) with his three concentrics for system performance measurement and evaluation, repeated here as Figure 3. He notes that "the outermost band is as yet undefined and is included thus far only in certain unique situations."

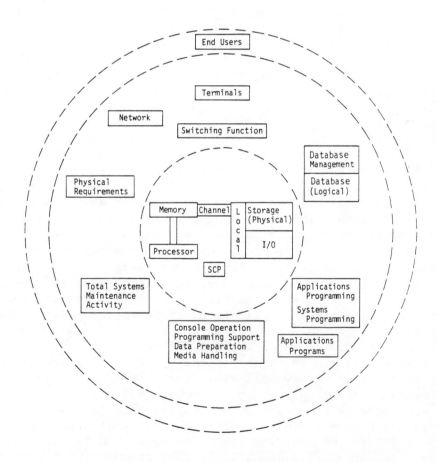

Figure 3. System Components and the End User:
The Conventional Perspective (MARCUS, 1977)

In today's design environment, models of the user-system interface, that is, descriptions of online information retrieval activities by end users, are somewhat more adequate than those employed in the 60s and 70s. The user is now considered to be one of the critical components of the system, if for no other reason than the successful working of the whole system in fulfilling its role depends upon how well the user manipulates the system. Thus, there is a new interest in how the user behaves when using the system, and some interest in shaping that behavior from the point of view of what is best for the system. As DWYER (1981) explains,

> *The interface between a person and a computer can be looked at*
> *from either side. Programmers tend to view it from the inside;*
> *they consider it their job to defend the machine against errors*
> *made by its users. From the outside, the user sees his/her*
> *problems as paramount. He/she is often at odds with this*
> *complex, inflexible, albeit powerful tool.*

This "inside" view, even when it is most sympathetic to the user's needs and abilities, has its inherent dangers. The sympathetic designer now wishes to care for the user's needs, and will, if only given enough time. The designer is human, after all, and can modify his system (when time permits) to make it easier for the user. Rare is the designer who thinks his system is not functionally powerful enough to handle the problem-solving domain for which it was designed. The danger in this approach is obvious: there is no guarantee that the designer's intuitions will match up with the real world activities and attitudes of system users. Referring to their reliance on "egocentric 'folk psychology'," MORAN (1981a) reminds us that "intuitions about complex psychological behavior (even about one's own behavior) can be remarkably deceptive."

The obvious antidote to continuous overdoses of intuition-based "theories" of user welfare is a commitment to empirical studies of user behavior and attitudes. If one is not in a position to conduct such studies, a review of the literature will lead one to fundamental findings relevant to improving the user interface, findings derived from systematically observed behavior of users of online systems. The scope of the findings based on sound empirical research is limited, however, to only a few aspects of human interaction with computers, and in some of these cases, only very general design principles can be supported by the evidence. The benefits to users of such research have come primarily in the form of improved design of the physical equipment associated with the interface, specifically, a variety of input/output devices, from touch-sensitive terminals to those which speak to the user.

Recognizing that the designers of the ten online catalog systems analyzed in this study have provided some ingenious user-oriented features, further progress in this direction may well ride on a commitment to acquiring conclusive evidence about user needs, behavior, and attitudes. This commitment will have to be shared by the designers, the users, and those who are responsible for both the costs and consequences of acquiring these online systems. As PENNIMAN and DOMINICK (1980) observe, "while lip-service always was given to 'user-oriented systems,' the user to whom the system was oriented existed primarily in the designer's mind and tended to be more systems-oriented than the actual user group."

Not only is the user component of the system the one least under the control
of the designer, the designer is usually wrapped up in the deadline-driven,
time-consuming development of the application itself. To carry out a
commitment to improve systems based on user behavior, the designer may have to
step out of his role as creator or developer of a particular system. He may
need encouragement to do so from users, from potential buyers, and from those
responsible for funding the ongoing research into the actual use of online
retrieval systems by an ever-widening population of users.

4.4 A Diversity of Online Catalogs at the Early Stage of Trial and Experimentation

The current state-of-the-art in the design of online catalogs can be
characterized as successful confusion. Much has been accomplished almost
overnight by isolated design teams. Some have achieved superb simplicity,
others have provided awesome search and retrieval power. Librarians speak of
the "card catalog," even with its archaeological layers of rules or variant
forms of organization, and justifiably anticipate a universality of
understanding about their subject of discourse. There is a common, shared
core of meaning regarding the card catalog as a medium for organizing,
storing, and providing for the retrieval of bibliographic information. This
is not the case with the "online catalog." Not only is the universality of
understanding not present at this time, neither is there commonality in
implementation or use.

There is no online catalog at this time, in the same sense that there is a
card catalog residing in libraries throughout the world. The online systems
reviewed, and others available in the marketplace, range from simple to
complex, functionally speaking, but among them all it is not yet possible to
discern a basic core of user features or a commonality in the utilization of
those features required of the user. They differ with regard to input
linguistics, access points, indexing methods, message style, output formats,
and the degree of assistance available to the bewildered, and often fearful,
first time user. Even experienced users of the major commercial and
governmental online search services experience difficulty when beginning to
use the basic capabilities of many of the online catalogs; guidance on how to
use these systems' special features to their greatest effect is usually not
provided.

Lest we seem to be too pessimistic, we acknowledge that online catalog design
has come a long way in a very short time, thanks to the intense efforts of
some very talented individuals and design teams. Some of these systems serve
the perceived needs of their local application very well. Furthermore, the
reader may wish to hypothetically design his own system, at least the user
interface component, by selecting and combining from among the features and
capabilities of the ten systems reviewed in this study. We anticipate that
this open sharing of design features, and other efforts like it, will
significantly advance the state-of-the-art in online catalog design.

4.5 New Models for Interface Design

Progress has been made on the research front as well. The issues have been refined, and a fuller accounting of the crucial variables necessary to an improved understanding of human-computer interaction has developed and now provides the direction for many empirical studies in the areas of man-machine communication and the information retrieval process. Ironically, online catalog developments have spurred many on to more rigorous analysis of user behavior with card or COM catalogs. Many questions remain regarding the optimal user interface, and some of the empirical data now being gathered and analyzed may provide the answers.

One thing is clear, our model of the information retrieval process is changing as we share insights and analyze the cumulating data together. There is now the hope that the future design of interfaces for interactive retrieval systems will be based on testable and confirmable theory. As BORGMAN (1981) outlines it, "An approach to theorizing in the area of human-computer interaction is to model the process, discern the causal processes behind the model, and explain why the process works as it does." The limited amount of such theoretical activity is explained in two ways by BORGMAN: (1) we have little understanding of how humans communicate with one another and are uncertain as to the appropriateness of applying these theories to human-computer interaction, and (2) the area of study is new and has thus far been an applied "science." Furthermore, the designers have been computer scientists or engineers rather than social scientists, and the need has been for a system that works in a specific application domain.

Describing the process, that is, patterns of purposeful behavior, of information retrieval in the use of online, interactive systems is a prerequisite for building a testable model of that process. Yet "description" depends on one's perspective along with an adequate organized collection of variables to serve as building blocks in the formulation of that description. Thus, model building is an iterative process that requires an open, questing mind particularly sensitive to new sources of evidence bearing on the systematic understanding of the activity in question.

The model illustrated in Figure 4 is offered by COCHRANE (1981) as "a better view of information retrieval for the 1980s." This depiction of the user-system environment and its major variables affecting online information retrieval brings us a long way from the traditional system designer's view expressed earlier by MORAN, MARCUS, and DWYER. The revised model proposed by COCHRANE is needed "because we have enough evidence now that it is the online user's behavior which can have such a heavy impact on the quality of information retrieval."

Referring to studies which show that user behavior must be shaped and guided to improve the retrieval process, COCHRANE lays this responsibility on the shoulders of the designers: "They should be inventive enough to guide the user to these opportunities." More importantly, new system design or changes in existing systems must take into account a multiplicity of system components and particularly the impact of any one of these variables on the others. The user-system interface has become the focal point for efforts to improve design and to assess the effectiveness of those improvements.

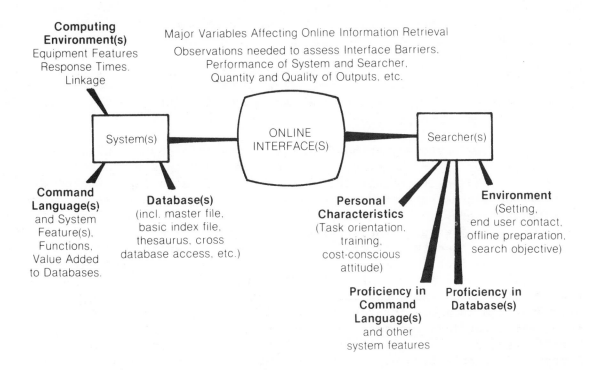

Figure 4. Major Variables Affecting Online Information
          Retrieval (COCHRANE, 1981)

COCHRANE's model is valuable because it identifies the major categories of
user variables which must be taken into consideration (such considerations to
be supported by research findings) when designing and/or evaluating an online
retrieval system. If this model has a deficiency, it may be its suggestion
that the user stands apart from the system as a whole, or its failure to
describe the components and dynamic qualities of the interface itself. The
interface is a complex process domain, and it is in that process that viewing
both the user and the computer as components of the overall information
retrieval system makes the most sense.

COCHRANE's model is an extension of an earlier version presented by FENICHEL
(1980-81) in a discussion of research issues on the man-machine interface.
FENICHEL suggests that we may divide the factors affecting the man-machine
interface into two major areas: "factors related to the system, and factors
associated with the searcher." This represents a giant step forward by
placing as much importance on the user-related variables as those pertaining
to the system. But her polarized approach may lead us away from consideration
of important but subtle complexities of the user-system interaction. The
properties and nuances of that interaction cannot be explained by an isolated
view from one side or the other of the interface.

FENICHEL is right on the mark, however, with her advice as to how we may begin
improving our online retrieval systems: "it is necessary to understand what
is actually happening at the man-machine interface in online systems." In
addition to presenting the comparative analysis of the ten online catalog
systems studied, it is the aim of this report to provide the reader with the

conceptual framework and terminology required for the understanding that
COCHRANE, FENICHEL, and others urge us to acquire. To this end we attempt to
extract the common structure from the user-system interfaces we have examined
prior to the in-depth comparison of their features (see section 4.7).

One of the better definitions of the user interface in interactive systems has
been offered by MORAN (1981b): "The user interface of a system consists of
those aspects of the system that the user comes in contact with--physically,
perceptually, or conceptually."

It may not seem obvious just how the user comes into contact with the
conceptual aspects of the system. The system's concepts would seem to be
those expressed in its architecture and software, including software which
receives and interprets the user's requests, and sends messages and displays
back to the user. Normally, the system's implementation is hidden from the
user who is not aware of the architecture or processing algorithms. MORAN has
something more than this in mind: inherent in the design of an interactive
system is some model of the information seeking and processing tasks and
goal-directed activities of the user population it is designed to serve. As
the user learns and uses the interactive system, he constructs a mental model
of the system as a problem-solving tool. The designer's model of the
information retrieval process is revealed to the user as the system permits,
facilitates, or thwarts his various actions and pursuits. It is this
conceptual organization of the system from the user's point of view that is an
integral part of the user interface. "The conceptual model is the knowledge
that organizes how the system works and how it can be used to accomplish
tasks" (MORAN, 1981a). To maximize effective use of the system, this model
must be taught to the user and reinforced by the behavior of the system.
Thus, the interface can be said to include all means of training and
documentation as well.

Prior to this training and use of a new system, the user has a model of the
information retrieval process--expressed by his habits, patterns of behavior,
and expectations about the organization of the catalog and the structure of
its bibliographic records--which he brings to the new system. If the system
designer's model is fundamentally different than the user's, a situation
occurs which might be called "cognitive incompatibility" or "model mismatch."
Confusion, floundering, and frustration on the part of the user are early
symptoms of "cognitive incompatibility." If the system matches the user's
understanding of the process at a basic level, but provides options and
capabilities which go beyond this level, user exploitation of the system's
power and diversity will depend on careful training, documentation, and online
or offline assistance available to the user on demand.

It is in this context that we can understand why designers create online
catalogs that emulate the card catalog, in whole or part. Searching the card
catalog, via author, title, or subject (if available) access points, is
assumed by some designers to represent the common model of information
retrieval. The desire is to provide the same access and manipulative powers
(however few) available at the card catalog. Other designs incorporate only a
small subset of card catalog features, for example, providing only author or
title search, and displaying only one "card" at a time.

The motivation is clear. We are in a period of transition when the computer
catalog does not have a proven track record, and the catalog user is most

familiar with the card catalog. But the assumptions about the user's information retrieval activities and expectations may be faulty. We suspect, rather, that the user employs different models of information retrieval depending on the kind of information store or processing system with which he is confronted. And surely we do not yet know how and why the card catalog user searches and manipulates it as he does. We have just begun to gain broad insights into this behavior, and a single model may not be able to account for it.

Early evidence, captured by computer monitoring of user-system transactions, suggests that users of existing online catalogs are searching in ways not possible with a card catalog (LARSON, 1981). Not only are the access points entered by the user different, the patterns of search behavior throughout a session vary considerably from those possible in searching an offline, nonautomated catalog. Some have already concluded that, "There is no way that the online catalog will only be accessed as was the card catalog" (COCHRANE, 1981). The exception to this of course, would be the use of an online catalog designed to be nothing more than a card catalog, with regard to its functional capabilities and access points.

4.6 No Ideal User Interface Exists

What is the correct model of information retrieval on which we should base our design of online catalogs, or on which we should base our decision in selecting an existing online catalog? Perhaps the question is misguided. It is not yet answerable if the answer is to be supported by conclusive evidence about the behavior of many classes of a wide population of online catalog users. We have studied systems which emulate the card catalog to one degree or another. We have studied systems which incorporate the features and complexity of the sophisticated commercial online services such as Lockheed's DIALOG. We have studied systems not designed for use by the new or casual direct end user. As we said earlier, no commonly understood (internalized in the minds of the users,) online catalog exists today. Major efforts (many sponsored by the Council on Library Resources) to gather and analyze data about online catalog user behavior, perceptions, and attitudes are now underway, and many of our questions will be answered in the near future. Data acquired from systematic observation and experimentation will replace the designer's goodwill and intuitions as guides to the design of many properties of the user interface.

In the meantime we return to principles and the fundamental understanding gained thus far. The design of the user interface must be grounded in the user's model of the information retrieval process. If this model is subject to change, the system may have to be flexible enough to accommodate this change. The designer must know what knowledge of information retrieval, what characteristic tasks, and what expectations of system performance the user brings to the online catalog system. The barriers to effective communication at the man-machine interface are becoming widely known, and cognitive incompatibility between the user and the system is a real and present deterrent to user acceptance of online catalogs. All of this supports the view that "the user interface is more than an add-on component; it penetrates deep into the computer system. The user interface must be considered early in the design process if it is to be really designed and not just happen" (MORAN, 1981a).

Figure 5, The User Interface in Online Information Retrieval, is offered not
as a replacement for COCHRANE's structural model of information retrieval
(Figure 4), but rather as an attempt to graphically illustrate and highlight
the new dynamic dimension of information retrieval in online, interactive
catalogs. The area of intersection represents the user-system interface. The
major activities and processes which take place at the interface are listed in
the shaded area.

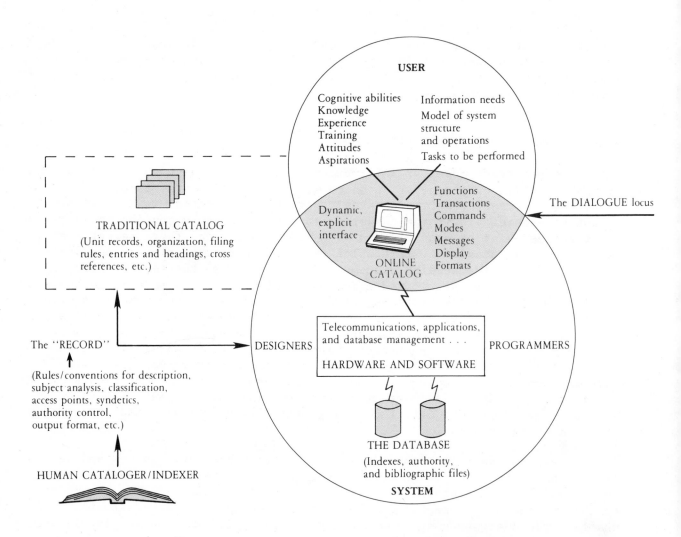

Figure 5.   The User Interface in Online Information Retrieval

Another purpose of this illustration is to identify the new human component
brought to the world of the catalog and its users, namely, the online system's
designers and programmers. It is they who design and implement the user
interface (dialogue techniques, command protocols, access points, prompts,
error messages, display formats) and thus they have a profound influence on
the nature, degree, and quality of access to bibliographic information.
Fortunately for the users of online catalogs, many of the designers have
evidenced a strong commitment to user-oriented interfaces. The variety of
user interfaces discovered among the ten systems studied indicates, however,
that we are far from reaching an agreement regarding the "feel" and properties
of the ideal user interface for searching online catalogs.

The interface is largely the creation of system designers, and thus is
familiar territory only to them in this new world of online catalogs. Users
of the commercial online search services of the last decade, primarily the
professional trained intermediaries, may feel somewhat comfortable in this
territory, but the new online catalogs are not being designed for their use
alone. These systems, to a greater or less degree, have been installed for
direct use by a variety of novice or casual end users. Some of the user
variables affecting the success of this endeavor are listed in the upper
section of Figure 5.

4.7 The Components of the User Interface

To achieve a deeper understanding of the commonalities and differences
existing among the ten systems studied, we found it necessary not only to
familiarize ourselves with the interface territories, but also to refine the
terminology encountered and extract the common structure of the interfaces.
The overall structure of the user-system interface may be divided into the
following parts or components. Each component may be said to consist of many
variables whose attributes in a given case characterize the dynamic
interaction experienced by the users of the system.

    1.   The physical component
        - input/output equipment such as VDU terminals, keyboards, printers, etc.
        - the physical structure of the workstation: desks, tables, lighting, etc.

    2.   The organizational component
        - the institutional setting, staff assistance, manual aids, peers, etc.

    3.   The personal component
        - in short, the user, in a bewildering variety of "shapes and sizes."
          (See Figure 5 and the following discussion on classes of users.)

    4.   The communications component
        - dialogue modes and techniques
        - the language of interaction: commands, prompts, messages, etc.

    5.   The functional component
        - operational control
        - search formulation control (includes access points)
        - output control
        - user assistance

The lists of variables, as indicated by the "etc.", are not complete, but
include the common options for the system designer. To illustrate how this
structural elucidation of the user-system interface aids analysis and
understanding of a given system, let us consider a hypothetical example.
(Numbers in parentheses refer to the interface components just listed.)

> *The SOC (Stupendous Online Catalog) system has been installed at
> the Plain City Elementary School Library (2) which has no
> library staff (2). Two touch-sensitive terminals have been
> placed on study tables in the library (1). No printers have
> been provided (1). A sign (2) directing the student (3) to the
> Principal's Office (2) if the computer does not work is taped to
> the table top. The touch-sensitive terminals determine the
> stages and direction of the search process (5) by employing a
> menu-selection dialogue technique (4). Each menu screen
> displayed includes guiding messages regarding the options
> offered for selection (4). The SOC system permits only exact
> title search (5), displays results in only a brief format (5),
> and provides no capability for the user to request assistance (5).*

Fortunately, the SOC system is an imaginative fabrication. But this example
not only illustrates the many complex issues surrounding the user interface in
online catalogs, it also serves to remind us of the new responsibilities (and
power) that currently are carried by the designers of these catalogs. The
many variables of the interface components can be mixed and matched in an
almost infinite variety of ways. Given any locally-defined set of constraints
or requirements (e.g., hardware or storage specifications, number of
terminals, system availability, cost ceilings, etc.), numerous options remain
for the design of the interface.

This comparative analysis of ten online catalog systems was limited in scope
to the communications and functions components (4 and 5) of the user
interface. Some basic understanding and common approach to all aspects of the
interface had to be attained to ensure the success of this research endeavor
at more than a superficial level. In the preceding chapter, the
classification of functional capabilities was presented, and a matrix format
was employed to permit comparison of the ten systems with regard to their
varying implementation of these capabilities for their users. In succeeding
chapters, the systems will be compared in more depth, with the topics being
dialogue modes, command language, indexing procedures, advanced search
features, display/print options, and user assistance features.

Human Communications with Computers:
A State-of-the-Art Review

5.1 Communicating with Computers

Both the user and the system bring varying amounts of knowledge and functional abilities to the interface. The system, presumably, also contains and provides access to information which may satisfy the information needs of the user. But, however large and well-organized the information store, and however diverse and powerful the system's functionality, a broad population of users may not be able to use it. There are many kinds of barriers or obstacles to the effective use of online interactive systems to obtain access to bibliographic information. The hardware may be inefficient or unreliable, the institution may not provide enough terminals, access points may be too few in number or kind, indexing procedures may be primitive or otherwise inadequate, and so on. The barriers to effective use of interactive systems (and the positive approaches to overcoming these barriers) discussed in this and the following two chapters are those which result from the interplay of variables which comprise the communications component of the user interface.

Since the advent of time-shared interactive systems about fifteen years ago, which GAINES (1981) labels the second revolution in the history of computer technology, human interaction with computers has more and more become characterized as a form of communication, analogous in varying degrees to human-human communication. This new dimension could not be claimed to be present in man's utilization of nonautomated machines or the early computers which operated in noninteractive modes. As BORGMAN (1981) observes, "The human-computer interaction has most of the elements of human interaction with other humans.... The human and computer must work as a team to solve a problem, and the information processing tasks must be shared between them." To accomplish this goal-directed activity, the human and computer partners "must be able to exchange meaningful information; this 'information passing process' is generically referred to as 'communication'."

BORGMAN'S paper reviews the theoretical approaches to studies of human-computer interaction which have been conducted in a wide array of disciplines. She reports that most writers accept the premise that interaction with interactive computers is a form of communication. Applying various theories and insights about human-human communication, many of the studies attempt to demonstrate the existence of the same or similar patterns and properties in human-computer interaction. Success in these endeavors is indicated not only by the demonstration of patterns of behavior common to both human-human, and human-computer communication but also by the willingness of people to carry on a conversation with a computer about some of the topics they ordinarily discuss only with other people.

5.2 The Personality of the Interface

There are good reasons to welcome what some may think is an unjustified anthropomorphic approach to the study of man's behavior with machines. The assumption that human-computer interaction is a form of communication has encouraged and directed expanded efforts in both methodological inventiveness and theory formation and testing. We have learned more about human-human communication and advanced the state-of-the-art by encouraging interdisciplinary, cross-fertilization of ideas and methods. As BORGMAN reports, there is not yet a common body of theory, nor has the "grand paradigm" emerged among the scientific community, but "one can see some common threads." Whatever one believes about the "personal" qualities of computers, studying humans and computers in their modes of interaction rather than studying each in isolation is apparently resulting in benefits to psychologists, social scientists, and computer scientists, alike. On a more practical note, these studies are producing insights for interface design which are being applied to increase the ease and convenience of use in many interactive systems.

There are empirical grounds for speaking of the "personality of the interface" or alluding to the behavioral characteristics of the system's interface. As DWYER (1981) observes, attributing personal qualities to a computer program is not illogical. Although a computer may have no native intelligence (and this issue resolves to one of meaning), "a program can be a projection of its programmer's personality." A program may or may not express the personality that we would like to experience in various modes of discourse undertaken for one purpose or another, a quality it also shares with humans.

In discussing proposed rules for programming good dialogue for interactive systems, GAINES (1981) suggests that, "This animistic view of the computer is a very useful one if not overdone--at times of doubt the question, 'well, what would I do?' is a good one." Hopefully, findings acquired from user studies will provide the answers to questions about the user's needs and preferences, and thereby replace the designer's intuitions as a source of guidance in the development of future interfaces. Nonetheless, GAINES's point is valid: "interactive programs do have a personality--usually some partial replica of that of their designer!" The state-of-the-art of dialogue design has advanced to the point, however, that the personality of the interface may range from that of a master (with the user as the slave) to a close approximation of a Socratic mentor. In what may be perhaps the worst of cases, the user is confronted at the interface with an indifferent deaf mute.

5.3 The Role of Conversational Dialogue in Human-Computer Problem Solving

What mode of communication does, or ought to, most appropriately characterize human-computer communications? Since the earliest days of commercial use of the new <u>interactive</u> computers, there has been a common agreement among computer and information scientists that the model employed should be that of human conversation. NICKERSON, et al. (1968) stressed the importance of distilling the common temporal and social properties from human-human conversation and incorporating them into the design of the interface. BASIC was designed at Dartmouth College in 1964 as a conversational programming language. Many works were to appear on the topic of "conversational computing" once advances in technology made it possible for users at remote terminals to be in direct communication with the host computer.

There are sound reasons why human conversation, even perhaps in one of its most refined manifestations--problem-solving dialogue--should be chosen as the predominant mode of communication in certain human-computer applications. Cooperative problem solving between two agents requires that the information processing tasks be shared between them. This, in turn, requires the exchange of meaningful information, that is, information responsive to feedback which may modify the subsequent response. In a specific, goal-directed problem-solving context, such mutual activity may be characterized as "transactional," or simply, interactive functional behavior. State-of-the-art interactive computer systems employing advanced database management software are particularly well suited for transactional interaction. In our Glossary we define "transaction" as "An operation or process in an interactive system consisting of a structured sequence of information and control exchanges between the user at a terminal and the system... to perform a particular functional objective. A transaction consists of a logical set of component tasks to be executed by the user and the system involving some interchange of information and control."

MEADOW (1979) has reminded us that "Online searching is probably as complex a task as is being assisted by computers today." In this problem-solving, task-sharing activity, something close to symbiosis between the human and the computer must be attained. The two performers must establish a close union and a goal-seeking interdependence. The mode of communications or information exchange most supportive of these symbiotic requirements appears to be human dialogue.

Dialogue is a form of purposeful, goal-directed conversation. (Conversation may also be, of course, undirected, or even "rambling.") The goal-directed dialogue may be required for certain problem-solving activities such as searching a bibliographic database to satisfy an information need.

What properties of dialogue make it the optimal form of communication for human-computer problem-solving activity? In addition to the symbiotic, purposeful attributes previously mentioned, STEWART (1980) reminds us that "A dialogue is by definition a two-way process.... [It] involves the sharing of knowledge by the exchange of information." Successful dialogues have these requirements:

-- Both parties must be able to send and receive information without undue constraint.

-- The language chosen as the carrier of the dialogue must facilitate the expression of subtle or complex ideas.

-- Accordingly, the interpretation and understanding of the language, its symbols and rules, must be shared to the same degree by both parties.

-- Each party must be able to grasp the context of meaning of the other party, and successfully follow or "keep up" when that context shifts or changes.

-- This, in turn, requires being responsive to the feedback of the other party and "modifying the communication so that it is better suited to the other party" (STEWART, 1980).

Mutual understanding is a key ingredient in good dialogue. If one party has difficulty in understanding the other, the partner will notice this and repeat, simplify, or otherwise clarify the message. The timeliness of message acknowledgment and response is also an important aspect of effective dialogue, as explained by HILDRETH (1981).

Warning us not to confuse a language as the medium of message transfer with the dialogue, SHACKEL (1980) suggests that "dialogue has a more dynamic implication, for human communicators, of interactive construction and modification of mutual understanding--an 'effort after meaning' as Bartlett used to say--somewhat akin to the concept of a Socratic dialogue." We are aware, of course, that current dialogue design capabilities are unlikely to generate and replicate truly Socratic intermediaries for the interfaces in interactive systems, but the fundamental distinction between language and its use in explicit dialogue accounts for the communications distinction in using an online catalog rather than a manual catalog. The new interface dimension is explicit, dynamic dialogue. We have tried to depict this difference in Figure 5.

Language can, however, impede the dialogue, and GAINES (1981) warns designers not to choose a new language completely alien to the existing situation. His second rule for programming user-oriented dialogue prescribes that we "use a model of the activity being undertaken which corresponds to that of the user, and program the interactive dialogue as if it were a conversation between two users mutually accepting this model." GAINES urges us to consider how language is actually used in daily affairs to achieve some desired result, so that all aspects of the dialogue between the user and the computer, "its vocabulary, its sequence, its consequences, appear natural to the user."

After their recent review of research on interface design, BRENNER, et al., (1980-81) report that there appears to be a consensus about the fundamental characteristic of a user-oriented system: "It should behave much like a human would and engage in a dialog with the user." They add, however, that no research to date has "conclusively" identified system features required to "optimize" the user-computer interface.

While admirable, the goals of this research (undefined in the BRENNER review) may be somewhat beside the point today. We are experiencing a period of intense development and deployment of online systems, and it is more realistic to encourage the inclusion of interface features that have come to be accepted as user-cordial through shared insight, if not actual consensus among designers and experienced users. The need now is to improve the interface, not "optimize" it once and for all time. Conclusive evidence is an appropriate requirement for hypothesis confirmation in pure research, but it is an unrealistic, misplaced requirement to apply to current development efforts. Ongoing research efforts can serve, however, as a continuing source of insight and guidance to the design and development process.

On the technical side, we are at a stage when software development techniques must catch up and keep pace with what we already know about good dialogue in particular, and user-oriented interfaces in general. As GAINES (1981) reports, there is not yet agreement among software engineers as to what constitutes good dialogue programming. "We are in a position today in <u>programming man-computer interaction</u> that we were with hardware design 30 years ago and software design 10 years ago--we are reliant on unsystematized 'craft' skills passed on erratically through fortunate 'apprenticeships'." (His emphasis).

5.4 Interface Barriers to Effective Use of Online Information Retrieval Systems

The need for improved dialogue design and programming, and the need for more "natural" interface languages, is poignantly expressed in the frustrating and discouraging encounters new direct end users commonly have with existing online retrieval systems. The design of effective, user-cordial interfaces for this new, rapidly expanding heterogeneous community of users is still in its infancy. What we are likely to experience today are modifications or extensions to the "conversational" interface of the last 10-12 years which was designed for interactive programming or information retrieval by information specialists--the trained intermediaries of this period. Retrievable "help" screens and improved error messages are typical of these enhancements. Such enhancements to the "classical" interactive interfaces of the last decade may alleviate the symptoms of user distress and ineffectiveness, but they do nothing to correct the underlying causes of these and related symptoms.

Given the knowledge and skills required to make good use of the online information retrieval systems of the 70s, the end user had little choice but to rely on trained intermediaries. The searcher not only must know a system's functional capabilities and be skilled in the use of its command language, but also be familiar with its databases, indexing policies, and their controlled vocabularies.

The effort expended by an end user to acquire this knowledge and to have these skills is not commensurate with the gain, especially for an infrequent casual end user. As SMITH (1980) observes, "Existing systems have properties which make them inconvenient for direct access by end users, properties which are often 'explained' by saying that 'the computer does not have any intelligence'." However, the installation and use of online catalogs by new or casual direct end users is expanding; thus it is imperative that we gain an understanding of the underlying causes of common interface problems and barriers to effective search interaction.

Much has been said about the general requirements for effective human-computer communication and its model, cooperative problem-solving human dialogue. But our experience with online catalogs is best explained by the observations of HAYES, et al. (1981): "Simply put, today's systems are not very good at communicating with their users. They often fail to understand what their users want them to do and then are unable to explain the nature of the misunderstanding to the user. In fact, it is the common experience of users of interactive systems, whether novice or experienced, infrequent user or regular, that communication with their machines is a time-consuming and frustrating experience." Why does this "man-machine communication barrier"

exist? Simply stated, according to HAYES, et al., the computer "lacks the
basic communication skills that come so easily to almost all of us."

Specifically, most online systems permit and respond routinely only to
commands comprising a narrow, rigidly governed, artificial indigenous
language, commands which must be entered with complete accuracy. If the user
fails to use the correct language, or makes a mistake when entering the
command, only a few systems will provide specific, informative error messages.
Even in these the user must go back and try again.

Communication between people is more understanding, forgiving, and flexible
than this. We are used to being understood by others even when we make minor
(sometimes major) errors in syntax or spelling, or even seem to wander "off
course." Another's ability to understand us even when we commit linguistic
errors surely is facilitated by the fact that the purpose of the discourse is
shared, and that the context of the stages of the dialogue are "tracked" and
adjustments made when shifts in context occur. Furthermore, we usually are
aware of one another's attitudes, personalities, and speech or writing habits.
Finally, if clarification is required, it can be requested and usually will be
supplied; also, if one party is getting too far "off track," he is usually
reminded of this and encouraged to return to the purpose or direction of the
shared activity. In a word, people are adept at focus tracking and focus
shifting, and are far more patient, forgiving, and supportive than most
computer systems.

The reader is apt to respond that all of this is well and good. After all,
the computer is a machine and not likely to become so human. The user must
learn new skills and this is a small price to pay for so sophisticated a tool.
Only a few commands must be learned, and if entered correctly, the system will
understand, obey, and respond accordingly. However, this view of
human-computer interaction, as MANN (1977) urges us to consider, is both
overly simplistic and archaic: "The dominant styles of man-machine
communications are so rigid, narrow, and alien to people's other
communications habits that achieving a suitable accommodation is often
unworkable. Thus many otherwise achievable benefits are lost."

Commands are a small and limiting subset of a person's communications
repertoire. A command language-driven dialogue with an inflexible computer
system reflects several problems of communication (SMITH, 1980, and MANN,
1977):

    --   Training and memorization of many rules and formats must take place
          before the user can begin using the system

    --   Many variations and extensions to basic features must be mastered
          before the system becomes an effective tool

    --   System is rigid and intolerant, and unable to function properly given
          minor "errors" in the user's input

    --   The system has no "working" memory, and thus doesn't know where it has
          been, what the user is up to, or where they might be headed together

    --   The user gets little or no assistance with search strategy or tactics.

5.5 Towards a User-Oriented Interface: Research and Development Efforts at the Crossroads

The state-of-the-art in research, as well as continuing development efforts, offers alternatives to this demanding, uncompromising, command language dialogue and the alien, intractable interface it presents to the user. HAYES, et al. (1981), in their quest for a "graceful" interface, have attempted to establish principles and techniques for designing a user-oriented interface to any interactive system or application. Beginning with the known and well-understood needs and conventions of human-human communication, they derive a set of "capabilities any gracefully interacting system should have." These include:

> -- Flexible parsing able to process the user's input even if linguistic errors are committed, and the ability to request clarification of the user's intent

> -- Focus tracking mechanisms that will follow the conversation, retaining context stages and shifts in direction or return to earlier stages

> -- Output compatible in detail and format with the user's requirements

> -- An explanation facility capable of (1) instructing the user how best to use the system's features, and (2) keeping the user informed of what the system is doing and why it is doing it

> -- Adaptive reaction and adjustment to the idiosyncrasies of each user, including the ability to adjust its "explanations" to the user's level of experience and proficiency.

HAYES, et al. (1981) remark that most of the software components and technology needed to build such an interface are currently understood and available.

In her review of artificial intelligence (AI) research and its implications for the direct end user of online systems, SMITH (1980) reports that AI "may offer ways to accommodate the 'casual' or 'naive' end user, who has not been trained in the use of an online system and may have need to use it only occasionally." Even now, however, available technology and software techniques allow us to "address the need for multiple levels of user interfaces" (SMITH, 1980).

A user-oriented interface for a given category of users can be designed "by augmenting the user interface capabilities of existing operational systems." Some of the systems studied in this research project have incorporated multiple-level interface features, as we will explain at a later point. Reports in the literature regarding the design and use of various user-oriented interfaces for new classes of users not experienced in the use of online systems may be found in the Project Bibliography under DOSZKOCS and RAPP (1979), DWYER (1981), GOLDSTEIN and FORD (1978), HAYES, et al. (1981), MARCUS and REINTJES (1979), MEADOW (1979), NEWMAN (1978), PENNIMAN (1981), RELLES and SONDHEIMER (1981), and SMITH (1980).

5.6 The New Heterogeneous Population of End Users: Implications for Interface Design

In his recent review of the state-of-the-art in online information retrieval, HAWKINS (1981) reports that direct searching by the end user is not yet feasible and the contributions of the intermediary are still required. "The substantial procedural differences among systems and the structural differences among databases seem to require the skills of a person who can devote much time to mastering the techniques of online searching." The important research issues he identifies under the heading of the user interface are the need for an intermediary, improved search strategy and search formulation, database quality, and the reference interview between the searcher and the user. Recognizing that the "user interface is crucial to the success of the search," HAWKINS agrees with those who believe that presently "the best mode of operation is to have the intermediary and the end user work together on the search."

This point of view may help to explain the concentration of design efforts in two areas: improved database organization and indexing, and increased functional power and flexibility for the trained professional searcher. The primary design goal has been the improvement of the quality of the results of information retrieval. Until recently, little effort has been expended to design an interface that would permit effective searching by the general end user.

The rapidly growing population of direct end users confronting a variety of communications barriers and the strenuous requirements for effective use of existing online retrieval systems has encouraged many designers to pursue a new direction in system design. As a design objective, improving the interface for use by untrained, new, or occasional end users is becoming more and more a top priority. The decision to develop online public access library catalogs forces the issue of a direct end user interface on the system designer in a rather dramatic manner. Existing interfaces must be modified and augmented to satisfy a new category of user requirements. Design efforts should now be focused on how the new or occasional end user may best communicate with the system to facilitate effective retrieval, and also, how the system may best assist the end user during the search process.

Design efforts based on these new end user requirements have been described as efforts to provide a "user-oriented interface." "User-oriented interface" is one of those satisfying, if not particularly enlightening, umbrella-like concepts. The remainder of this section will consist of an explication of this popular concept, as well as a consideration of some fundamental problems encountered when incorporating its many dimensions into actual interface design.

GOLDSTEIN and FORD (1978) suggest that "user-oriented interface", as commonly used, implies "a concern for optimizing the interface for the end user, making it user-oriented." So far, so good. But these authors believe that the term, as commonly applied to efforts to improve the interface properties of large scale bibliographic retrieval systems e.g., DIALOG, ORBIT, BASIS, or BRS, also implies "the optimization of a single interface for a large, heterogeneous user population."

Herein lies an "intractable problem," according to GOLDSTEIN and FORD. This heterogeneous population consists of many, different classes of users, and any attempt to design a single, optimal, interface for all user classes is somehow logically ("a contradiction in intent") impossible. Thus, "different classes of users are not, by and large, reflected in the actual user interface." Realistic interface design efforts will stem from the recognition of the need to provide a user-oriented interface for more than one class of user. And, according to GOLDSTEIN and FORD, advances in hardware technology not only make it possible to provide "user-cordial" interfaces for an arbitrary number of user classes, but the user having access to an intelligent terminal "may have his own customized interface."

Much has been written in the last year or two about the growing heterogeneous population of new computer users, which includes those individuals we define as direct end users of online library catalogs. Many dimensions have been used in descriptions of this heterogeneity: age, educational level, interests, experience with computers, nature of information need, frequency of computer system use, etc. Attempts to describe the common characteristics of these new users are usually couched in negative terms:

-- They have little or no programming or other computer skills.

-- They have little or no experience in online information retrieval.

-- They have received little or no training on the use of a given system.

-- They will not use the system frequently.

-- They will not use the services of an intermediary.

This approach to user classification has led, however, to a simplistic, dichotomous characterization of online users according to those that have computer skills, training, and experience and those that don't: "Although a sizeable proportion of the end-user population will be skilled personnel..., an increasing proportion will be individuals who have little or no specialist skills in computing. For these individuals, interactive systems will be simply one type of resource which they can call on while pursuing the wider objectives of their occupation or profession" (BARNARD, et al., 1981). This latter class of users has been described as "casual," "naive," "general," "occasional," and "discretionary." The other class consists of the trained, skilled, experienced expert in the person of the computer or information scientist.

This bi-level classification of interactive computing system users leaves us with no less of an "intractable problem" for interface design than that problem situation described by GOLDSTEIN and FORD. The class of nonexpert, infrequent (or beginning) users still remains a rather large, heterogeneous population. Perhaps all that has been gained by this simple classification scheme is the wider recognition that systems designed for effective use by experts are not suitable for use by nonexperts. The challenge of discovering the relevant user requirements for many kinds of users in this remaining nonexpert population is still before us.

The simple experienced/inexperienced (or expert/nonexpert) approach to user requirements and interface design is likely to result in the development of systems oriented to only two rather narrow categories of users. At the level of theory, this bi-level view has led to the conclusion that "the requirements of experienced users on the one hand, and of the beginners or incidental users on the other hand, are contradictory" (STIBIC, 1980).

After presenting a long list of the "characteristic properties of a user-friendly online system for a broad users population," properties which may be translated into user requirements for interface design, STIBIC intuitively assigns some of these requirements to the experienced/expert user class and others to the beginner or occasional user class. A member of the latter class wants, for example, a simple, transparent, helpful system. He is not willing to learn complicated rules and will not use many commands or parameters. The inexperienced user prefers clear advice as to what to do at every step and specific error messages in natural language. On the other hand, according to STIBIC, an experienced user finds typing frustrating and prefers only essential messages in concise form. He prefers complex, comprehensive coded commands, and desires the display of output data in a concise, orderly form enabling quick overview.

Studies of user behavior and attitudes have shown that a simple bipartite division of user needs, practices, and preferences cannot be supported by the data. The experienced user also dislikes learning complicated rules, uses only a familiar subset of command capabilities, and would often welcome assistance from the system. The inexperienced user equally appreciates a brief review of multiple output data in concise form. Additional findings based on sound research methods may invalidate many other theories supported only by the intuitions of the designer. In the meantime, the danger lies in the expanding development of two kinds of inflexible systems: one for the expert, and one for the beginner or novice. The beginner will not be able to use the expert's system, and the expert will not want to use the beginner's system. In most cases, they do not now have a choice. Either user will be lucky to find a system in any given location specifically designed for his level of expertise and experience.

Perhaps the fundamental error in this polar approach to the design of user-oriented interfaces is the mistaken assumption that expertise or naivete are global attributes of a given user or user class. A user may be proficient with some parts of the system, but incapable of using other features. A class of users will not share all of the class's defining properties equally, at all times. The level of motivation, for example, may not always remain commensurate with the level of training or experience, across all users within a specific class. The most adequate characterization of the heterogeneous population of new online system users is offered by STEWART (1980):

> *Of course there are more than experienced users and new users.*
> *There is frequently a continuum with people at many different levels*
> *as they gain experience, learn, forget after being absent, use only*
> *limited parts of the system and so on. The dialogue needs to be*
> *able to accommodate this range at any point in time.*

5.7 Designing User-Oriented Interfaces for Different Classes of Users

Advances in artificial intelligence research support the hope that a single system will be able to accommodate all users on this continuum by adapting dynamically with time to the user's changing levels of experience and varying learning needs. Such a system would be highly intelligent and flexible, capable of learning enough about a given user to tailor the interface dynamically during interaction with that user.

The more common approach taken today is the design of online systems oriented specifically for a given class or category of users of an interactive computing application, such as bibliographic retrieval. The functions provided, the kind and amount of user assistance, and the dialogue techniques designed into the interface, reflect the designer's interpretation of the characteristic properties of the user class for whom the system is intended. This interpretation rests, in turn, on an implicit or explicit classification of users of online information retrieval systems.

Generally speaking, users of an online bibliographic retrieval system may share many bibliographic information needs (for known items, materials for topical interests, etc.), but may vary along many other dimensions needed to characterize a particular type of user. Therefore, any classification of users involves a decision as to which dimensions are relevant to the online application in question. For example, users of an online catalog may be classified by probable frequency of use, degree of computer literacy, prior information retrieval abilities or habits, availability or tolerance for training in the use of the system, educational level, and so on.

Common dimensions under which users are grouped together include frequency of system use, proficiency in the use of the system's features, and prior information retrieval skills and habits. Specific systems are designed for users characterized by one or another mix of these dimensions. Thus, we find systems which have been designed primarily for the occasional, moderately proficient user, previously experienced only in the use of a manual card catalog. So the interface is designed to emulate the card catalog (or the designer's model of search activity in a card catalog).

Other systems have been designed for a user who is experienced in online retrieval or other computer applications, is willing to undergo training in the use of the new system, and is predicted to use the system on a frequent, demand basis. These systems function and have an interface very much like the major vendor online retrieval systems such as DIALOG or BRS.

Translating the requirements of different classes of users into interface features and actual system design is no easy task. At this early period in the development of online catalogs, the problem is compounded at the start (the classification of user types) by a common conceptual confusion in the use of various dimensions employed to classify system users. Frequency of use, degree of experience, and proficiency in use are often assumed to amount to the same thing for purposes of classification. Yet a refined analysis of user behavior and attributes reveals significant differences among these dimensions. Consider these three dimensions with their well-known poles, as continuums along which users may be characterized at any given point in time:

	I.	II.
1.	Infrequent use...............	Frequent use
2.	Inexperienced...............	Experienced
3.	Naive (non-expert)...........	Expert (in proficiency)

Users who fall to the left of column II characterizations are frequently labeled "beginner," "novice," "naive," "casual," or "occasional" users. The casual or occasional user is sometimes considered to be best characterized as between the dimensional poles. The matter is not so simple, however, for surely a well-trained, infrequent user of an easy-to-use system could have at least a moderate degree of proficiency in the use of the system. Occasional use of a complex, difficult system may keep a user at the naive stage of proficiency. Experienced users may not use a system with equal frequency, and may vary considerably among themselves in the degree of proficiency in full use of the system's features. An adequate classification of users must take these various combinations of attributes into account.

A user's experience varies not only in degree, but also in what he/she is experienced with, relevant to the design of an interface oriented to a particular user class. "Relevant experience comes in three categories" (MARCUS, 1976). First is the category of experience with computers, especially online, interactive systems. Second is experience with the bibliographic retrieval function, both manual and online methods. Third is experience with the subject area or discipline of the data to be retrieved. Online retrieval systems designed for use by professional intermediaries or expert users in general, can be explained in part by the apparent decision that the first and second categories are relevant for defining this class of users.

The "casual" or "occasional" user is not well defined within the dimensions of experience and frequency of use alone. Designing for this user class must include considerations of motivation as well. SCHILLING (1979) defines two types of casual users relevant for interface design, or as he puts it, "coping with the casual user."

The first type of use defining a unique user is "infrequent but mandatory." This occasional use is due to a basic requirement of the user's job or profession. Although use of the system may be infrequent, the task at hand can be accomplished in no other way. "The emphasis of any such system, if user satisfaction is a requirement, must be on ease-of-use."

The second type of use defining a unique user is "infrequent but optional." This user views the computer system as one way of satisfying his information needs. Motivation to use the computer system will depend largely on receiving output or results superior to those possible using offline methods and tools. In addition the value of the output for the user must be "disproportionally higher than the effort of the input."

Similar analyses of other dimensions (educational level, purpose in using the online catalog, availability for training sessions, etc.) relevant to the classification of users would prove equally revealing and possibly fruitful for system design decisions.

In this discussion we have tried to indicate the present state-of-the-art in designing online interfaces for different classes of users. Current planning and development efforts for online catalogs reflect a simple, bi-level classification of users based on an uncritical and sometimes confused reference to a limited number of user-relevant dimensions of measurement and evaluation. The user interface encountered in any given system (i.e., the dialogue techniques, command functions, access points, display formats and options among these) is a reflection of the designer's views regarding the relevant, characteristic properties of a particular user class, and the designer's decisions regarding the interface's communications and functional features most appropriate for, or best "fitted" to, a user in that class.

Faced with the necessity of designing systems for particular user classes, large scale online catalog development efforts have dealt with this problem by pursuing one of two possible alternatives:

1. One system with a single unchanging interface for one defined user class.

2. One system with two or more interfaces, each designed for a different kind of user (usually based on experience or system use proficiency). The user selects the desired interface or dialogue mode.

A third design solution to the problem of the heterogeneous population of end users is reflected in many experimental systems, but may be considered because state-of-the-art hardware/technology and software engineering can support many of the user-oriented features explored in separate research efforts.

A single system can now be developed incorporating both an adaptable and an adaptive, collaborative interface capable not only of accommodating multiple types of users, but also adaptive and flexible enough to facilitate and support effective use by a user on STEWART's (1981) continuum whose levels of proficiency or frequency of use change over time. Such an online system would take into consideration the online interaction lifetime of the user, a lifetime that is not likely to unfold and develop in a steady, linear, progressive manner. The design focus would not be on classes of users, but on the developing user. These users would learn the system unaided (except by the interface features) from the start of use and grow in proficiency and skill, but at variable rates and in a discontinuous manner. Dialogue modes or techniques, command capabilities and syntax, and additional interface features which would comprise an adaptable, collaborative online catalog system will be explained and illustrated in the following sections and in chapter 6.

5.8 Guidelines for the Design of a User-Oriented Interface

The development of online bibliographic retrieval systems for direct end use is in the earliest stages of a trial period. In very few cases has the online catalog actually replaced previous forms of the catalog for a particular user population. HAWKINS (1981) has characterized the decade of the 70s as the period of infancy for the large scale vendor supplied online retrieval systems whose interfaces were designed for the intermediary user. Extending the metaphor, most online library catalogs have just been conceived; those born, are still tied to their creator by the umbilical cord.

This early period of online catalog development provides an excellent opportunity for the forming of agreements among user communities, if not a broad-based consensus, regarding the prerequisites for system design which will ensure effective use of online catalogs by a changing population of end users. These agreements should be based on the findings of the many online catalog user studies and research efforts (both underway and proposed), comparative analyses of recently developed online systems, and review of current state-of-the-art system capabilities.

Current online systems greatly under-exploit the existing techniques and capabilities supportive of a user-oriented interface. It is hoped that comparative studies such as this will encourage the rigorous exchange of ideas on the development of user-oriented systems among system designers, library planners, and related decision-makers at various forums in the near future.

In the meantime we deem it appropriate to offer a number of attributes which may be included in the design of a "user-oriented" interface. As promised earlier in this chapter, these attributes summarize our explication of the term. A review of the recent literature on the user interface in online, interactive systems discloses many lists or sets of proposed "criteria," "principles," "standards," or "guidelines" for the design of "user-oriented," "user-cordial," or "user-friendly" systems. The reader is directed to the following sources for reviews and compilations of these design guidelines and principles: GEBHARDT and STELLMACHER (1978), RAMSEY and ATWOOD (1979), SHNEIDERMAN (1980), SMITH (1980), STIBIC (1980).

Our attempts to compile an exhaustive list of properties of the user-oriented interface, or guidelines for its design, from a review of the literature seemed endless, given the many viewpoints and varieties of expression encountered. Analysis of the lists we created began to reveal a pattern of higher-level categories of attributes recommended or prescribed for the user-oriented interface. One category would be emphasized by one writer, another category by a different writer. Some attributes were obviously related to and subsumed under more broadly understood properties. Based on the insights acquired from our considerable use of ten online catalog systems throughout the duration of this research project, we have organized the many proposed user-oriented attributes into five "guideline clusters." (See Figure 6.) No claim is made for the completeness of the list of attributes within each cluster, and we are aware some attributes could be included in more than one cluster. Figure 6 is offered as an aid to organized review and discussion of the many criteria that have been proposed for the design of a user-oriented, cordial, or friendly user-system interface.

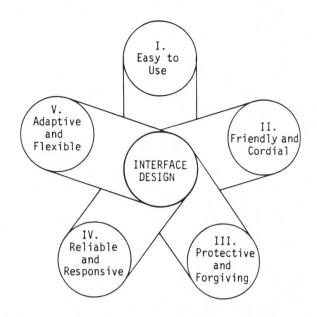

I. Easy to Use

- Easy to access and begin use
- Easy to understand basic functions/capabilities
- Easy to learn command use
- Easy to enter commands/data
- Easy to grow, advance, in use
- Easy to remember how to use over time
- Easy to refresh/relearn how to use

II. Friendly and Cordial

- Supplies specific, positive, informative and corrective error messages
- Prompts user when system is ready for input
- Requests clarification if unable to interpret user's command/response
- Immediately acknowledges receipt of user's command/request
- Keeps user informed of system's processing status or activities
- Provides "point of need" user assistance when requested
- Assumes directive control/initiative only when user requests or permits
- Provides for user's assumption of control any time during the dialogue

III. Protective and Forgiving

- Compensates for common linguistic errors by user
- Accepts common synonyms for command or parameter words
- Requests user confirmation before executing costly, dangerous, or irreversible operations
- Provides user ability to back up and recover after committing an error in logic or the use of a functional capability
- Retains point of progress when user errs or requests specific help
- Enables fast, convenient correction of input errors prior to execution
- Provides standard prompts as reminders of routine procedures
- Prohibits user damaging system or accidentally destroying search progress

IV. Reliable and Responsive

- Scheduled system availability not less than institution's user access periods
- System downtime not more than 2% of scheduled availability
- System actions are regular, predictable, and non-catastrophic
- User's work progress saved if system crashes
- System response time maintained within a range of a few seconds
- System response time for similar transactions remains uniform over time

V. Adaptive and Flexible

- Provides user selection of default values for parameters, display formats, etc.
- Provides user selection of dialogue mode and system message length
- Provides user capability to select content, format, and sorting sequence of display/print
- Provides a modular command language with developmental syntax and "add on" functional extensions to accommodate changing user ability levels
- Monitors user's proficiency with commands and functions, and supplies prompts when need for assistance is detected
- Adapts dynamically with time to accommodate user's changing need for guidance with search strategy/formulation, and provides guidance when appropriate

Figure 6. Guideline Clusters for the User-Oriented Interface

6

6.1 Two Approaches to Interface Design for the Online Catalog
6.2 Command-Driven or Menu-Driven? A False Dichotomy
6.3 A Classification of Dialogue Modes and Techniques
6.4 Eclectic Dialogue Composition
6.5 Dialogue Characteristics of Ten Online Public Access Catalogs
6.6 The User-Adaptable, Collaborative Interface

Human Communications with Computers: Dialogue Modes and Techniques

6.1 Two Approaches to Interface Design for the Online Catalog

Creating the ideal interface or mix of interfaces for the new heterogeneous population of direct end users of bibliographic retrieval systems will require a unique synthesis (based on cooperation and shared commitment) of all the best intellectual and technical resources currently reflected in various research programs and online design efforts. This will not occur overnight; the institutional underpinnings and broad-based sanctions required to support and encourage such a massive, cooperative development effort have not yet taken form. What we are seeing in the meantime are many relatively isolated online catalog development efforts; many wheels are being invented over and over again. The proprietary interests of commercial competitors may explain some of this isolated development, but most of the institutions currently developing online systems are not-for-profit institutions. Competition among some of these institutions is as rife as it is among the for-profit vendors. Systems are being developed in isolation and relative secrecy. Only when the product is installed are "outsiders" welcomed to visit and view the marvels of the newly born online system.

As discussed in section 5.7, individual design efforts to build a user-cordial interface for new direct end users of online catalogs follow one of two approaches:

1.   A single interface for a given class of users (the definition of the intended class varies), and

2.   Dual or bi-level interfaces for two distinct classes of users (implicitly defined as the "experienced/expert" class and the "beginner" or "occasional use" class).

Although time and cost constraints are invoked in justifications of the first approach, determinations of the all-important user class to be served remain vague, obviating any systematic effort to discover the relevant user requirements of that class. Typical class definitions are "public library users," "academic library users," "researchers," "casual users," and "experienced users." Among those institutions choosing the first approach (one user, one interface), including those designing for the "same" class of users, a wide range in the variety of user interfaces has been provided. Systems designed explicitly for the same class or category of user offer different kinds and amounts of assistance to the user, vary considerably in

the rigidity of input syntax, offer messages ranging from the coded or cryptic
to the verbose, and employ fundamentally different kinds of dialogue
techniques.

6.2 Command-Driven or Menu-Driven? A False Dichotomy

Even though a variety of interfaces has been designed for online retrieval
systems, discussion with designers inevitably reveals their belief that the
interface-design decision reduces to a choice between two alternatives: (1)
command-driven dialogue, or (2) menu-selection dialogue. These are the terms
used most frequently to classify the fundamental types of user interfaces.

Command-driven dialogue is represented by the "classical" online retrieval
system interface developed in the 70s by the major search system vendors (e.g.
DIALOG and BRS). Commands are entered in an artificial language by a trained
user; system response is limited to simple prompts, error messages (terse),
postings, and the display of user-selected index/thesaurus terms or search
results. No "discussion" takes place between the system and the user, and the
system is passive until commanded by the user. A broad array of commands may
be provided, giving the user increased control and flexibility.

Successful efforts to improve the cordiality and ease of use for the
experienced searcher have included simpler, more natural command languages,
and more informative error messages. However, due to the training and/or
experience required for the effective use of command-driven systems, designers
faced with a population of new or casual users unable or unwilling to undergo
this special training often have opted for an entirely new means of
human-computer communication: the menu-selection technique.

With menu-selection, users do not have to learn a specialized language and
laboriously type commands at a terminal keyboard. Instead the system offers a
series of menus listing choices for commands, parameters, and display formats.
The user simply indicates his choice from the displayed list, usually by
typing its line or entry number. It is possible with some menu-driven systems
for the user to complete a lengthy session having only to enter numbers and/or
depress a few simple function keys (e.g., "YES", "NO", "RETURN", "MORE"). The
system retains control of the dialogue, as the user can only select from the
menu being currently displayed on the screen.

Several problems exist with this simple classification of dialogue which
includes only two types, command-driven and menu-driven. The term
"command-driven" is misleading because either technique enables the user to
input commands to the system. A command is a user-entered request at the
terminal for the execution by the computer of a specific operation (e.g.,
database search, brief display of results, index display, etc.).
Command-entry methods include typing a predefined character string on a
typewriter-like keyboard, depressing a special function key, or responding to
a question or option list displayed on the screen by touching an appropriate
point on the screen or typing a number from the option list. Differences
among command input methods are differences of format or style.

However, command-driven and menu-driven dialogue modes or techniques have
commonly been viewed as mutually exclusive. It has been thought that an
interactive system could be characterized by one or the other, but not both.

The properties of <u>control</u> and <u>flexibility</u> are frequently used to explain this distinction.

In a traditional menu-driven approach, a hierarchy of menus is presented to the user. After the initial selection is made, the system displays a new list of alternatives within the area previously selected and the process is repeated until all the information that is required for a complete transaction has been elicited from the user. After this multiple-screen selection process is complete, the system responds to the user's request. With a system employing only this dialogue technique, the user has little control over the transaction sequence. The designer has determined all the choices that are required in "typical" search and retrieval transactions, and has structured the sequence of menus according to a predetermined, linear path. The flexibility to choose either an alternative path or the desired commands at any time is denied the user who must go through the full menu-selection process as presented by the system. On the other hand, the classical "command-driven system" provides greater control and flexibility for the user. The user may choose a direct path to the retrieval goal (if the right command and parameters are known), or proceed circuitously in a nonlinear manner, backing up, changing direction before a search sequence is complete, etc.

This emphasis on the properties of control and flexibility has led to a confusion of <u>levels</u> of meaning regarding the concept of human-computer dialogue. We suspect that the original concern with control and the division of dialogue into two mutually exclusive types has its roots in the paternalistic and protective instincts of system designers faced with untrained end users. The unstated goals were two: (1) protect the system from misuse, and (2) lead the naive user unerringly through the mechanics of the system, once the system has elicited the intent and objective from the user (through the use of questions or menu lists).

However, both in theory and practice, command languages and menus, as dialogue <u>techniques</u>, may be seen as mutually supportive components of the same interface. Menus can be (and are) used in a limited way in a user-initiated command language dialogue to inform the user of multiple choices at a given point. The user may select from the menu, or ignore it and enter a command of his own choosing. In fact, a menu is just a way of presenting choices and asking questions. The system may also ask a singular question, requiring that the user answer by filling in a blank or indicating "YES" or "NO". The point is this: when a dialogue technique is removed from exclusive association with the locus of control, system or user, that technique may be used in combination with other techniques throughout the interactive dialogue to most effectively communicate with a given class of users.

Fortunately, the designers of the ten online catalog systems reviewed in this research project share this insight. Our early attempts to characterize the dialogues of the ten systems as either command-driven or menu-driven proved inadequate simply because other techniques were discovered in the dialogue patterns of each of them. Also, the question of control was answered in experience; it shifts from time to time within a given system, and is always limited to no more than a set of commands appropriate to the user chosen logic of the search transaction (e.g., one would not choose to view a portion of an index of single terms, then command the system to display one of them in full MARC format!).

6.3 A Classification of Dialogue Modes and Techniques

A new dialogue classification scheme or structure had to be constructed to account for the richness and variety of communication modes at the interface. Our experience with multiple online retrieval systems and reviews of the research-based literature uncovered many dialogue techniques, including many variants of those best known.

Current discussions of dialogue modes and techniques can be very confusing. Menu-selection is used to mean anything from the overall mode of control, to a specific terminal device (touch-sensitive screens). Commands are assumed to belong to only one dialogue technique (formal, artificial programming or query languages). Figure 7 represents our attempt to analyze the conceptual territory of human-computer dialogue, and to clarify the meaning of key concepts as that meaning is reflected in actual dialogue implementation.

Discussions of dialogue modes (styles) or techniques of interaction often confuse levels of meaning, on the one hand, or confuse software-based properties of dialogue with physical devices, on the other. At the highest level, as depicted in Figure 7, the general modes of dialogue are distinguished by the predominant locus of control, user or computer. This locus of control may fluctuate during the actual use of some online systems, or may be fully integrated and shared according to the level and progress of the dialogue in an adaptive system.

Interactive dialogue may also be divided into user-to-system and system-to-user communication. In the latter case, system communication may be classified as directive, suggestive, or passively silent. We have used the notion of prompting to characterize these three types of dialogue. Among the many meanings of "prompt" are "to move to action," "cue," "urge," and "to assist by suggesting something forgotten or imperfectly learned." System prompts may serve various purposes: to indicate system readiness for input, direct the user to the next required action, suggest a course of action, warn the user of a dangerous or erroneous action, ask the user what to do next, or simply seek clarification of a user request or response.

Directive prompts belong to the general category of dialogue mode that is computer guided and controlled. This type of dialogue is based on a preestablished course of action, and consists of messages which direct the user to a required action or forced choice. Examples are:

ENTER AUTHOR'S LAST NAME:

DO YOU WISH TO ADD TO YOUR SEARCH? (YES/NO):

LINE NUMBER?

TYPE CALL NUMBER IN THIS FORMAT (Format shown)

21 RECORDS RESULT FROM YOUR SEARCH REQUEST. DO YOU WISH TO DISPLAY ALL RECORDS? (YES_NO_)

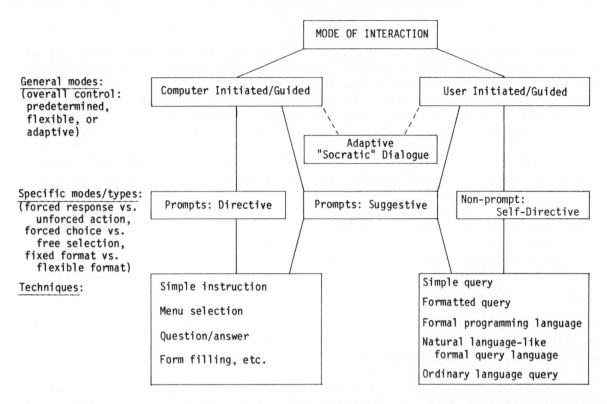

Figure 7. Dialogue Classification

Suggestive prompts inform the user of possible action(s) which may or may not
be taken. The user is free to pursue the suggested course of action, select
from among a specific set of choices offered, or pursue an unstated course of
action in a self-directed manner. Guidance on how to proceed frequently
accompanies these suggestions for further action. Examples are:

PRESS RETURN (OR TYPE NS) TO SEE THE NEXT SCREEN.

FOR A REVIEW OF COMMANDS TYPE "HELP" OR "?"

TO DISPLAY THE RESULTS OF YOUR SEARCH CHOOSE ONE OF THE AVAILABLE FORMATS:
1. SHORT 2. MEDIUM 3. LONG 4. MARC

YOUR SEARCH RESULTS EXCEED THE MAXIMUM FOR RETRIEVAL. LIMIT YOUR RESULTS
BY ADDING A DATE OR FORMAT QUALIFIER TO YOUR SEARCH STATEMENT.

ENTER "BIB" TO SEE A DISPLAY OF THE FULL RECORD.

SEARCH TERM NOT FOUND IN INDEX.
DO YOU WISH TO SEE ADJACENT TERMS?

NO RECORDS MATCHED THE SEARCH. TRY THE TERM SEARCH; IT'S MORE GENERAL AND
MAY GIVE BETTER RESULTS.

TYPE i TO RETURN TO INDEX. TYPE e TO START OVER. TYPE h FOR HELP.

YOU MAY START A NEW TITLE, AUTHOR, OR SUBJECT SEARCH FROM ANY SCREEN.

Suggestive prompts are usually found in a user-guided dialogue mode, but may
appear at some points in a dialogue that is predominantly computer guided.
The tone or format of a prompt may not be sufficient to distinguish the
directive from the suggestive. However, the system's response, in the form of
an error message, a reiteration of the prompt, or command execution, will
indicate whether a user action taken following a prompt has been permitted.

Systems which limit messages to the user to terse, noninstructional error
messages, input readiness symbols, or screen labels (e.g., "Page 1 of 2",
"More") are classified as "non-prompt" in their dialogue mode. In this mode,
no assistance or instruction is provided in the system-to-user dialogue. In
these systems, interaction is primarily controlled by a self-directed, trained
user. The user-to-system dialogue may, however, employ several different
dialogue techniques, including formatted argument entry (e.g., matched-code,
derived search keys) and formal command languages with a rigidly governed
parametric structure.

Dialogue techniques should not be confused with dialogue modes simply because
the same technique (i.e., how the interaction is structured and actually
performed--giving orders, taking orders, offering choices, asking questions,
filling in blanks, etc.) may be used in either the user-guided or
computer-guided mode. The system may present a menu list or ask a simple
question either of which the user may be free to ignore. A suggestive message
may accompany a menu-controlled dialogue, explaining, for example, the meaning
of each choice offered, but the user may be permitted to respond only by
selecting an item from the menu.

6.4 Eclectic Dialogue Composition

MARTIN (1973) describes and illustrates twenty-three dialogue techniques, and
HEBDITCH (1979) describes eight techniques of system/user dialogue. Yet
variants of many of these can be found in use in existing interactive systems
(HEBDITCH suggests that a "pedantic" approach could yield as many as fifty).
Our use of the ten online systems participating in this project revealed not
only "hybrid" dialogues (dialogues with two or more modes or techniques
occurring at various points throughout the session) but also mixed techniques
(e.g., one search argument input prompt employed a one-line menu, a fill in
the blank, and a YES/NO question prior to executing the search). The
dialogues in existing online catalog systems may be best described as
eclectic. Multiple modes and techniques are employed in each; only the mix of
techniques and mode of predominance varies from system to system.

We are witnessing a period of rapid change and experimentation. In addition
to the traditional input methods, eclectic online interaction between user and
system may now utilize touch-sensitive screens, hand-held keypads, and even
natural language voice input devices. Knowing when and where in a dialogue to
employ the various techniques appropriate for a given class of users,
regardless of the terminal equipment available, is knowledge still to be
discovered. "Just as a composer follows a set of harmonic principles when he
writes music, the system designer must follow some set of principles when he
designs the sequence of give and take between man and machine" (HANSEN, 1971).
The theory of dialogue composition has not been written; the world of online
information retrieval has not yet benefited from its Bach or Beethoven.
Dialogue composition is still an unprincipled, if sometimes imaginative, art.

6.5 Dialogue Characteristics of Ten Online Public Access Catalogs

Some of the many dialogue characteristics by which the ten participating
online systems may be compared are listed in Table 7. Nine of the ten systems
employed a user-initiated command language, user-guided dialogue at the
interface. None of the ten employed menu selection as the primary dialogue
technique. This may reflect the belief that the menu-driven, computer-guided
mode is too slow and inflexible for anyone except the beginning user.

Dartmouth College and the University of California have chosen the design
approach where one online system offers two independent interfaces. Each
system provides a user-entered, parametric, command language interface for the
experienced user (Dartmouth uses the BRS/SEARCH protocols), and each also
provides a computer-guided dialogue mode for the new or occasional user not
proficient in the use of the command language. The choice of modes belongs to
the user and may be exercised at any time during a search session. The
computer-guided mode in both systems employs multiple dialogue techniques
(menus, question/answer, fill in the blanks, suggestive prompts, etc.), and
thus both represent truly eclectic interfaces.

The online catalog of the Claremont Colleges was the only system reviewed
which provides a computer-guided dialogue mode as its primary dialogue mode.
All searches are entered by the user in response to various directive prompts.
An open space is provided for entering the search argument after the user
selects a search type. If the search type selected is a call number search,
the exact entry format is indicated. Using special codes, the user may
directly enter several record display commands. An introductory menu listing
available "help" displays is provided; each display may be retrieved simply by
selecting its number from the menu.

Two of the many features of a user-adaptable interface are the provisions for
user selection of dialogue modes and the desired length or comprehensiveness
of system-supplied messages (other adaptable interface features include user
selection of default values or use of an automatic instructional assistance
mode). As Table 7 indicates, only the Mankato State University online system
provides the capability of selecting a desired system message length. As
previously described, both the University of California and Dartmouth systems
offer the user a choice of dialogue modes. (Systems which permit user
selection of default values will be identified in later chapters.)

6.6 The User-Adaptable, Collaborative Interface

In their discussion of interface design prerequisites for ensuring that an
inexperienced user can make effective use of online systems, MARCUS and
REINTJES (1976) propose this principle: "A good system should train an
inexperienced user how to become an expert user in time. Therefore, the good
system should also allow for modes of operation that are efficient for the
expert user and a mechanism for conveniently switching from beginner to expert
mode at the user's discretion."

Table 7. Dialogue Modes and Techniques

DIALOGUE CHARACTERISTIC	California, University of	Claremont Colleges	Dartmouth College	Mankato State University	Mission College	Northwestern University	OCLC	Ohio State University	Pikes Peak Library District	RLG/RLIN
Dialogue mode can be selected by user	X		X							
System message length can be set by user				X						
Computer-guided mode	X[1]	X	X[2]							
User-guided mode	X		X	X	X	X	X	X	X	X
User-initiated formal command language	P	s	P	P	P	P	P	P	P	P
Menu selection	s[1]	s	s[2]						s	
Prompts, directive	s	P	s							
Prompts, suggestive	s	s	s	s	s	s	s	s		s
Preformatted form or line filling		s								

X = Dialogue characteristic applies to system

P = Primary

s = Supplementary

NOTES: 1. The "LOOKUP mode", for the new or occasional user, leads the user along the retrieval path with menu selection and prompt techniques.
2. Dartmouth's "User Cordial Interface" mode combines menu selection, question-answer, and directive prompt techniques to lead the user through the retrieval process.

A flexible interface has been thought of as most appropriate for the experienced user, and too confusing for the novice or casual user. However, a given user will experience changing levels of proficiency along the novice/expert continuum over time. System adaptability reflected in a flexible interface implies the ability of the user to choose from among several modes of interaction those best "tailored" to his current level of proficiency.

A straightforward way of implementing this interface flexibility is to present an introductory, profile-eliciting display to the user. From such a display, the user's selection of the desired modes and default values may be ascertained by using any of a variety of dialogue techniques (e.g., menu selection, multiple choice, question/answer, fill in the blank). If the user is unhappy with his choices at some point in the search session, a simple

command ("BEGIN", "PROFILE") could be entered to recall the introductory mode
selection display. More sophisticated programs could be used throughout a
session whereby the computer could elicit and construct a complete, detailed
profile describing the user's level of experience, degree and kind of
proficiency, etc. Similar programs are currently operational in the health
sciences; for example, medical histories of patients are constructed solely
through a question/answer interactive session between the patient and the
computer.

However designed and implemented, a user-adaptable interface represents an
alternative design solution to those discovered among the ten online systems
reviewed (one system, one interface, or one system, two independent
interfaces). Permitting the user to tailor the interface's operational
features to his level of experience and need for computer guidance would
include a dialogue mode selection option and the opportunity to set system
default values for such things as search field parameters and display formats.
MARCUS and REINTJES (1976) suggest additional interface options which a user
may select to design his own interface for a given session (they present the
options as mutually exclusive pairs):

1. *VERBOSE/TERSE. These modes relate to the length and
   comprehensiveness of system dialog. There could
   conceivably be more than two modes along this spectrum, but
   it may be more important to switch among these modes for
   individual messages than to establish a whole third level.*

2. *INSTRUCTIONAL/SERVICE. These modes relate to how much
   emphasis in the system dialog is put on instruction versus
   the provision of retrieval service as such. At one extreme
   there could be a completely tutorial mode whose sole
   purpose is to instruct. In general, there may also be more
   or less prompting and other instructions given in and
   around service operations.*

3. *INTERPRETED/STRICT. In a STRICT mode the system does
   exactly what the user requests. In the INTERPRETED mode
   the system goes beyond exactly what the user requested.
   For example, in a search in STRICT mode only the term as
   given by the user is searched, whereas in INTERPRETED mode
   an attempt is made to extend the search to terms related
   morphologically (e.g., as by stems) or semantically (e.g.,
   as by thesaurus relations in a Master Index and Thesaurus).
   As a second example, in the translating interface
   situation, a request that could not be translated exactly
   is, in STRICT mode, indicated as such to the user, whereas
   in INTERPRETED mode an attempt is made to find an
   approximate translation.*

4. *AUTOMATIC/ASSISTED. In AUTOMATIC mode the system simply
   goes ahead and automatically does what it thinks best for
   the user, whereas in ASSISTED mode the user is allowed, and
   encouraged, to assist the system in making decisions. For
   the examples mentioned in (3) immediately above, in the
   AUTOMATIC mode the system itself decides how to extend the
   search or make the translation whereas in the ASSISTED mode
   the system simply lays out for the user the options and
   lets him choose.*

5. *HIDDEN/EXPOSITORY*. *How much should the system tell the
    user about what is going on? In the EXPOSITORY mode the
    system exposes a great many details (e.g., all the steps of
    a login process in connecting to a remote host through the
    translating interface). In HIDDEN mode the system assumes
    that the user shouldn't (needn't) be concerned with the
    details (e.g., simply report the success or failure of the
    aforementioned login process).*

Although the existing online catalog systems offer the user little interface
flexibility, there seems to be a growing agreement among designers that, given
the variation in requirements of users of any particular system, it is
impossible to design a single, unchanging, interface which will suit all
users. Attempts are being made to include user-oriented interface qualities,
from among those listed in Figure 6, in the design of particular,
single-level, online catalog systems.

If an online catalog is ever to gain acceptance as a worthy replacement for
previous forms of the catalog, we believe that it will have to incorporate the
qualities listed in Guideline Cluster V (Figure 6). Specifically, the system
will have to provide a dialogue which is compatible with the user's level of
experience and proficiency. A system with a permanently fixed level of
dialogue cannot satisfy a community of users with a wide range of experience.
An experienced user will not want to waste time in a search and retrieval
session, plodding through tedious prompting or question/answer displays. This
entails multiple levels of communications from the verbose and instructional
to the "non-prompt" and self-directive, which may be selected by the user or,
with the inclusion of certain artificial intelligence techniques, determined
dynamically by the system as the user-system dialogue progresses.

Descriptions of experimental systems with adaptive, collaborative facilities
may be found in the following published literature: CROFT (1981), GOLDSTEIN
and FORD (1978), MARCUS and REINTJES (1976 and 1979), MEADOW (1979), and
NEWMAN (1978). SMITH (1980) reviews the implications of this research and
experimentation for improved end user use of online systems.

GOLDSTEIN and FORD (1978) remind us, however, that providing a "user-oriented"
interface is not dependent on the products of advanced artificial intelligence
(AI) research:

> *The user interface is, in reality, a matter of format; this
> includes the choice of command language as well as display
> formats. Hence the different interfaces are the result of
> subjective decisions by system designers as to the best format
> for the end user. The technology, today, allows us to separate
> the retrieval capabilities (operations) ...from the format
> (interface) presented to the end user.*

The choices of command formats, display formats, retrieval capabilities, and
related features made by the designers of the ten online catalog systems
analyzed in this research project will be reviewed and compared in the
following chapters.

7

7.1 The Use of Command Languages as a Dialogue Technique
7.2 Is There a Model Command Language?
7.3 The Conventional Model of Command Languages for Information Retrieval Systems
7.4 Design Criteria for User-Oriented Command Languages
7.5 Command Languages in Ten Online Public Access Catalogs

Human Communications with Computers: Command Languages

7.1 The Use of Command Languages as a Dialogue Technique

In section 4.7 we identified these components of the user-system interface:

1.   The physical component

2.   The organizational component

3.   The personal component

4.   The communications component (which includes dialogue techniques and the language of interaction)

5.   The functional component

In chapter 5 we presented a state-of-the-art review of research and development efforts for improving human comunications with computers. The problems and promises of designing effective, problem-solving dialogues for various classes of users were analyzed and summarized. Dialogue was characterized as a structured, goal-directed mode of communication akin to human conversation, especially as it is manifest in shared, problem solving activities. Such activities require, at least, a sharing of knowledge and insights attained by the meaningful exchange of information.

A distinction was made between human-computer <u>dialogue</u> and the <u>language system</u> which is the <u>medium</u> of communication and the "carrier of the dialogue," so to speak. SHACKEL (1980) explains this distinction:

> *Strictly, language is the underlying structure, with its various*
> *components and the rules and procedures for linking them,*
> *whereas dialogue is the interactive usage of a mutually agreed*
> *language between the communicators so as to exchange*
> *information.... While language is the transfer medium, dialogue*
> *has a more dynamic implication, for human communicators, of*
> *interactive construction and modification of mutual*
> *understanding.*

Language can facilitate or impede effective dialogue, either in system-to-user or user-to-system communication exchanges. System messages may be couched in a language incomprehensible to the user. User requests or commands may be

interpreted by the computer differently than the usual human interpretation of
that particular language construct. At the present time, languages which
computers can understand are different from the natural languages of humans.
As computer languages become more "natural-like," they still comprise only a
small subset of natural languages in terms of functionality, and richness and
complexity of expression. Even if a computer language is easy-to-learn and
easy-to-use, the dialogue it supports may be poor in expressive capabilities
or rigid and unforgiving in its interpretation and acceptance of
user-to-system messages and requests.

In chapter 6 we analyzed and classified dialogue modes and techniques (see
Figure 7). In either the computer-guided or user-guided dialogue modes,
dialogue may be further divided into user-to-system communication and
system-to-user communication (or information transfer). Special purpose
languages have been designed by computer scientists and designers for both of
these unidirectional forms of communication. More and more these computer
languages resemble the ordinary English we speak and write. No longer do
users have to converse with the computer in its native machine language or
receive error messages in hexadecimal or some other coded form.

Additional distinctions must be made, however, if we are to understand the
problems confronted by the user of today's computer languages. In a
particular system, the language may be adequate (e.g., expressive,
comprehensible) at one side or level of the dialogue, but inadequate or
problematic at the other. Languages must be carefully selected or designed to
serve two major roles in human-computer communications:

1. In user-to-system communication, the language must facilitate the
    entry of commands or requests by the user, or the provision of data
    requested by the system. A command or sequence of commands instructs
    the computer to execute the operations required for the performance
    of the desired function. A request may only state the results
    desired by the user, not the step-by-step method of execution. This
    difference has led to a distinction between "nonprocedural" and
    "procedural" command languages. In reality, the difference is usually
    one of degree. Command languages vary in the amount of procedural
    language (e.g., verb-object clauses) which is explicit rather than
    implicit.

2. System-to-user communication includes prompts, diagnostic and error
    messages, and "help" facilities. As previously indicated in chapter
    6, prompts may be classed as suggestive or directive. More
    specifically, they may serve to direct (the user must follow), guide,
    query, warn, inform, induce or convince. These are among the typical
    speech acts of shared problem solving. Error messages range from
    reporting a mistake on the part of the user, to describing what it is
    and where it occurred, to explaining how to correct it and avoid
    making it again in the future. "Help" messages, when retrieved or
    automatically displayed, range from brief, simple reminders of
    correct entry procedures, to extensive computer-aided tutorial
    packages. This "side" of the dialogue has developed in recent years
    to be much richer and more natural in expressive capabilites than the
    user-to-system side of the dialogue.

In terms of user-to-system dialogue, most online public access catalog systems can be classed as command language systems (see Table 7 in chapter 6). In most command language systems, a command-execute cycle describes the interaction: the user enters a command which the system immediately executes, the user enters another command, and so on.

Command language systems may be described and analyzed at two levels, the semantic level and the syntactic level. At the semantic level, one may speak of the objects or data structures (records) and the operations on these objects (search, display, sort). The user brings to the system some conception of the structure and organization of its records, and some notion of the operations which may be performed on these records. These files, records, and the operations which may be performed on them represent the system's functional capability.

At the syntactic level, possible operations on these records are expressed by the command language. Command languages are constructed from a few linguistic elements, and are governed in use by a few rules and conventions for combining those elements. Commands are imperative statements (explicit in a command language dialogue) issued by the user to the system specifying an operation or operations to be executed for the performance of a function. Syntax defines what the user must say to the system, and how he must say it, to get the system to execute the required operations.

The semantics of the commands indicate what each command means and under what circumstances each is to be used. Speaking of the computer-based constraints on user-to-system dialogue, MORAN (1981) explains:

> The syntax is constrained by the conventions of the computer's
> interface language, and the semantics are determined by the way
> the computer interprets the statements from the user.

Special purpose command languages, generally known as query languages, have been invented for use in information retrieval systems. A query language permits the user to translate his image of the database, the structure of its records, and his notions of what a computer can do by way of searching and retrieving, into an expression of what he wants done. Since the user brings some notions of the information store (database) and the computer's capabilities to the query process, the semantics and syntax of the query language should be designed to accommodate these conceptions. Although limited in syntax and vocabulary when compared to natural languages, query languages should not feel uncomfortably unnatural. Otherwise, all but the mandatory user may simply refuse to use them.

Unlike natural language discourse among humans, there is no generally adopted syntax reflected in the command language systems employed by the majority of the OPACs. Yet most designers agree with GOLDSTEIN and FORD (1978) that constructing a command language and system message facilities is merely a matter of format design, largely independent of the system's functional capabilities. The variety of syntactic requirements placed on the user for evoking the same function in different OPACs is evidence that system designers cannot agree which command language format is the optimal format for a wide variety of users.

7.2 Is There a Model Command Language?

We narrow the scope of this question (in this section) to considerations of
the linguistic elements and structure of a command language. Our analysis of
commands takes place at the <u>syntactic</u> level rather than the <u>semantic</u> level
(which focuses on the functional capabilities and logical relationships of
commands).

A <u>model</u> command language for information retrieval purposes may be constructed
either <u>descriptively</u> or <u>prescriptively</u>. These two approaches are frequently
confused in discussions of command language design. The descriptive approach,
properly applied, would involve collecting those linguistic attributes common
to most query languages in use, and presenting them in a format independent of
any particular language in use. This descriptive model would best be used for
hypothesis formation and testing regarding user needs and preferences for a
command language.

The prescriptive approach to model building or selection includes the aim to
recommend, explicitly or implicitly, a single model as the optimal command
language system for a particular application and/or user class. The
prescriptive model may be constructed from a designer's insights and
imagination, or a particular command language in use may be selected and
prescribed (at least structurally) for all similar applications (e.g.,
information retrieval) supported by different computer systems.

The problem with the descriptive approach to model building is that a wide
variety of query languages may be found in use, especially in online public
access catalogs. Any attempt to collect those linguistic attributes "common"
to most of them would involve an arbitrary decision to omit variations found
in several OPAC systems. The implications of this variety for descriptive
model building and hypothesis testing are obvious: different models must be
employed in repeated experiments until one is found to best "fit" the user's
needs, abilities, and preferred practices.

In discussions of command language design, the descriptive and prescriptive
approaches are often confused and merged. Recommendations for the design of
future command languages often refer to the "classical" or "conventional"
model of command language systems, or some subset of the properties of this
conventional model. This conventional model is usually selected from an
existing command language which, with minor enhancements, is recommended as
the <u>standard</u> language or optimal <u>common</u> command language for users who must
access and use heterogeneous retrieval systems. However, research findings do
not yet support the prescription of the conventional model as the most
effective command entry technique.

The common assumption behind today's standardization efforts is that a model
(prescriptive) exists which should guide future command language design
efforts, at least at the syntactic level. The Common Command Language
specified for EURONET's search services, the ANSI Z39-G draft recommendations,
and the language employed in the CONIT system's "virtual interface" to
heterogeneous systems share this assumption. They have adopted or recommended
common, "standard" command languages that are strikingly similar in
syntactical properties. This model command language is, in reality, the
conventional model exemplified by the query languages of the major vendor-

supplied information retrieval services developed in the 70s. These services include DIALOG, ORBIT, and BRS. Surface variations appear in the query languages of these three systems, but the underlying syntactical structure and elements are the same and all three languages represent the conventional model that has been proposed as the standard for information retrieval command languages.

This conventional model is described in the next section; however, it should be noted in advance that not all the OPACs we have used employ command languages derived from, or compatible with, the conventional model. Although we support standardization efforts in principle, we believe that conclusive evidence gained from interface experimentation and other user studies must determine the "model" command language to be adopted as the standard for bibliographic retrieval in online public access catalogs.

The description of conventional query languages will serve to identify the categories (at the syntactic level) important for comparing and evaluating the different languages employed by OPACs and other information retrieval systems. Until more evidence is brought to bear on the design of good query languages for OPACs, we may consider what appears to be a consensus among researchers and designers regarding the general requirements for a user-oriented command language:

1. Criteria or specifications for the design of a command language should be consistent with guidelines or principles for the user-oriented interface, such as those listed in Figure 6 (section 5.8).

2. Specifically, a user-oriented command language must be easy-to-learn, easy-to-use, and easy-to-remember for the casual and occasional user of the system.

7.3 The Conventional Model of Command Languages for Information Retrieval Systems

Until recently, the majority of online information retrieval systems have employed specially constructed command languages as their primary dialogue technique, hence the misleading usage of "command-driven" or "command-based" to classify these systems. Whatever dialogue technique is used, all online retrieval systems are command-based. A command instructs the system to execute one or more operations. In a user-initiated, command language-based system, an artificial language with a controlled vocabulary of keywords governed by rules for their combination is used to issue commands and requests to the system. This language is usually explicitly procedural, to a greater or lesser degree. It is used as a dialogue technique to tell the system precisely what to do to achieve some desired result.

In the conventional model, commands are imperative statements issued by the user to the system. Specifically, the command string is patterned after English imperative verb clauses. MEADOW and COCHRANE (1981) describe the conventional command syntax:

> *In general, a command to an information retrieval system is an*
> *imperative sentence, consisting of a verb and an object of the*
> *verb, such as <u>begin eric</u>. Sometimes the object is a compound*
> *one, such as <u>print au, ti</u>. Continuing the analogy to natural*
> *language, the object could be a clause made up of one or several*
> *phrases. It is also possible to have no object, just the*
> *verb.... It is even possible for the verb to be implicit and to*
> *state only the object.*

Commands having verbs and simple or compound objects may also have additional
elements which qualify the command action (the verb) or the object of the
action. These various options may be illustrated using the structural
analysis of command statements proposed by MARCUS and REINTJES (1976).

A command consists of a command <u>name</u> followed by one or more <u>arguments</u>
followed by a command <u>terminator</u>. The arguments or other command elements are
separated by <u>delimiters</u>. <u>Operators</u> may be used to form compound object
arguments, and <u>qualifiers</u> may be used to modify arguments. A command is
defined by its arguments which are specifications of objects used by commands.

> *Many commands require arguments to qualify the function that is*
> *to be performed, or to specify the objects upon which the*
> *operations are to take place (HUCKLE, 1981).*

As an illustration of this structural analysis of commands, consider the
following:

FIND TI JOY OF COOKING

"FIND" is the command name. What follows is the argument. "TI" is a reserved
keyword which qualifies a search parameter, in this case indicating the field
to be searched (title). "JOY OF COOKING" is the search term or object.
Spaces are used as delimiters, and presumably depressing the carriage return
key serves both as a command terminator and the end-of-message indicator.
When commands are "stacked," semicolons are commonly used to terminate one
command and separate it from the next command.

More complex command statements having additional elements may be analyzed
with this approach.

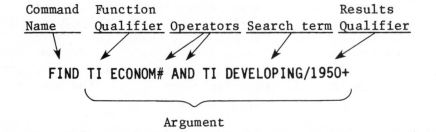

In this command statement, spaces are used as delimiters, but special
punctuation ("/") is used to indicate a sub-argument restricting the results
of the main argument. Special characters are used to indicate truncation
("#") and "equal to or greater than" ("+"). The rules may permit abbreviation
of the command name to "F" or "FIN." The command name is a common English
word which clearly indicates the action to be taken, and the Boolean operator

("AND") is entered explicitly. The characters may be entered in either upper or lower case.

This structural analysis facilitates the identification of <u>critical issues in the design of command languages</u> and the evaluation of existing languages. Many of these critical issue categories which follow are equally pertinent to the evaluation of command languages that do not conform to the conventional model.

1. <u>Command names</u>
    What should be the choice and grammatical form of command names when their explicit entry is required?

2. <u>Format (phrase structure)</u>
    Should the structure be analogous to natural language phrase construction? Should the entry order of argument elements be fixed or flexible?

3. <u>Parameter qualifiers</u>
    Should search field or display format qualifiers, for example, be expressed by keywords or special characters?

4. <u>Abbreviation rules</u>
    Should abbreviations be permitted for all commands and qualifiers? Do these abbreviations need to be uniform in character length?

5. <u>Punctuation</u>
    In addition to serving as delimiters, what role is required for punctuation? Should punctuation replace English words or their abbreviations to indicate command functions or parameter qualifiers?

6. <u>Special characters</u>
    Since special characters require complex keyboard manipulation, should they be avoided by using simple keyword mnemonics (e.g., "TR" rather than "#", "GT" instead of ">")?

7. <u>Explicit/Implicit entry and default values</u>
    Which elements of the command may be omitted under certain conditions? Should the user have the option to explicitly override system-supplied default values for a command or qualifier?

8. <u>Compound/Multiple phrase arguments</u>
    Should the system permit the entry of a compound or multiple phrase argument in a single command statement?

9. <u>Developmental syntax</u>
    Should the language permit the use of advanced, special features by simple extensions to the basic commands, or require the user to learn another set of commands for complex operations?

These categories comprise the major areas of investigation and concern for researchers and designers who wish to provide new or casual end users an easy-to-learn, easy-to-use, effective command language for communicating with the computer. Any of the categories listed may serve as a focal point when comparing the properties of different command languages used in today's OPAC systems. While the use of a set of commands comprising a formal query language is seldom the only means of supporting user-to-system dialogue, each of the OPACs analyzed in this study employ, at least as a supplemental command entry technique, a command language consisting of controlled keywords or symbols governed by rules for their use and combination.

7.4 Design Criteria for User-Oriented Command Languages

Some of the barriers to effective communication with interactive computer systems were discussed in chapter 5, and a summary list of guidelines for the design of user-oriented interfaces was presented in Figure 6. These "guidelines" are a structured compilation of the current opinions of researchers and designers regarding the properties which should be designed into any user-oriented, user-cordial interface. Criteria or standards for the design of command languages should be derived from, or be consistent with, these interface guidelines. No standard method or formula exists yet by which interface guidelines can be uniformly translated into specifications for the design of command languages. However, the increasing number of studies of effective interfaces for various user classes promises to provide the missing links between the general guidelines and actual dialogue specifications. These studies include attempts to define and measure "ease of use" factors (REISNER, 1981 and KRICHMAR, 1981), identification of the most frequent causes of error in the use of commands (LEDGARD, et al., 1980 and HUCKEL, 1981), and the psychological constraints affecting command language comprehension and retention in memory (SHNEIDERMAN, 1980). A useful, comprehensive analysis of design criteria for the syntax of query languages may be found in GEBHARDT and STELLMACHER, 1978.

While additional experimental research and studies of user behavior and preferences are needed, especially in the use of online catalogs, there is a growing consensus on a number of the critical issues inherent in designing user-oriented command languages. Figure 8 includes those command language design criteria (or principles) on which we found a great deal of agreement in our review of the literature and in our many conversations with researchers and designers of OPACs across the country. We coined some of the keywords, and take responsibility for the expression of their meanings. We hope these criteria will suggest specific questions that may be raised when comparing different command languages, and hope that some of the criteria listed will instigate controlled experiments on command language ease of use and effectiveness for searching online catalogs.

I. Semantics

1. Completeness The set of commands
    provided must be capable of evoking all
    the functions required in the user's
    model of the task domain.

2. Functionality The operational
    interrelationships among the commands
    must be flexible enough to be compatible
    with a variety of user activity patterns
    in online information retrieval.

3. Singularity Each function should be
    represented by only a single, distinct
    command, and no command should be capable
    of evoking multiple functions.

4. Modularity A basic, simple subset of
    the language, capable of evoking the
    fundamental functions, should be provided
    for the new or occasional user. The
    design structure must be hierarchical,
    permitting the learning and use of
    specialized extensions to the basic
    subset to develop in a linear manner.

5. Variety Extensions to the basic command
    core representing specialized and more
    sophisticated features should be provided
    for the experienced user.

6. Linearity The structure of the basic
    command core and its extensions should
    permit the user to proceed in a left to
    right, top down, manner.

7. Optionality Alternative ways of
    expressing commands during input should
    be supported, consistent with the syntax
    criteria listed below. This would
    include the use of abbreviations,
    flexible argument order, and user
    designation of default values for
    commands and parameters.

8. Simplicity Any complexity introduced
    should result only from the extension of
    the basic command core to include more
    powerful or refined capabilities, and
    should not result from the meaning of the
    commands or the syntax governing their
    use.

9. Consistency Command words should have
    the same meaning in all contexts, and
    syntax decisions should be applied
    uniformly throughout the language.

II. Syntax

1. Natural language structure The
    structure of the command statements
    should be patterned on familiar, natural
    language phrase structures.

2. Natural language keywords Command
    keywords should be short, familiar words
    chosen from the user's natural language,
    and should clearly express the specific
    action being commanded.

3. Abbreviations Self-evident
    abbreviations should be permitted, but
    governed by easy-to-remember, uniform
    abbreviation rules.

4. Punctuation Punctuation required for
    command construction should be kept to a
    minimum and be limited to universally
    familiar symbols. Blank spaces should
    serve as delimiters.

5. Argument position The positioning of
    arguments following a command word should
    be flexible and not governed by a
    predefined, rigid ordering of components.

6. Syntax compatibility Command syntax
    should be compatible with display syntax.

7. Default states Default states for
    commands and parameters, as well as the
    capability to set or reset them, should
    be provided for the user.

8. Special function keys The user should
    not have to learn specialized keyboard
    techniques. The use of special function
    keys or control key combinations should
    be kept to a minimum. Entry in either
    upper or lowercase should be permitted.

Figure 8. Criteria for the Design of User-Oriented Command Languages

7.5 Command Languages in Ten Online Public Access Catalogs

Although the command languages reviewed in this study were designed to
facilitate access to bibliographic records in library catalogs via the
traditional (and other) access points of author, title, and subject, little
similarity exists in command language vocabulary or syntax. The command
languages analyzed range from the simple and terse, to the powerful and
complex. When classed by types of users for which they were apparently
designed (e.g., technical staff, public service librarians, academic patrons),
the differences in vocabulary and syntax are even more striking. We have
observed what one author has called "command language sprawl" (BEECH, 1980):

> *In the absence of any accepted criteria for curbing command
> language sprawl, the progressive designer has a wealth of
> opportunities... Now consider the stronger requirement, which
> is not for the improved design of a variety of command
> languages, but for consensus to develop about the syntax and
> semantics of a single language (or at most a very few languages)
> which would ease the life of users of multiple systems, whether
> used directly or via networks. (author's emphasis)*

What follows are brief sketches of the command languages employed in each of
the ten OPACs included in this study. We do not attempt to list here all the
functional capabilities which may be performed by the use of each system's
commands. Our comments on each of the systems are based upon the command
language analysis presented in sections 7.2 and 7.3. Some of the OPACs
conform very closely to the conventional model described in section 7.3.
Other OPACs reflect interesting variations to the conventional model in their
command languages, and some depart from it altogether. When reviewing the
command language of a particular online catalog, the reader is encouraged to
raise the critical design issues identified in section 7.3 and to apply the
criteria for a user-oriented command language (Figure 8) when evaluating that
language.

Figures 9-11, which precede these sketches, illustrate the phenomenon of
"command language sprawl." They indicate the variety of syntax requirements
and options for entering a search command for the same record across the ten
systems.

```
                       SAMPLE RECORD:
                       Commoner, Barry
                       The poverty of power: energy and the economic crisis.  1976.
```

California, University of

COMMAND mode:

FIND PA barry commoner

FIN PA b commoner

FIN PA commoner

FIND PA commoner,b

FIN PA commoner, barry

   The LOOKUP mode for "new or occasional" users prompts the user with menu options (for type of search) and instructions like: "Type AUTHOR'S name below or type HELP, then press RETURN." Entry of the search term is as flexible as when in the COMMAND mode.

Claremont Colleges

ENTER CODE LETTER;D FOR CODE LIST;H FOR HELP:A
ENTER AUTHOR (AS MUCH AS KNOWN) AT LEAST 3 CHARACTERS.
INCLUDE COMMAS, SPACES, PERIODS ONLY IF PRESENT IN THE
RECORD; LAST NAME FIRST (EXAMPLE: HENLE, JAMES M)
----
commoner

[optional search statements]:

commoner, b

commoner, barry

Dartmouth College

  "USER CORDIAL INTERFACE":

Search type? A)uthor, T)itle, S)ubject, or O)ther: A
Search statement: barry commoner
Checking terms...
Do you want to add more to your search statement?
  Y or N: N
(BARRY WITH COMMONER).ME,AE.
Do you want to execute this search (Y or N)? Y
Searching...

[optional search statements]:

commoner barry

commoner

  BRS PROTOCOLS:

BRS - SEARCH MODE - ENTER QUERY
   1_: COMMONER ADJ BARRY

Mankato State University

AU commoner barry

AU commoner b

AU commoner

AU commoner,barry

Mission College

A=commoner barry

A=commoner,barry

A=commoner b

A=commoner

Northwestern University

A=commoner,barry

A=commoner,b

A=commoner

A=commoner barry

OCLC

comm,bar,

comm,ba,

comm,b,

Ohio State University

AUT/commonbar

AUT/comm-

Pikes Peak Library District

A/commoner,b

A/commoner

RLG/RLIN

FIND PN barry commoner

FIN PN b commoner

FIN PN commoner

FIN PN commoner,b

FIN PN commoner, barry

Figure 9. Command Input Syntax Comparison Chart *
(Author Search)

* A variety of options is shown; examples are not exhaustive. Some terminals
  require character input in upper case.

SAMPLE RECORD:
Commoner, Barry
The poverty of power: energy and the economic crisis. 1976.

California, University of

   COMMAND mode:

FIND TI poverty of power

FIN TI poverty

FIN TI poverty of power energy

FIN TI energy poverty pow#

F TI power economic crisis

   The LOOKUP mode for "new or occasional" users
prompts the user with menu options (for type of
search) and instructions like: "Type TITLE words
below or type HELP, then press RETURN." Entry of
the search term is as flexible as when in the
COMMAND mode.

Claremont Colleges

ENTER CODE LETTER;D FOR CODE LIST;H FOR HELP:T
ENTER TITLE (AS MUCH AS KNOWN) AT LEAST 3 CHARACTERS.
----
poverty

[optional search statements]:

poverty of power :/energy

poverty of power

poverty of

Dartmouth College

   "USER CORDIAL INTERFACE":

Search type? A)uthor, T)itle, S)ubject, or O)ther: T
Search statement: poverty energy
Checking terms...
Do you want to add more to your search statement?
  Y or N: N
(POVERTY WITH ENERGY).TI.
Do you want to execute this search (Y or N)? Y
Searching...

[optional search statement]:

poverty of power

   BRS PROTOCOLS:

BRS - SEARCH MODE - ENTER QUERY
   6_: POVERTY.TI. AND POWER.TI.

Mankato State University

TI poverty of power

TI poverty of power energy

TI poverty of po#

TI poverty of #

Mission College

T=poverty of power energy

T=poverty of power

T=poverty of

T=poverty

T=pov

Northwestern University

T=poverty of power

T=poverty of pow

T=poverty

OCLC

pov,of,po,

pov,of,p,

pov,o,p,

pov,o,po,

Ohio State University

TLS/povepower

Pikes Peak Library District

T/poverty of power energy and the economic crisis

T/poverty of power

T/poverty

RLG/RLIN

FIND T poverty of power

FIN T power poverty

FIN T poverty

FIN T power

FIN T poverty AND pow#

Figure 10. Command Input Syntax Comparison Chart *
(Title Search)

* A variety of options is shown; examples are not exhaustive. Some terminals
  require character input in upper case.

SAMPLE RECORD:
Commoner, Barry
The poverty of power: energy and the economic crisis. 1976.

California, University of

   COMMAND mode:

FIND PA commoner AND TI poverty

FIN PA commoner AND TI power

F PA commoner AND TI economic crisis

F TI poverty AND PA barry commoner

   Once in LOOKUP mode, user may choose either 1.
AUTHOR/TITLE search or 2. SUBJECT search. Selecting
1, user is prompted to enter AUTHOR's name, then
prompted to enter TITLE words.

Claremont Colleges

Not applicable

Dartmouth College

   "USER CORDIAL INTERFACE":

Search type? A)uthor, T)itle, S)ubject, or O)ther: <u>A</u>
Search statement: <u>commoner</u>
Checking terms...
Do you want to add more to your search statement?
  Y or N: <u>Y</u>
Search type? A)uthor, T)itle, S)ubject, or O)ther: <u>T</u>
Search statement: <u>poverty of power</u>
Checking terms...
Do you want to add more to your search statement?
  Y or N: <u>N</u>
(COMMONER).ME,AE. AND (POVERTY WITH POWER).TI.
Do you want to execute this search (Y or N)? <u>Y</u>
Searching...

   BRS PROTOCOLS:

BRS - SEARCH MODE - ENTER QUERY
   10_: <u>COMMONER.ME. AND POVERTY.TI.</u>

Mankato State University

CO commoner poverty

CO commoner,poverty

CO commoner pov#

Mission College

AT=commoner/poverty

AT=common/poverty

AT=com/pov

AT=commoner/pow

AT=commoner/energy

Northwestern University

Not applicable

OCLC

comm,pove

com,pov

com,pove

Ohio State University

ATS/commpover

Pikes Peak Library District

Not applicable

RLG/RLIN

FIND PN commoner AND T poverty

FIN PN b commoner AND T power poverty

FIN T poverty of power AND PN commoner

FIND PN commoner AND T power

Figure 11. Command Input Syntax Comparison Chart *
(Author/Title Search)

* A variety of options is shown; examples are not exhaustive. Some terminals
require character input in upper case.

The University of California

MELVYL, the University of California OPAC, employs a command language (in the
user-guided COMMAND MODE, but not the user-prompted LOOKUP MODE) which closely
resembles the conventional model described in section 7.3. Command names are
familiar English words (verbs) which clearly indicate the function to be
performed. The verb-object phrase structure of natural language is generally
followed, and blanks are used as command element separators (delimiters).

```
FIND PA HENRY EDELMAN
FIN PA SMITH, JOHN
F TI MONEY AND PA PORTER
BROWSE SU ENERGY OR ECOLOG#
DISPLAY 1, 8-10 LONG
DIS SUB 1-10
```

The index to be searched must be initially specified by using a controlled
mnemonic qualifier (e.g., PA for personal author, SE for series, UT for
uniform title) following the command verb. In Boolean searches, the index
qualifier for additional terms to be combined may be omitted (except when the
initial index is personal author). The system will assume all keywords are to
be searched for in the index explicitly named.

All command words may be abbreviated to the first three characters. FIND,
DISPLAY, and HELP can be abbreviated to the initial character ("?" may also be
entered for HELP).

Names of personal authors may be entered in either direct order or inverted
order. Since the searching of other indexes (except the numbered indexes) is
keyword searching, the words may be entered in any order. MELVYL assumes that
a Boolean "AND" has been inserted between the words. If another logical
operator is desired, it must be entered explicitly by the user. The order of
the elements following the display command (format, record number(s)) is
flexible.

Keyword truncation to as few as two characters is indicated by the use of the
special character, "#". This symbol may only be used at the end of the
keyword character string.

Compound search arguments in a single command are permitted by the use of
Boolean operators. After the completion of a search, the search may be
modified on a new line by adding on another argument (index and keyword)
preceded by a Boolean operator. Results may be limited by the publication
date by entering AND DATE 1979-, for example. Consider the following
dialogue:

    ->   f su organic chemistry

          Search request: F SU ORGANIC CHEMISTRY
          Search result: 1037 records at UC libraries

    ->   and su date 1980-

          Your modification would have produced zero results.
          Your previous result remains in effect.

          Search request: F SU ORGANIC CHEMISTRY
          Search result: 1037 records at UC libraries

          and date 1979-

          Search request: F SU ORGANIC CHEMISTRY AND DATE 1979-
          Search result: 97 records at UC libraries

    ->   dis sub 1-20

          Search request: F SU ORGANIC CHEMISTRY AND DATE 1979-
          Search result: 97 records at UC libraries

          1.
          Subjects: Nuclear magnetic resonance spectroscopy.
                           Chemistry, Organic.

          2.
          Subjects: Isomerism -- Congresses.
                           Carbohydrates -- Congresses.
                           Carbohydrates -- Chemical synthesis -- Congresses.
                           Heterocyclic compounds -- Congresses.
                           Chemistry, Organic -- Congresses.
                           Carbohydrates -- chemical synthesis -- congresses
                           Molecular Conformation -- congresses
                           Stereoisomers -- congresses
                           Carbohdrates -- congresses.

A special display feature permits the user to select a single field or block
of fields to display for each record retrieved (e.g., dis 245 1-5, or dis sub
1-20).

The RETURN key, when depressed, serves both as a command terminator and the
end-of-message signal. Command stacking is not permitted.

The command language of MELVYL provides a great deal of variety, optionality,
and functionality (see Figure 8 for the meaning of these terms). It is a
modular language that is consistent and reasonably simple given the amount of
variety and optionality it provides the user.

Claremont Colleges

Claremont's OPAC command entry system may be classified as a hybrid consisting of both unprompted command entry and directive prompts which either instruct the user to enter a search command or indicate the type of search argument to be entered. The unprompted commands that may be entered directly by the user are output control commands, with the exception of the "/" command which returns the user to the new search mode prompt. No search can be entered without a prior response from the user to this initial prompt:

ENTER CODE LETTER;D FOR CODE LIST;H FOR HELP:

Searches are initiated when the user enters a single character code after the colon (e.g., A, for author, T, for title, C, for call number). The system then responds with a directive, instructional prompt for the type of search selected, and the user may enter the search term on the next blank line (see Figures 9 and 10).

The review list of single character search codes must be explicitly retrieved by entering the code letter D at the end of the universal prompt line shown above, or by selecting the first "help" display from the menu of user assistance displays which is retrieved when H is entered.

Each directive search prompt includes some information on how to enter the search term. The entry of the code letter T produces this system prompt.

ENTER TITLE (AS MUCH AS KNOWN) AT LEAST 3 CHARACTERS

With the exception of the limited Boolean search (code E), keyword or component word searching is not permitted. The user must enter three or more characters of the author, title, or subject phrase as it was entered in the cataloging record (except initial articles). The author search term is entered last name first, and if included, the first name must follow the last name and a comma. However, an exact match is retrieved only if spaces and punctuation are included in the search term precisely as they appear in the stored record.

Additional unique prompts are supplied with the subject/author/title Boolean search and the call number searches. After selecting the Boolean search (code E), the user is prompted in this manner:

```
ENTER CODE LETTER;D FOR CODE LIST;H FOR HELP;E
BOOLEAN SEARCH *** SUBJECT ENTRY
WITH KEYWORDS IN AUTHOR AND/OR TITLE
ENTER FIRST SEARCH KEY:
HENLE
ENTER SECOND SEARCH KEY:
INFINITESIMAL
ENTER SUBJECT (3 CHARACTERS OR MORE OF THE ENTRY)
------------------------------------------------------
CALCULUS
```

If a call number search is requested, the user will be prompted with the proper format for entering the components of the number.

No prompts are provided for the use of the following commands:

    *USE "/" (SLASH) TO STOP CURRENT SEARCH MODE (ENTER NEW OPTION)
    *USE "@" KEY TO OBTAIN A FULL DISPLAY OF THE RECORD LAST SHOWN.
    *USE "J" FOLLOWED BY ONE NUMERAL TO JUMP FORWARD 1-9 ENTRIES.
    *USE "K" FOLLOWED BY ONE NUMERAL TO JUMP BACKWARD 1-9 ENTRIES.
    *USE "C" TO DISPLAY CIRCULATION DATA ABOUT ENTRY.
    *USE "SPACE BAR" TO SEE NEXT ITEM.
    (Extracted from a help display)

These commands may be used after a record has been retrieved and displayed
following a search. Since a single record is always retrieved and displayed,
even if it is not an exact match, the user may move forward or backward, "card
by card," in the selected file by using the J and K commands. In addition,
fast forward and fast reverse scanning may be requested by entering F or R
immediately after the initial search code (e.g., AF or TR).

With the exception of the F and R commands which qualify a search command,
only single character search commands may be entered. Most of these commands
are somewhat mnemonic (exception: Y for series search). All search commands
must be entered in the character position immediately following the colon at
the end of the universal search prompt. If a blank space is inserted, the
system will read that as a command symbol and return an error message.

When the user has begun a search and is prompted for the search term, no other
command may be executed at that point. Any command name entered, including
the "/", will be interpreted as a search term and so processed. Only after
the search is completed and a record is displayed may the user enter one of
the non-search commands ("/" is used to request a return of the searching
prompt line). As with many systems which employ menu or prompt dialogue
techniques, a degree of searching flexibility is exchanged for greater
simplicity and explicit user guidance.

Claremont's OPAC dialogue is computer-guided only to a point. After a single
record is retrieved and displayed, the user faces a "silent" screen. To
proceed, he must remember the code and meaning of such commands as "/" and
"@". Dialogues designed for the novice or infrequent user must be consistent
in their expectations of the user's ability to remember unfamiliar command
names or symbols and strict rules for command/argument entry.

Dartmouth College

The Dartmouth College OPAC offers the user a choice of dialogue modes. BRS
has created a database for Dartmouth using OCLC transaction tapes, so the user
can search directly on BRS using that retrieval system's powerful search
features. In addition to the BRS mode, an easy-to-use "user interface" (as it
is called on the help displays) for the inexperienced searcher is available
("to help you communicate with BRS"). This user-cordial interface guides the
user through the search process using a combination of brief menus, directive
prompts, and questions to which a simple "yes" (Y) or "no" (N) may be answered
(see Figures 9-11).

To select the user-cordial mode for searching, displaying results, and other
functions, a special function key (known as "the RED key") must be depressed
followed by one of the codes below. After the code is entered, the RETURN key
is used as a command terminator and end-of-message signal.

    S: To start searching
    P: To list search results
    X: To get special list options (output formats)
    D: To display previously executed search statements
    E: To get explanations
    H: To get Help
    L: To logoff (resets system for next user)
    Q: To quit (terminates the program)

Once a selection from this list (displayed on an introductory screen or the
Help (H) display) has been entered, the system assists the user with the
search (or display, print, etc.) through instructive prompts and questions.
If the search command is entered, the system responds with the series of
statements shown in Figure 9. The user is requested to enter a search type.
Only a single character code is required (e.g., A, for author, S, for
subject). After entering the search code, a prompt for the argument is issued
by the system. Since the system undertakes keyword ("free text") searching in
designated fields, the user is given a great deal of flexibility in entering
the search terms. An author search statement, for example, may be entered
last name first, or in a straightforward manner. Punctuation is not required,
and blanks are used as separators. Each user-entered message is sent to the
system by depressing the RETURN key.

When a multiple word statement is entered, the system supplies the logical
operator "WITH" to join the separate words. This search will be processed to
find records which have these words, in any order, in the same field. The
user does not have to explicitly enter the qualifiers for the field(s) to be
searched. The system assigns these (e.g., main entry and added entry fields
for the author (A) search) automatically for author, title, and subject
searches.

Compound search statements may be constructed in response to prompts for
additional search types (which indicate the fields to be searched) and/or
search terms. In the user-cordial mode, compound search arguments are
processed by the system as being joined by the AND Boolean operator. As shown
in Figure 11, the system supplies all the logical operators used. The user
merely chooses a search type and enters search statements.

Word truncation is available to the user in either the "interface" or BRS
mode. The special character, "$", is used as the truncation symbol (e.g.,
COMPUT$).

To display search results in the special "user interface" mode, the RED key
followed by P must be depressed. The system then prompts the user for the
number of the search for which the results are to be displayed. A brief
display format is provided by the system which includes location (library and
call number), main entry, title, imprint, series (where applicable), and
subject information. If the user wishes to view a shorter or longer record,
the X command must be entered. A menu of four display formats (title only,
brief, standard, and full) is displayed from which the user may choose one by
entering the first character of the format name.

To summarize, although the "user interface" features comprise a limited subset of BRS retrieval features, the user does not have to remember special command names or apply the rules of a rigid, detailed syntax. Punctuation is not required, and all commands are issued by responding to questions or by entering single-character mnemonic codes. However, some special features not usually provided in easy-to-use, computer guided systems are available to the user. These include word truncation, the use of word proximity (WITH) and Boolean (AND) operators, and the capability provided to the user to view previously executed searches, or select from among four display formats.

The experienced user may select the BRS search mode by depressing the RED key followed by C, then entering ..SEARCH followed by depressing the RETURN key. This command will return the standard BRS search prompt:

BRS - SEARCH MODE - ENTER QUERY
    1_:

BRS has published excellent system reference guides and brief command guides which explain the features of the retrieval service and the correct entry formats for commands. Only a brief summary of the command language syntax is presented here.

The BRS command language is a unique variation of the conventional model discussed in section 7.3. The user must select functional modes of interaction (e.g., ..SEARCH, ..LIMIT, ..PRINT, ..SAVE) by entering special commands. These commands instruct the system to activate the special processing functions and put the user into the selected mode of operation. The user remains in the selected mode until he explicity selects another mode. Once in search mode, for example, all commands are assumed to be search commands. The command verb is always implicit, and only the object of the verb is required for explicit entry.

The system prompts the user for each search statement by displaying a line number (user entry follows the colon):

1_: genetics

Compound search arguments may be entered using either Boolean or positional (word proximity) operators.

2_: genetics and plants

Operators must be entered as words (e.g., OR, WITH, ADJ) and preceded and followed by spaces. If no operator is inserted between the keywords, the system assumes the OR relationship. Several operators may be used in a single search statement.

3_: genetics and plants with mendel

Nested search logic may be employed using parentheses to indicate the relationships between terms. The parentheses tell the system which segments of the compound search statement to process first.

4_: (genetics and plants) not mendel

The use of special features on BRS requires learning a detailed scheme of
punctuation and syntax rules that must be rigidly applied. To qualify a
search argument by the field or fields to be searched, mnemonic field (called
a paragraph by BRS/Dartmouth) labels accompanied by decimal points must be
entered:

1_: genetics.ti. and plants.ti.

If multiple fields are to be searched, the qualifiers must be separated by
commas:

2_: genetics.ti,su. and plants.ti.

Searching on a truncated keyword requires the use of the special character,
"$". This symbol is placed immediately after the stem with no spaces
separating it from the stem. The user may also specify the maximum number of
characters that are to follow the truncated word:

3_: develop$ and politics

4_: develop$4 and politics

In multiple-element search statements, the elements must be entered in a
precisely specified order. This usually requires the use of controlled
labels, special characters, and punctuation. Consider, for example, this
print request:

2_:..print 1 au,ti,im/doc=1-6

The user has requested a display of records one through six retrieved in set
one. Only the author, title, and imprint information is desired.

To use the BRS search commands and procedures, with their complex rules for
abbreviation, punctuation, and syntax, the user must receive training of some
sort and use the system frequently enough to remember these rules. Even so,
there are many opportunities for error in the entry of commands and search
statements.

The "user interface" however, with its simple entry requirements combined with
several special BRS features, provides an attractive and useful interface
alternative to the new or casual user of the library's catalog. It is also an
excellent illustration of the eclectic dialogue approach. The user may enter
commands through a special language to select a functional mode. Menus are
used to suggest choices, directive prompts tell the user when to enter the
search term, and questions are used to elicit specific information or
decisions from the user. The Dartmouth "user interface" employs these various
techniques in a highly structured manner. Other combinations of these
dialogue techniques provide varying degrees of search flexibility and user
guidance.

<u>Mankato State University</u>

The OPAC at The Mankato State University employs a user-guided dialogue mode
and a user-initiated command language as a command-entry technique. For the
most part, search commands are entered without prompts (e.g., menus,
question-answer, instructional prompts) after the user entry cue is displayed
(">"). After a search is completed, the number of records which match the
search term (i.e., postings) is displayed. The user is then prompted to
display from 1-20 of the retrieved records. The display prompts are terse and
do not include instructions for requesting special formats, e.g.,

TYPE DI NMBR to display a specific record /NS to display next screen

This terse, generally unprompted (especially with the more advanced features)
dialogue is supported by an extensive system of "help" screens which may be
retrieved at either a "brief" or "detailed" level.

Commands generally consist of two parts, a command name or code (called
"search ID" by Mankato staff) and a search term (or argument). The command or
search code is always a two-character code. At least one space must separate
the search code and the search term. In a few cases, only the search code is
entered. The special function key, NEW LINE, serves as a command terminator
and end-of-message signal.

Five basic search types are supported by the Mankato OPAC: author, title,
combined author/title, subject, and term (keyword) searching. The following
are examples showing the various command formats.

```
AU AMERICAN LIBRARY ASSOCIATION
AU JOHNSON JOHN E
TI ONE DAY IN THE
CO TWAIN LIFE
SU BIBLE CONCORDANCES ENGLISH
TE EXISTENTIAL
```

The Mankato OPAC is unique in that it offers the user two kinds of command
entry formats. In addition to the above command formats, the user has the
option of entering a truncated (derived) search key. In fact, when a user
enters searches in the manner illustrated above, the computer creates the
truncated version. (At an early stage of development, this computer-truncated
search key was displayed to the user prior to the postings message.) This
precise search key format is offered as an option because it may require fewer
characters for the user to enter.

The truncated search key format varies with search type (this form does not
apply to term searches):

Search	Format	Example
Author	8,5,1	AU JOHNSON,JOHN,E
Title	6,3,3,2	TI POVERT,OF,POW,EN
Author/Title	6,6	CO COMMON,POVERT
Subject	8,3,3,2	SU INFORMAT,STO,AND,RE

When entering commands in the untruncated format, up to four words will be
searched in the title and subject indexes, and up to three words in the author
index. The author search may include personal or corporate authors. If a
personal name is entered, the last name must be entered first, followed by the
first name and middle initial. Spaces are used as delimiters.

In a title search, initial articles should be omitted from the search term.
If entered, the computer issues a warning that initial articles are not
indexed, but it may continue to execute the search as entered, with the
leading article as part of the search term.

When entering a subject search in the untruncated format, only the first four
words of a Library of Congress Subject Heading may be entered. All
punctuation between these words, except spaces, should be omitted when
entering the search. The computer constructs a search key to search the
subject index (8,3,3,2).

Term searching, commonly known as "keyword" or "free text" searching, may be
done on all searchable fields or on specific groups of fields:

        TE PSYCHOLOGY   (General term search)
        AT BROOKINGS   (Corporate/conference name term search)
        TT BEHAVIOR   (Title term search)
        ST EXPERIMENTAL   (Subject term search)

Boolean operators (AND, OR, NOT) may be used to relate keywords to each other:

ST LIBRARIES AND AUTOMATION AND BIBLIOGRAPHY

The general subject search could not limit this set of results to
bibliographies, as "bibliography" is the fifth word in the LC heading. In
relating keywords, Boolean operations are performed from left to right on the
search argument as entered, thus switching terms in a compound argument may
have important consequences for the results to be retrieved.

Many additional search features are available for the experienced searcher,
including the capabilities to build and combine sets, and to save them or
purge them. It will be useful to review the command syntax of two of these
special features, truncation and limiting search results.

Three types of truncation are permitted when searching the Mankato OPAC. Both
word and statement (multiple word) truncation use the special character "#";
embedded (unknown) character or word truncation, uses the special character "?".

Word truncation is available on all five basic types of searches. The symbol
"#" must be placed immediately after the stem to be searched:

TT ELECTRIC#

Statement truncation is permitted only on a title or subject search. When
only a limited number of words in a title or subject heading are known, the
symbol "#" may be entered as a separate word at the end of the argument:

SU CHEMICAL SUBSTANCES

Note that a blank or comma must separate the truncation symbol from the preceding word.

The special character "?" is used to denote unknown letters in words, and may be used in all five basic searches.

        TE WOM?N
        AU HORO?ITZ

The symbol "?" also may be used in title searches to denote missing words. If so used, the "?" must be separated from the other words by blanks or commas.

        TI BEYOND ? AND DIGNITY

When a search retrieves more matches than desired, the results may be reduced or "limited" in three ways; by date of publication, by type of library material ("format"), and by language. Each of these three limiting commands must be used <u>after</u> a search is completed and the postings displayed. Including them in the original command, through multiple phrase arguments or command stacking, is not permitted.

Two-letter command codes are employed for all limiting commands. They are simply entered on a new line to limit the results of the previous search, e.g.,

        GT 1970   (restricts to post-1970 dates)
        EQ 1975   (restricts to 1975 date)
        FO SE   (restricts to serial publications)
        LA FRENCH   (restricts to French language text)

The syntax required of the display (DI) command is consistent with the syntax of the search commands. The two-character mnemonic code is followed by the record number or range element, and then by a format designator, if the format is to be explicitly specified. The elements are separated by spaces. If a range is specified, the brief, one-line format is displayed for each record (date, title, and author), by default. If the display of a single record is requested, the user may specify the format from several available, including "short," "medium," and "long" formats. The system assumes the "medium" format if none is explicitly specified.

        DI 5   (displays record number "5" in medium format)
        DI 5-12 (displays records "5-12" in brief format)
        DI 2 L   (displays record number "2" in long format)

(These formats will be discussed in chapter 9 and are illustrated in Appendix C.)

The command language employed by the Mankato OPAC offers the user a great deal of variety, optionality, and flexibility. The traditional command verb is implicit in the search commands, but the search codes are mnemonic and result from a uniformly applied abbreviation rule (two characters). Punctuation has been kept simple (usually spaces suffice), and few special characters are employed. When the user forgets the special extensions to the basic commands, or the correct form for entering them, a complete set of help displays is available for the user's assistance.

Mission College

The ULISYS OPAC at Mission College employs a user-guided dialogue mode and a
user-initiated command language as a command entry technique. The search
commands available for searching are entered unprompted (except by the user
entry cue, "?") throughout the dialogue. Suggestive prompts indicating
display options are provided after retrieved results, and are initially
displayed in a brief, one line format (call number, author, title). However,
all search and display commands must be entered explicitly. The user is free
to initiate another search immediately after the display prompts are presented
by the system.

A ULISYS command statement generally consists of a one- or two-character
mnemonic code indicating the search or display type, followed by the special
character, "=", then the search term or record number to be displayed.

```
A=DEWEY JOHN
T=HUMAN NATURE AND CONDUCT
S=SOCIAL PSYCHOLOGY
BI=4
ST=4
CN=BF57.D4
AT=DEWEY/CONDUCT
```

The command verb is implicit in both search and display command statements.
In a search command the "equals" sign instructs the computer to search the
specified index (author, A, for example) for all records which match the term
entered. The display command, BI=4, instructs the computer to display record
number "4" (previously displayed in the brief, one line format) in a full,
detailed bibliographic format (similar to a traditional card format).

ULISYS assumes that searches are truncated searches unless the user explicitly
indicates that an exact search is to take place on the term entered. If an
exact search is desired, the search term must be followed immediately by the
qualifier, "/E".

```
T=ROOTS/E
S=CHILDBIRTH AT HOME/E
```

If the exact match qualifier is omitted in the first case, the system will
retrieve all records having titles that begin with "ROOTS" (initial articles
are excluded in the index). In the second example, the subject search,
S=CHILDBIRTH AT HOME/E, will retrieve titles having that assigned subject
heading, but titles assigned the heading, CHILDBIRTH AT HOME--CONGRESSES, will
not be retrieved.

When entering an author search, the personal author's last name must be
entered first, followed by either a blank space or a comma if the first name
is also entered. If only the last name is entered, all records matching that
name in the author index will be retrieved, whatever additional name or
characters follow it. Corporate authors are included in the author (A) index
and are to be entered in a straightforward manner (e.g., Dow Chemical
Company).

The combined author/title search permits the user to enter the author's last name and any word in the title. The terms are separated by the special character, "/".

AT=DICKENS/CITIES

Either term may be truncated in this limited Boolean search. All records matching the author term are retrieved, and from among this set, those also having the keyword (e.g., CITIES) anywhere in their titles are displayed.

ULISYS is forgiving in accepting blanks for commas and other punctuation in search terms, and will ignore blanks separating the command (CN=) and the search term proper. However, if the user begins a search term with an initial article, the system will search on that article and miss the title desired. In building the indexes, initial articles are omitted. Thus, a search for "THE BELL JAR" will return all titles beginning with "THE.." (most likely "THEATER....") but not "BELL JAR." In all commands, word order is inflexible and the elements of a command must be entered in the specified manner.

Pikes Peak Library District

After selecting "Inventory" from an introductory menu of files and programs (e.g., "Courses," "Calendar," "Clubs," "Agencies," "Welcome"), the entry prompt is displayed ("PPL>") and the user may begin to search the online catalog. The dialogue is user-guided from this point on; no suggestive prompts are displayed by the system. A simple command language is employed for entering searches and requesting displays.

<pre>
                    Public Dial-Up Access
                         > Menu <
                   For HELP enter "?selection"

        AGENCIES   COURSES   CALENDAR   GOODBYE

        INFO   INVENTORY   TERMINAL   CLUBS

        WELCOME
  Program:
</pre>

Entering HELP at any point while searching the catalog will retrieve this display:

<pre>
        Command choices:
            A/data = Author search
            B/data = Barcode search
            C/data = Call number search
            E/   = Expand this record
            F/   = Forward
            L/data = LCCN search
            N/   = Next author/title
            S/data = Subject search
            T/data = Title search
            X/   = Exit program
</pre>

No other help display is available in the "INVENTORY" program, but a failure
to enter the search command correctly will cause this same display to be
retrieved automatically.

All search commands consist of a single character followed by the "/" and the
search term. The system forgives spaces entered immediately after the search
code and prior to the search term.

        A/UNIVERSITY OF DENVER
        A/VONNEGUT
        T/SUCCESSFUL COIN HUNTING
        S/ENERGY POLICY UNITED STATES

An author search may include a personal author's name or a corporate author.
In the former case, the last name must be entered first. If the first name is
included, a comma must separate the last and first names. The corporate
author term must be entered in natural order omitting initial articles.

Title phrases are entered in the order they occur in the record, omitting
initial articles. Up to fifty characters will be processed by the system in
the attempt to match the search term with an index record. Both the author
term and the title term may be truncated at any point. No explicit symbol is
required.

The system matches the character string entered as the search term with the
first record in the designated index that contains that string as the leading
characters. If an exact match is not found, the next record with the search
term string as its leading characters is displayed. If no match is achieved,
the next record in sequence in the searched file will be displayed. For any
search (assuming correct command entry), a single record is retrieved, match
or no match.

For example, the search "T/RISE OF CIVILIZATION" retrieved the title, "RISE OF
COMMUNIST CHINA." The search "S/WORLD WAR II" retrieved a record assigned the
subject heading, "WORLD WAR III."

If an author, title, or subject search does not produce an exact match, it may
place one near the desired point of reference in the selected file. The
display commands, F/ and N/ enable the searcher to browse through the file.
F/ enables the searcher to move sequentially (as though card by card) through
the file under the heading in which it was entered. For example, after
retrieving a record from the A/VONNEGUT search, the F/ command, entered by
itself, will enable the searcher to see all copies of all titles by the
author, Vonnegut.

The N/command enables the searcher to move through the selected file, heading
by heading. For example, N/ entered after the first record by "VONNEGUT K" is
displayed will cause the first record filed under "VONNEGUT M" to display. In
the title file, F/ will cause additional copies of the same title (just
displayed) to be displayed. N/ will jump the searcher to the next title in
the file. Knowing the sequence in which the file is sorted is all-important
for the effective use of these commands.

The F/ and N/ commands are especially useful in browsing the call number file. F/ displays the next title assigned the basic number entered, e.g., C/410. Entering the N/ command increments the basic number by one each time it is entered. Of course, the F/ command, entered successively, would reach the point attained were the N/ command entered instead.

The record retrieved when a search command is executed is a brief record which includes the call number, author, title, LC card number, bar code number, holding library, and circulation status information (in some cases the subject is included). If a more detailed, bibliographic display is desired, the user may expand the short record to a MARC-like display (including tags and subfield codes) by entering the E/ command (no search term required).

After each single record is displayed (no multiple listings are displayed), the system returns the user cue for a new search or display command. The entry of X/ returns the original menu of programs and files.

The Pikes Peak OPAC is a simple, easy-to-use system. There are few commands to memorize, and the abbreviations and basic syntax are uniform. Powerful search features have not been included in this system. It is a system largely designed on a model of card catalog use. Circulation data is routinely provided with the display of bibliographic records. However, the browsing mechanics would be enhanced if the user were given the ability to move backward in the file and/or to view related records in a more immediate manner.

Northwestern University

The OPAC at Northwestern (LUIS) combines user-entered commands, suggestive prompts, line number selection, and retrievable help displays in an eclectic dialogue mode which provides author, title, and subject access to the database of bibliographic records. Although the search commands must be explicitly entered in a precise manner (e.g., A=FAULKNER), guidance is provided to the user at each stage of the retrieval process. At the lower part of the screen, each display includes standard prompts to assist the user throughout the search and retrieval process. An example of a LUIS Author/Title Index Display follows. This display is produced when 2-17 records match the search term.

```
LUIS SEARCH REQUEST:  A=COMMONER

 AUTHOR/TITLE INDEX -- 7 ENTRIES FOUND

  1 NU:COMMONER BARRY +ALTERNATIVE TECHNOLOGIES FOR POWER PRODUCTION PREP (1975

  2 NU:COMMONER BARRY +BALANCE AND BIOSPHERE A RADIO SYMPOSUIM ON THE ENV (1971

  3 NU:COMMONER BARRY +CLOSING CIRCLE NATURE MAN AND TECHNOLOGY (1971

  4 NU:COMMONER BARRY +HUMAN WELFARE THE END USE FOR POWER PREPARED FOR T (1975

  5 NU:COMMONER BARRY +POLITICS OF ENERGY (1979

  6 NU:COMMONER BARRY +POVERTY OF POWER ENERGY AND THE ECONOMIC CRISIS (1976

  7 NU:COMMONER BARRY +SOCIAL COSTS OF POWER PRODUCTION PREPARED FOR THE (1975
```

TYPE LINE NO. FOR BIBLIOGRAPHIC RECORD WITH CALL NO.

TYPE e TO START OVER.   TYPE h for HELP.

TYPE COMMAND AND PRESS ENTER

The standard suggestive prompts are generally of three types: (1) instruction for the most likely step(s) to be taken from the given bibliographic, introductory, or help display, (2) instructions for additional valid commands which may be entered from the display, including "H" for help, and (3) the command entry cue, "TYPE COMMAND AND PRESS ENTER." The first two prompt types vary from display to display. The third is constant and indicates where all commands must be entered. The prompts are suggestive rather than directive, because following them is optional, and a new author, title, or subject search may be entered from any screen.

LUIS provides a small set of commands governed by a few simple rules of syntax. Most command symbols or codes consist of a single character. These symbols are mnemonic in that they are the display, paging action, or search type they reference, e.g.,

        S= (command code for LCSH subject searching)
        T= (command code for title searching)
        I   (retrieves previously displayed Index Display)
        M   (more: displays next record or more titles where appropriate)
        D   (command code to obtain circulation status)

Five types of primary searches may be conducted on LUIS: author (A=), title (T=), Library of Congress Subject Heading (S=), Transportation Library Subjects (ST=), and Medical Subjects (SM=). Broad access is provided under the author and title searches, as main and added entries are indexed. The author index includes personal, corporate, and conference names, as well as uniform titles.

An author search is entered by using the command code "A=" followed by the search term.

```
A=BRITISH JOURNAL OF DENTISTRY
A=EMERSON, RALPH W
A=ELIOT T
```

In the case of a personal author, the last name must be entered first. A comma or space or both may be used to separate the last and first names. A middle initial or name may be entered only if the first name is spelled out. Initial articles must be omitted for corporate names and titles.

A corporate or conference name may be truncated. No special symbol is required.

In a title search, words are entered in their natural order, omitting initial articles.

```
T=TAO OF PHYSICS
T=SUN ALSO RISES
T=WALL STREET JOURNAL
T=CHRISTIAN SCIENCE
T=JOURNAL OF EDUC
```

A portion of a title may be entered. Truncation as a feature occurs by default. No command is explicitly entered. The user may not override this default and request an exact search on the term entered. This means that the term "CHRISTIAN SCIENCE" will retrieve all title records which begin with that phrase, e.g., "CHRISTIAN SCIENCE IN THE TWENTIETH CENTURY."

Subject searching in LUIS requires that the user enter a heading or a portion of a heading from one of three controlled subject heading lists: the Library of Congress Subject Headings (LCSH), the Transportation Library's Subject Headings (TLSH), and the Medical Library Subject Headings (MESH). For example:

```
S=ENERGY POLICY--UNITED STATES
ST=URBAN TRANSIT
SM=ELECTROCARDI (truncation requires no explicit command)
```

Three types of displays may result from a search:

1. Guide Displays - the Author/Title Guide displays when more than seventeen records match the search term. This display indicates by record number major portions of the alphabetical sequence of records matching the search term. The Subject Heading Guide lists the headings which match the search term and those headings which are alphabetically near.

2. Index Displays - the Author/Title Index displays when 2-17 records match the search term. This display includes single line brief records consisting of the institution code, author, title and date (for a book) or place of publication (for a periodical). The Subject/Title Index lists titles (plus date, location, and call number) for which a subject heading selected from the previous Subject Heading Guide has been assigned.

3.   A <u>Bibliographic Display</u> – displays automatically when only one record
     matches the search term. This display of a single record includes
     author, title, imprint, location and call number, and holdings
     information.

The following is one possible result of searching for titles under a subject
heading:

LUIS SEARCH REQUEST: S=ENERGY POLICY -UNITED

BASIC BIBLIOGRAPHIC RECORD -- NO. 89 OF 148 ENTRIES FOUND

Commoner, Barry, 1917-

   The poverty of power : energy and the economic crisis / Barry Commoner. -- 1st

ed. -- New York : Knopf : distributed by Random House, 1976.

HOLDINGS IN NORTHWESTERN UNIVERSITY LIBRARY

LOCATION: main

CALL NUMBER: 333.7;C734p

LOCATION: core (copy 2)

CALL NUMBER: 333.7;C734p

LOCATION: main (copy 3)

CALL NUMBER: 333.7;C734p

TYPE m FOR NEXT RECORD, d FOR CIRCULATION STATUS (FIRST WRITE DOWN CALL NO.)

TYPE i TO RETURN TO INDEX, g TO RETURN TO GUIDE, e TO START OVER, h FOR HELP.

TYPE COMMAND AND PRESS ENTER

Several simple display manipulation commands assist the user in narrowing the
search to a desired record or in browsing through multiple index listings.
For example, "B/" and a number enable the user to select a line entry on the
Index Display. This will produce the standard bibliographic display for that
record. "I/n" enables the user to request a block of sequential index entries
from the Guide Display. This produces an Index Display. A simple "I" or "G"
will restore the previously displayed Index and Guide displays respectively.
"M" may be used to retrieve more brief title entries from an Author/Title or
Subject/Title Index, or to retrieve the next bibliographic record from the set
which matched the search term.

The "D" command is used to switch the user to the circulation subsystem from a
bibliographic record display. The user is then prompted to enter the call
number to receive information on the circulation status of the item. To
reenter the catalog access subsystem, the user must enter LUIS.

The use of the help command code, "H", will retrieve one of seven help displays, each relevant to the point the user has reached in his search. The "E" command retrieves an introductory display which summarizes database content and explains the use of the search commands, including "D", which retrieves circulation information.

LUIS is a simple, easy-to-use OPAC. Prompts guide the user through a search, and several help displays are available for additional assistance. The search codes are suggestive of their search type and are easy to remember. Each search code is always followed by the "=" sign and the search term. Keyword access to title and subject is not provided, but all search terms may be truncated. LUIS provides only one extended display format, but offers the user the means to retrieve status information on the item's availability.

Ohio State University

Except for certain logical constraints inherent in the search process, the user of Ohio State's LCS OPAC controls the dialogue with the computer. User-to-system communication is achieved solely through the explicit entry of commands employing a complex, detailed command language. No menus, directive prompts, or question/answer formats are used for the selection or entry of commands. The user communicates with the system by entering a command code and a search key or term. The command code is always a three letter code followed by a slash (/). The code identifies the type of search or display requested. (The paging commands are two letter codes followed by a number or the plus or minus signs.) The search key required for an author/title or title search is a combination of letters or numbers. These keys must be constructed according to a preestablished format from natural language names or terms. The author and subject search commands do not require rigidly constructed search keys. The words or name components may be entered in their normal form.

System-to-user communication is limited to terse error messages and suggestive prompts of two kinds. After general searches retrieve multiple titles or headings (name and subject), paging prompts appear beneath a listing of one line entries. Such prompts are useful because LCS employs three different paging codes (PG, PS, PD), depending on the type of search conducted. Another prompt appearing with the paging prompt suggests the special line number search most logical at that stage of the search.

PAGE 1 of 3   FOR PRECEDING PAGE, ENTER PS-; FOR FOLLOWING PAGE, ENTER PS2
ENTER TBL/ AND LINE NO. FOR TITLES

If no other page selection is possible, the search by line number prompt appears by itself beneath the multiple listing.

Two single record display formats are provided in LCS. A brief record format includes author, title, date, location, call number, and availability information. This brief format displays when the user requests a detailed search by line number (DSL/) or by call number (DSC/). A "full bibliographic" display is available for most titles added to the database since 1974. The full bibliographic record by line number (FBL/) command is used to retrieve this display. When a record is displayed in either of these formats, no

prompt appears at the bottom of the display (or elsewhere on the screen). The
user is free (and unguided) to conduct another search at this time.

The search commands available to the LCS OPAC user are:

          ATS/   (author/title search)
          AUT/   (author search)
          TLS/   (title search)
          SUB/   (subject search)
          SPS/   (shelf position search)
          SAL/   (see also by line)
          DSC/   (detailed search by call number)
          DSL/   (detailed search by line number)
          TBL/   (title search by line number)
          FBL/   (full bibliographic record by line number)

Using the LCS OPAC requires a familiarity with many different commands and a
variety of rules for using them. Acceptable syntax and punctuation varies
from command to command. Only a few commands will be discussed here to
indicate the requirements placed on the user when entering various commands.

Derived search keys are required for title and author/title searches. The
match-code for these search keys is 4,5. In other words, four letters from
the author's last name must be entered, followed by five letters from the
first significant word of the title:

          ATS/TWAIHUCKL
          TLS/HUCKFINN

No punctuation is required in the search key unless a name or word has fewer
than the required number of letters. When this is the case, spaces must be
entered to complete that component of the search key. However, if the second
word of a title is not known the key may be completed with hyphens.

Derived keys are not required for subject or author searches, but they have
their own entry requirements.

The subject term must be entered exactly as it appears in the Library of
Congress Subject Headings, e.g.,

          SUB/WOMEN'S WRITINGS, AMERICAN
          SUB/CHEMISTRY, ORGANIC

When conducting a personal author search, the author's last name must be
entered first, followed by a space, then the first name. Corporate or
conference names are entered in their natural order, with spaces separating
the words:

          AUT/HUNT HOWARD
          AUT/RESEARCH LIBRARIES GROUP

LCS places a large number of words on two stoplists (words that may not be
entered in a search), one for the English language, and one for foreign
languages. Words on these lists may not be used in title or author/title
search keys, but any word except an initial article may be used when entering
author or subject searches.

Most searching in the LCS OPAC takes place in stages. General searches are
processed for author or title terms, and all records matching the search key
or term are displayed in a one-line, multiple-listing format. The system then
prompts the user indicating the correct command code to enter to retrieve a
single record by its line number (e.g., DSL/8). The user has the option of
entering a request for the full bibliographic record (FBL/8) when its
availability is indicated by the code, FBR, at the end of a single line entry.

Although keyword searching and Boolean capabilities are not provided in LCS,
some special features which augment the basic commands are available. Title
search terms may be truncated after the first word by entering hyphens.
Several options exist for limiting the results of a search. General searches
(e.g., TLS/ and ATS/) may be restricted to monographs only, or serials only.
The commands are entered in this manner:

TLS/EDUCPSYCH/SER
ATS/ASSOCOMPU/MONO

When serial titles are retrieved, a specific volume or year of the serial
title may be selected by limiting the detailed line number search in this
manner:

DSL/6,V=12   (volume 12 of the serial)
DSL/6,Y=1949 (year 1949 of the serial)

The commands must be entered exactly as indicated, with no intervening spaces.

Command stacking is permitted when using the detailed or full bibliographic
search commands:

DSL/3/5/7
FBL/2/4/6

Searching the LCS OPAC effectively requires the user to learn and remember the
many search command codes, derived key formats, and rules of syntax and
punctuation. The limited prompts are helpful once a search is underway, but
no other online assistance in the form of an introductory display or
retrievable help display is provided.

OCLC

Dialogue with the OCLC online catalog system may be characterized as
user-guided. The dialogue technique employed for user-to-system communication
combines a specially constructed language for search and display commands with
the use of two special function keys on the OCLC terminal. The OCLC command
language bears no resemblance to the conventional model discussed earlier in
this chapter. Unlike systems which use a command name or code to indicate a
specific search transaction, OCLC employs precisely structured search keys to
retrieve records from the bibliographic database. A search key consists of
one or more groups of characters (letters, numerals, punctuation) formatted
according to specific rules.

When a bibliographic record is entered into the OCLC database, the system
creates keys from information in certain fields of separate index files. Each
index file is a collection of search keys derived from a specific category of
information, such as author, title, and ISBN. The keys for each index are
characterized by a distinctive format. When the user enters a search key, the
system determines which index file to search, according to the distinctive
format of that search key.

Search keys for the "number" index files, assigned by OCLC or national
services (e.g., OCLC control number or ISBN), have a prescribed number of
characters. Some of these "number" search keys also have distinctive
punctuation.

INDEX FILE	SEARCH KEY FORMAT	EXAMPLE	SEARCH KEY
(NUMERIC KEYS)			
OCLC Control Number	number sign (prefix), 1 or more digits	1300106	#1300106
LCCN	1 or 2 digits, hyphen, 1 to 6 digits	72-4519	72-4519
Government Document No.	gn:, 1 or more characters	GA 1.13:MWD-76-109	gn:ga11376109
ISBN	10 digits	0-87779-329-8	0877793298
ISSN	4 digits, hyphen, 4 digits	0024-2527	0024-2527
CODEN	5 or 6 characters	AISJB6	aisjb6

Search keys for "derived" index files (name and/or title) are constructed from
words in name and title fields. These keys have two or more groups of
characters, separated by commas. Each component group represents a separate
name or title word. Search keys for each index file have a distinctive number
of component groups and consequently, a distinctive number of commas.

INDEX FILE	SEARCH KEY FORMAT	EXAMPLE	SEARCH KEY
(DERIVED KEYS)			
Title	3,2,2,1	Journal of population research	jou,of,po,r
Name/title	4,4	Goldenberg, I. Ira Build me a mountain	gold,buil
Personal Name	4,3,1	Strong, Anna Louise	stro,ann,l
Corporate Name	"=" (prefix) 4,3,1	Pittsburgh Carnegie Library	=pitt,car,l

Certain groups in these search keys have a fixed length, that is, a required number of characters must be present (unless an indexed word has fewer characters). Other groups have a variable length for the number of characters to be included.

REQUIRED NUMBER OF CHARACTERS

Index File	Group 1	Group 2	Group 3	Group 4
Title	3	at least 1, not more than 2	at least 1, not more than 2	1
Name/Title	at least 3, not more than 4	at least 3, not more than 4	--	--
Personal name	4	at least 1, not more than 3	(optional), not more than 1	--
Corporate name	4	at least 1, not more than 3	(optional), not more than 1	--

To retrieve a record from the database, the user enters a search key at the "home" position (upper left corner of screen) and then depresses the function keys labeled "DISPLAY REC'D" and "SEND." A search key using name or title data often requires searching through successive screens to locate a single record when multiple records are associated with the same key. If a search key retrieves more than one record, the system displays a summary list of truncated and/or collective entries. Each line entry is numbered on the summary display, and the user may view a more detailed display by entering the line number at the "home" position and then depressing the "DISPLAY REC'D" and "SEND" function keys.

If the user's search key retrieves two or more records, the system displays entries in an abbreviated format. If the abbreviated records will fit on two screens or less, the format used is the "truncated" format. A truncated record includes author, title, place, and date of publication.

If the display of truncated records would require more than two screens, the system performs an extended search. The results of an extended search may be grouped into "collective" records. Each collective record entry displayed on the screen represents multiple records. Each collective entry consists of some data that the set of records have in common, such as the initial portion of author or title fields. A collective entry appears in uppercase letters and is followed by a number in parentheses that indicates the number of records represented.

A collective display is a single-screen display that may also include one or more truncated entries. A line number search on a collective entry will produce a truncated entry display. A line number search on a truncated entry will produce a display of the full bibliographic record. A typical collective entry display follows:

```
To see title for a COLLECTIVE ENTRY, type line#, DEPRESS DISPLAY RECD,
SEND.

 ▶ 1  On the usability of narrative interviews in sociological field
research as illustrated by an example of research in community power
structure.    Schutze, Fritz.    n.p.    1970 ¶
 ▶ 2  ON THE USE OF   (31) ¶
 ▶ 3  ON THE USE OF M (13) ¶
 ▶ 4  On the use of non-linear systems in the estimation of nutritional
requirements of animals.   Monroe, Robert James,   Raleigh, N.C.,   1949 ¶
 ▶ 5  ON THE USE OF O (2) ¶
 ▶ 6  ON THE USE OF P (5) ¶
 ▶ 7  On the use of quaternions in simulation of rigid-body motion.
Robinson, Alfred C   Wright-Patterson Air Force Base, Ohio, Springfield,
Va.  1958 ¶
 ▶ 8  ON THE USE OF R (3) ¶
 ▶ 9  ON THE USE OF S (5) ¶
 ▶10  ON THE USE OF T (23) ¶
 ▶11  ON THE USE OF W (4) ¶
 ▶12  ON THE USEFULNESS OF   (2) ¶
 ▶13  ON THE USES OF   (3) ¶
```

OCLC Collective Entry Display

If a derived (name and/or title) search key retrieves 100-1500 records, the
system displays a "group" display:

```
BUL,,,/1960-1980 ¶
   ▶  1   Books              1960-1967   27 ¶
   ▶  2   Books              1968-1971   29 ¶
   ▶  3   Books              1972-1974   28 ¶
   ▶  4   Books              1975-1979   32 ¶
   ▶  5   Maps               1972         1 ¶
   ▶  6   Media Materials    1973-1977    2 ¶
   ▶  7   Serials            1960        21 ¶
   ▶  8   Serials            1961-1962   44 ¶
   ▶  9   Serials            1963-1964   48 ¶
   ▶ 10   Serials            1965-1966   47 ¶
   ▶ 11   Serials            1967        32 ¶
   ▶ 12   Serials            1968        43 ¶
   ▶ 13   Serials            1969        35 ¶
   ▶ 14   Serials            1970        30 ¶
   ▶ 15   Serials            1971        23 ¶
   ▶ 16   Serials            1972        41 ¶
   ▶ 17   Serials            1973        36 ¶
   ▶ 18   Serials            1974        25 ¶
   ▶ 19   Serials            1975-1976   46 ¶
   ▶ 20   Serials            1977-1978   39 ¶
   ▶ 21   Sound Recordings   1973-1978    2 ¶
```

OCLC Group Record Display

A group display categorizes retrieved records by record format type and by
year of publication. Each numbered set in a group display may represent up to
ninety-nine records.

OCLC provides several commands which permit the user to "backup" to a general
display from any more specific display, or to return to the previous screen or
display. These commands are:

   ps   (to return to the previous screen)
   tr   (to return to display of truncated entries)
   co   (to return to display of collective entries)
   gp   (to return to group display)
   bib   (to return to a single record after viewing
         symbols of libraries that hold copies)

Additional screen manipulation commands include "ns" (next screen) and "s1" or
"s2" (screen one or screen two).

If the user wishes to obtain location information for a bibliographic item
whose record is displayed, several related commands may be used to retrieve a
display of institution symbols for libraries that hold copies of the item.
Each symbol represents one OCLC participating institution that has cataloged
that item using the OCLC Cataloging Subsystem. These commands, followed by
the user depressing the function keys, "DISPLAY REC'D" and "SEND," retrieve
the holdings symbols in the following groupings:

dhs (locations within the state)
dhr (locations in the region: state and
      contiguous states)
dha (all locations)
dh (locations selected by the system, depending
     on the number and geographic proximity of
     holding institutions)

If a derived search key retrieves 51-1500 bibliographic records, the system
responds with a message which offers the user the choice of continuing the
search (a YES/NO query), but also suggests that the retrieval set be reduced
by qualifying the search key by record type, or by a year or a range of years.
A derived search key may be qualified by entering a slash (or slashes)
followed by the qualifier(s) immediately after the constructed search key.
For example:

    hemi,ern,/mss/1971-80   (manuscripts of Ernest Hemingway
                                 published between 1971 and 1980)

    rodg,okla/sco   (Richard Rodgers' scores of the musical, OKLAHOMA)

The OCLC online catalog was designed to be searched by trained library
technical staff in the normal performance of their cataloging, serials
control, interlibrary loan and other related tasks. A wealth of literature
has been produced to support the training and effective use of the OCLC
system. However, no online instruction or assistance is provided for the new
or casual user on the operation of the system or the rules for entering the
various search commands. When the OCLC system is used for public access,
usually either printed instructions are provided, or the user is directed to a
library staff member for assistance.

RLIN

Searching the RLIN online database requires the user to initiate and guide the
dialogue through the use of precisely defined command words, from responses to
suggestive prompts, or through the use of several function keys for selecting
and moving between display screens. When the command entry cue (":?")
appears, the user must employ RLIN's formal command language to initiate a
search. After the retrieval of one or more records, the system may display a
command prompt for a suggested action (e.g., ":MUL?" for the multiple,
abbreviated record display, or ":+?" for a display of the next screen of the
record displayed). If the user chooses to enter the prompted command, only
the SEND MESSAGE key need be depressed. If the user does not want to enter
the prompted command, he is free to use the formal command language to enter a
command, or he can depress one of the special function keys on the RLIN
terminal (+B, -B, +, -) which permit moving between retrieved screens and
records.

RLIN's command language conforms closely to the conventional model illustrated
in section 7.3, and resembles the previously discussed command language of the
University of California's OPAC. The command language vocabulary (e.g., names
for indexes and display formats) of these two systems is not uniform, but the
two languages share a common syntactical structure. For example, minor
variations exist in rules for command abbreviation, and in the elements of a
command statement which are implicitly expressed at the time of command entry.
In RLIN, the DISPLAY or DIS command may be omitted when entering the name of a
desired display format and/or record number. Search and display commands may
be abbreviated down to the first three letters only.

In response to the command, SHOW INFORMATION (or SHO INF), RLIN displays this
summary of search, display, and information commands:

Information display

Searching
 FINd <index> <value> - initiates search
 AND, &   - restricts search   AND NOT, &~, ~ - restricts search
 OR, | - expands search   RESume - continues search in next file

SELect FILes <file>,... - Determines which files are to be searched

Display
 MUL - Multiple record display   FUL - Fully tagged display
 LON - Long, card-like display   CAT - Cataloged holdings display
 PAR - Partial record display   PRI - Primary cluster member display

SET DISplay <display name> - sets default local-version record display

Information
 SHO NEWs - RLIN system news
 SHO CHAnges - Subsystem-specific news
 SHO INFormation - [this display]
 SHO SETtings - User status information
 SHO INDexes - Index information

Uppercase letters indicate permissable command abbreviations.

Entry of the SHO INDexes command retrieves a display which lists RLIN's
searchable indexes:

:? SHO IND

Index display

General indexes	BKS	FLM	MAP	REC	SCO	SER
PN, PE - Personal name & exact personal name	x	x	x	x	x	x
TP, TW - Title phrase & title word	x	x	x	x	x	x
RT - Related title phrase						x
CP, CW - Corp. name phrase & corp. name word	x	x	x	x	x	x
SP, SD - Subject phrase & subdivision	x	x	x	x	x	x
LCCN - LC Card number	x	x	x	x	x	x
CLS - LC and Dewey classification	x	x	x	x	x	x
GC - Geographic class code	x	x	x	x	x	x
DOC - U.S. Government document number	x	x	x	x	x	x
ISBN - International standard book number	x	x	x	x	x	x
ISSN - International standard serial number	x		x		x	x
CODEN - Coden						x
PUB - Publisher or issuing agency				x	x	
NUM - Publisher/issue number				x	x	

Local Indexes
CAL - Call number   ST - Record Status
LDN - Library Data Number   UST - Unit Status
ID - Record ID   ADD - Added records   SAV - Today's saved records
UID - Unit ID   UPD - Updated records USV - Today's saved units

RLIN provides both keyword and phrase (from the left as entered in the record,
omitting initial articles) searching in title and corporate name fields.
Keyword searching on subject headings is not permitted. Keywords or words in
phrases may be truncated from the right, using the special character, "#".
Some typical search commands follow:

      FIND PN BONHOEFFER, DIETRICH
      FIND TW CYBERNETICS AND PN WIENER
      FIND CW TELEPHONE AND TW ELECTR#
      FIND SP PSYCHOLOGY# BIBLIOGRAPHIES
      FIND TP COMMUNIST MANIFESTO
      FIND PN HOFFER OR HOEFFER
      FIND PN ANTHONY BURGESS

Truncation usually increases the results of a search, but RLIN provides a
subject searching feature which permits the user to find works with a certain
bibliographic form such as bibliographies. When conducting a subject phrase
search, the user may enter the truncation symbol between the main term and the
form heading to retrieve works that have been assigned a subject heading with
the desired form subheading (see the fourth command in the previous examples).

In search commands, the command verb and index name must be explicitly
entered. However, when requesting the display of a record from a multiple
retrieval set, the DISPLAY command is assumed. Only the desired format and
record number may be entered, as the following example illustrates:

```
:+? FIND PN HAWKINS AND TW NATURE

FIND PN HAWKINS AND TW NATURE - 4 clusters in BKS

1) Cocker, Edward, 1631-1675.  COCKER'S DECIMAL ARITHMETICK : (The sixth
   edition. London : Printed for J. Darby [and 2 others] 1729.)
NJRG (c-9114 NjR)

2)  Hawkins, David, 1913- THE INFORMED VISION; (New York, Agathon Press;
      distributed by Schocken books [1974])
DCLC (c-9110 DLC)    CSFX (c-9660 CSf)    CSUG (c-9660 CSt)    CTYG (c-9610 CtY)

3)  Coke, Edward, Sir, 1552-1634. THREE LAW TRACTS:  (London, Printed by His
     Majesty's Law-Printer for J. Worrall, 1764.)
CUBL (c-9344 CU-L)

4) Hawkins, David, 1913- THE LANGUAGE OF NATURE; (Anchor Books, 1967.)
CSUU (c-9667 CSt)
:? LON 4


Cluster 4 of 4

Hawkins, David, 1913-
   The language of nature; an essay in the philosophy of science.  By David
Hawkins.  Illustrated by Evan L. Gillespie.  Anchor Books, 1967.
   461 p.

   1. Science--Philosophy 2. Science--Methology I. Title.

   ID: CSUSU1728539-B              CC: 9667       DCF:
   CALL: Q175.H357
:?
```

The LONg display format resembles the traditional catalog card format, and the
FULL format produces a fully tagged MARC record display. A special display
feature permits the specification of a single field or block of fields for
display from a retrieved record. For example:

```
:+? FUL 2 6XX

Cluster 2 of 113

650  Ø Anthropology$xPhilosophy.
650  Ø Social evolution.
650  Ø Man$xAnimal nature.
600 1Ø Marx, Karl,$d1818-1882.
600 1Ø Darwin, Charles,$d18Ø9-1882.
:+B?
```

The FUL command must precede the designation of the record number and field or
fields.

Default values for the display formats may be "set" by the user. When this
default is set, the use of the DIS command, alone, will result in a display of
the first or "current" record of a user's search results in the default
display format. When only a single record is retrieved, it automatically
displays in the system-supplied display format (PRImary, which includes the
symbols for all RLIN institutions that have used the record to catalog a
bibliographic item).

To summarize, RLIN's command language includes a natural language-like
vocabulary and phrase structure. Mnemonic labels are assigned as index names.
Blank spaces are used as command element separators (slashes are used to
separate commands when commands are "stacked" for entry at the same time).
Commands may be abbreviated, uniformly, to the first three letters. Except
for the DISPLAY command and the format default value, commands and index names
must be entered explicitly by the user when the command language is employed.
The use of special characters may be limited to the truncation symbol "#", and
special function keys are provided on RLIN terminals to permit selection and
movement between record and screen displays.

Once again, several dialogue techniques are employed to effect communications
between the user and the computer system. RLIN employs a formal command
language, suggestive prompts, line number selection from a displayed list, and
special function keys to support a user-guided dialogue between the searcher
and the online retrieval system.

Variations in the Quality of Online Access to Bibliographic Records

8.1 Key Factors Affecting the Quality of Online Access

Many factors play a role in determining the kind, extent, and quality of access to bibliographic records in online catalogs. Among the major variables to be considered are:

1. the fields selected as searchable (parts of the record by which it can be accessed),

2. the kind and format of data elements in the indexes to the database,

3. command capabilities available to the user,

4. search term processing methods (index lookup and matching), and

5. the content and format of index and bibliographic record displays.

This list is not exhaustive and no attempt is made here to rank these variables in order of importance or weight in influencing the degree and quality of access in online catalogs. This chapter analyzes the first four of these access-determining variables and reviews the various approaches and methods implemented in the ten OPACs included in the study. The next chapter discusses output control and display options.

As a point of reference, Figure 12 depicts the major hurdles facing the end user along the way to successful retrieval in online catalogs. Most of these hurdles are unique to <u>online</u> access. Highly design dependent, they may enhance online bibliographic retrieval or further compound the traditional problems of access to bibliographic records. Some of these "help or hinder" categories have been discussed elsewhere in this report. This chapter focuses on access points, index construction, authority control, and specialized search and retrieval capabilities.

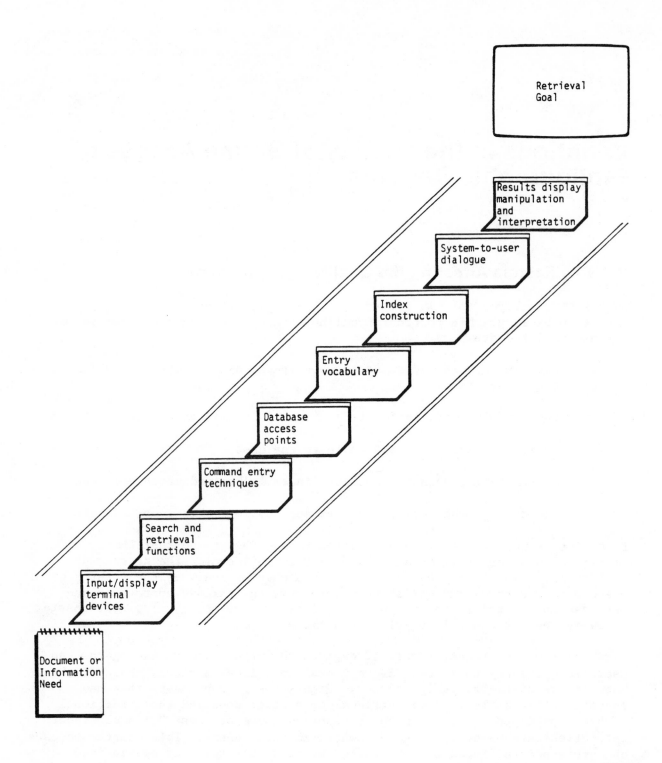

Figure 12.   Obstacles/Aids Along the Online Catalog Access Path

Reports of online catalogs encountered in the recent literature often fail to
make certain required distinctions when search capabilities and access points
are discussed. We think the distinctions outlined in the following
search/access classification scheme are useful for analyzing and evaluating
varieties of access in online catalogs.

1. Search categories or genres

    Search categories are general approaches or routes to retrieving
    bibliographic records from the database through author fields, title
    fields, subject-rich fields, classification numbers, and standard
    identification numbers (e.g., LCCN, ISBN), or by broad parameters
    such as language, publisher, date of publication, and type of
    material. Thus, subject searching capabilities may include access by
    indexed subject headings, title keywords, or call numbers.

2. Access points

    Access points are specific searchable fields in the bibliographic
    record. More precisely, they are words or phrases, extracted from
    fields and/or subfields, that have been entered into an inverted
    index file. As unique index records, these words or phrases serve as
    access points to the record or records from which they were
    extracted.

3. Access methods

    These are the different methods or operations for processing a search
    term (number, word, or phrase) either against various kinds of
    indexes, or among indexes. Keyword, phrase (e.g., title, subject
    heading), and derived abbreviated key represent three kinds of
    indexes. An exact, character-by-character match of a search term
    with an index record is one method of access; a truncated search in a
    keyword or phrase index is another. Combining search terms with
    Boolean logic operators, and requesting specific word locations and
    positions in the record(s) are additional methods of access.

4. Search mechanics

    "Search mechanics" is defined by BATES (1981) as "the methods and
    operations by which a database or service is accessed and a search is
    performed--i.e., the 'how to'." Search mechanics are access methods
    viewed from the user's side of the interface and constitute the
    functional component of the interface. Search mechanics include what
    we have called "command capabilities" in Figure 2 and Tables 2-6.
    The mechanics of a search are to be distinguished from the
    formulation of a search (one or more search statements), and from the
    strategy or plan which explains that formulation.

8.2 Indexing and Access Points

Replicating the functions and access points of the card catalog has been a
guiding principle in the design of today's online catalogs. Library catalog
planners and developers generally agree that setting and accomplishing this

"at least as much as the card catalog" objective is fundamental to user
acceptance of the online catalog. Online catalogs that do not provide all of
the traditional access points are considered inferior to the card catalogs
they supplement or replace. Reviewing the development of the PHOENIX online
catalog system at the University of New Brunswick, ALLEN (1982) expresses this
shared attitude in this manner:

> *A catalogue, like any library service, performs a number of
> functions. If a system is replaced by another which performs
> fewer functions, or performs the same functions less adequately,
> user dissatisfaction is inevitable. With this in mind, we set
> out to provide all functions of the card catalogue at least as
> well as the card catalogue did... Our attitude has been that we
> should replicate the functions and services of the card
> catalogue, while developing as many additional capabilities as
> possible to supplement traditional functions.*

During this period of experimentation and transition, it is not surprising
that increasing numbers of librarians are encouraging designers of online
catalogs to keep their feet on the bedrock _functional_ foundation of the card
catalog. However, this is regrettable because we know so little about how the
card catalog is used, or, equally important, why many library patrons do not
use the card catalog. An online catalog may encourage users to search or scan
related records in ways not attempted by users (and by definition, nonusers)
of the card catalog. The online catalog which offers a variety of _access_
methods (e.g., truncation, Boolean, and word proximity searching) and
additional title and subject _access points_ (e.g., keywords, embedded phrases,
and call numbers) will be searched in ways not possible in the card catalog.
The well-known virtues of the card catalog should not be ignored by designers
of online catalogs, but a well-designed online catalog can provide more modes
of access and more effective retrieval than possible in earlier forms of the
catalog.

Increasing the number and kind of access points is generally believed to be a
primary way of improving access to bibliographic records. Most of the OPACs
included in this study provide multiple access points, including title,
author, and subject fields. Table 8 registers the search categories or access
points provided by each of the ten OPACs, and invites comparisons between
individual systems. However, such comparisons can be misleading. The quality
of access in any form of catalog cannot be ascertained solely by counting its
search categories and access points. Additional factors such as the quality
of the indexing, the presence or absence of cross-references, and the
provision of useful search capabilities must be taken into account before
judgments can be fairly made regarding the extent and quality of access.

Equally important as the number of access points in a particular system is the
kind of access provided, namely, the "search categories or genres." Table 8,
which includes both access points (e.g., ISBN and government document number)
and search categories (e.g., title, author/title, subject), indicates which

Table 8. Access Points

ACCESS POINTS*	California, University of	Claremont Colleges	Dartmouth College	Mankato State University	Mission College	Northwestern University	OCLC	Ohio State University	Pikes Peak Library District	RLG/RLIN
Personal author	X	X	X	X	X	X	X	X	X	X
Corporate author	X	X	X	X	X	X	X	X	X	X
Title	X	X	X	X	X	X	X	X	X	X
Author/Title	X		X	X	X		X	X		X
Subject	X	X	X	X	X	X		X	X	X
Call number		X	X		X			X	X	X
LC card number	X		X	X	X		X		X	X
ISBN	X		X	X	X		X			X
ISSN	X		X	X			X			X
Government document number			X				X			X
Other control number	X^3		X^1	X^1			X^1	X^4	X^5	X^2
Additional access points	X^8	X^8	$X^{7,8}$	X^8	X^9	X^8	$X^{6,8}$	X^8		$X^{7,8}$
Free-text term search	X^{10}	X^{10}	X^{11}	X^{10}						X^{10}

X = Access point available to user

NOTES: 1. OCLC control number
        2. RLIN control number
        3. 1 and 2
        4. Title number
        5. Barcode number
        6. CODEN
        7. 6 and others
        8. Series title
        9. Course/instructor
       10. On selected fields
       11. Full text and selected fields

* In some systems, access points (usually names) are combined under a single search command.
  In others, the specific index must be identified with the search command.

systems provide, for example, subject or call number searching. However,
Table 8 does not reveal precisely which fields of the bibliographic record
have been rendered searchable by inclusion in an index. Table 8 does not tell
us, in the case of author and title search categories, which indexed field
belongs to which search category. We do not know at this point how the
indexes are constructed, nor do we know if cross-references are included.
These are some of the vital factors which affect the quality of online access.

In an online information retrieval system, the user-supplied search
formulation is matched against the index records of the database. If a
"match" occurs, that is, the logical requirements of the search are satisfied,
either the index records or the bibliographic records they reference are
retrieved and displayed to the user. The search formulation may consist of a
single word, number, or multiple-word phrase to be matched in an index, or it
may require the combination of two or more terms to be matched in one or more
indexes. With today's database management and retrieval systems, indexing
renders the fields of a record (or more precisely, the data in those fields)
searchable. Search terms are processed in various ways against one or more
indexes. If no match occurs, there can be no retrieval.

Online catalogs provide a wide range of indexes to their bibliographic
databases. No uniformity in the kinds and contents of indexes provided exists
at this time. The kinds of access points (fields) included in a given index
varies from system to system. Some OPACs combine related but different access
points (e.g., personal and corporate names, or even uniform title main entry)
in a single index and search category, such as "author." Other OPACs
segregate indexes rigorously by field, providing separate indexes for personal
author, corporate author or conference name, uniform title, series, etc. When
searching, the user may be required to specify the precise index to be
searched. In the latter case, the user at least knows the type of field(s)
which will be searched when a word or phrase is entered as the search term.

For effective retrieval, it is not only essential to know the index in which
various searchable fields are included, but also which fields are indexed at
all. Fields indexed in one system may not be indexed in another. For
example, name, title, and series added entries are not universally indexed in
online catalogs. In some systems, joint authors, illustrators, etc., are not
indexed. In others, the uniform title and/or the title traced differently
(which may include a subtitle) are not indexed. Rarely is a subdivision of a
subject heading indexed independently of the entire subject heading or its
component words. Most OPACs do not yet index the notes fields of the record
(5XX in the MARC format). Most notably missing in the eyes of the subject
access enthusiasts are the formal contents notes (505) and the summary or
abstract notes (520).

Various indexing policies and practices were discovered in our use of these
OPACs. However, the user often is not informed in a direct manner which
fields are not searchable (e.g., joint authors), or which index to search when
the principle of segregation has been applied to the indexing of related
fields (e.g., title in field 245, uniform title, or series title). These
shortcomings may lead a user to believe that an item is not in the library's
collection, when in reality, the author or subtitle entered by the user was
not indexed for online access (both may be in the cataloged record), or the
wrong index was specified in the search argument. These omissions and
inconsistencies in indexing practices may lead to the demand for

simplification (from the user's point of view) and standardization as the population and mobility of online catalog users increases.

8.3 Authority Control

In the preceding section it was noted that a user-supplied term not entered in the index being searched would result in a "non-hit" and no record would be retrieved. However, there are two possible exceptions to this situation, and both are unusual features in the online catalogs that are operational today. In the Claremont and Pikes Peak OPACs, at least one record is always retrieved and displayed to the user. If no match occurs on the search term, the system retrieves and displays the next record ("following" the absent record) represented in the file being searched. Browsing capabilities are provided in both systems to permit moving among records in the file (e.g., title, call number) without the necessity of entering another search.

If the user-supplied search term is not in the index being searched, it may be linked to one that is, and the match will be made on the latter term yielding, perhaps, a successful retrieval. This automatic switching of a search term not indexed to a related term that is indexed is made possible by the presence of an online authority control system. A link is maintained between an indexed name or subject heading and certain variant forms of the name or subject heading. These variant forms are included along with the standardized form in an authority record. An index which is under authority control will accept certain variant forms of a heading that is indexed. Two design options exist at this point: either the system can switch terms automatically and process the retrieval on the "authoritative" form of the heading, or the system can display a special "see" reference to the user. For example:

> The name you entered, Holt, Victoria, is entered in this catalog under, Plaidy, Jean. Do you wish to continue this search? (If "YES" press the RETURN key.)

Switching from the term as entered without informing the user can cause confusion when records are displayed which do not contain the name or subject entered as a search term.

Full online authority control requires not only an online file of authority records with cross-references ("see" and "see also"), but also links between the bibliographic records and the authority records. Such links permit the global modification of all headings (e.g., names or subjects) in the appropriate bibliographic records, and also provide the basis for the automatic switching from a variant form entered in a search argument to the authorized heading. A record retrieved in this manner would display the uniform, authoritative form of the name or subject in the authority-controlled field or fields.

The following is a name authority record retrieved from OCLC's Name Authority File. This file, built and maintained by loading the Library of Congress name authority tapes, may be searched online by a user who wishes to discover the authoritative form of a name or other names under which a person has authored one or more works.

```
Rec stat: c Entrd: 801128 Used: 810116
Type: zBib lvl: x Govt Agn:    Lang:      Source:
Site: 011 InLC: a Enc lvl: n Head ref: a Head: cc
Head status: a Name: a Mod rec:    Auth status: a
Ref status: b


- 1 010        n  80028245
- 2 100 10 Hunt, E. Howard q (Everett Howard), d 1918- w
n010801115aacann-----nnnn
- 3 400 10  Dietrich, Robert w n002800423aanann-----nnnd
- 4 400 20  St. John, David w n003800423aanann-----nnnd
- 6 400 10  Hunt, Everett Howard w n005800423aanann-----nnnd
- 7 400 10  Hunt, Howard, d 1918- w n011801115aaaana-----nnnd
- 8 500 10  Baxter, John w n007800423aanann-----nnnd
- 9 500 10  Davis, Gordon w n008800423aanann-----nnnd
-10 670      His East of farewell, 1942. w n009800423aanann-----nnn
```

The 100 field contains the authoritative form of the author's name. The 400
fields contain variant ("see from") forms, and the 500 fields contain related
names for which "see also" references could be generated.

Authority file control over the name and subject indexes of an online catalog
has been deemed either a highly desirable or a required feature by those
planning for online catalogs. According to library consultants BOSS and
MARCUM, "The prevailing opinion is that a fully automated, interactive
authority control system should be required." BAUSSER (1981a) reports that a
"consensus" exists on the desirability of online authority control, and
MATTHEWS (1981) reports that participants in the Consortium to Develop an
Online Catalog (CONDOC) ranked online authority control for names and subjects
(with cross references) fourth among forty features.

Full online authority control exists in only one of the online catalogs
included in this study (The University of California's MELVYL system), and
this authority control is limited to names. A display of a portion of a name
index retrieved by the BROWSE command will include related names when these
are included in the name authority file. For example:

-> browse pa howard hunt

Browse request: BROWSE PA HOWARD HUNT
Browse result: 2 author names found in the personal author index

1. Hunt, Howard Francis, 1918-, ed
2. Hunt, Howard, 1918-
   ALSO KNOWN AS:
      Dietrich, Robert
      St. John, David
      Hunt, E. Howard
      Hunt, Everette Howard
      Hunt, E. Howard (Everette Howard), 1918-

An online authority control system which includes the capability of switching
the user-supplied variant name to the authoritative choice and form is not an
unmixed blessing, as the following example of a personal author search on
MELVYL illustrates:

Search request: FIND PA DAVID ST. JOHN
Search result: 8 records at UC libraries

1. Hunt, Howard, 1918- THE BERLIN ENDING; A NOVEL OF DISCOVERY. 1973
2. Hunt, Howard, 1918- GIVE US THIS DAY. 1973
3. Hunt, Howard, 1918- THE SORCERERS BY DAVID ST. JOHN. 1969
4. Hunt, Howard, 1918- UNDERCOVER : MEMOIRS OF AN AMERICAN SECRET... 1974
5. Hunt, Howard, 1918- WHERE MURDER WAITS / Gordon Davis i.e. H. Hunt. 1965
6. St. John, David, 1949- HUSH / David St. John. 1976
7. St. John, David, 1949- THE SHORE / David St. John. 1980
8. Wright, Charles, 1935- WRIGHT, A PROFILE / new poems by Charles... 1979

The user wanted, presumably, a work or works published under the name, David
St. John. Perhaps a friend recommended a novel by this author. The above
response to the request, FIND PA DAVID ST. JOHN, is displayed in the brief,
REVIEW format available in MELVYL.

During the routine search for a work or works by the author of interest, no
message explaining the name switch is provided. The user, who may not
understand the librarians' rules for choice and form of entry, or is unaware
of the machinations of online authority control, cannot help but be confused
by this display. A clue to the mysteries of authority control may be noticed
in record number 3 in the previous example, but it is more likely that the
user would pursue the retrieval and location of works authored by the poet,
David St. John, born in 1949. Some information regarding the relation of
names may be obtained using MELVYL's BROWSE command, but this command
represents an optional, special purpose capability which may not be used by
many searchers. In either case (BROWSE or FIND), providing the user more
explanatory information about the catalog's use of "see" and "see also"
references would be useful.

The LCS online catalog at The Ohio State University has recently begun to
include "see" and "see also" references for selected subject headings when a
portion of that index is displayed. LCS and the other systems (except MELVYL)
do not have online authority control for names. Five of the systems do not
provide a term selection browsing capability in a name or subject index (see
Tables 6 and 10). This underscores the call for future design improvements in
this area. Online catalogs that do not provide "see" and "see also"
references for term selection deprive the users of aids that they may have
grown accustomed to (and benefitted from) when searching the card catalog.

8.4 Index Construction Techniques

Whether they combine or fully segregate index files in their stored databases,
today's OPACs provide a range of indexes for searching their machine-readable
databases. Regarding the desirable number of indexes, some espouse the
principle, "the more the better." Others choose to keep it "simple," arguing
that anything more than author, title, and subject (perhaps) index searches

will confuse the user. However, as we have seen, the individual fields that
are consolidated under each of these search categories may vary considerably
from one system to another. Thus, there is the need to distinguish between
search categories and actual access points (fields or data elements indexed
and searchable).

Indexes for online access to catalog records are usually constructed by
extracting data elements from the fields designated as searchable. There are
many methods by which a computer can extract data from machine-readable
records to build and maintain online indexes. Computer-constructed indexes
have been called "automatic indexes," and they have become common in online
retrieval systems:

>   An *automatic index* can be defined as a group of words or phrases
>   chosen from a text by a computer for the purpose of providing
>   terms to facilitate the location and retrieval of information,
>   or sometimes to provide insight into the kind of information
>   given in a text (EARL, 1970).

Various algorithms (software programs) have been applied for extracting data
(single words or phrases) from fields and manipulating that data for inclusion
in an index. No uniform approach producing standardized index records was
discovered in the indexing practices of the operational online catalogs. The
same bibliographic record stored in the LC MARC format will be indexed
differently (that is, the content and structure of the index record) from OPAC
to OPAC. However, the computer catalog will usually attempt a
character-by-character match of the user-supplied search term with an indexed
data element (internal character or word truncated searching is an exception
to this). Thus, the same type of search for the same record, using a uniform
search term, in different OPACs may produce different results. Hence it is
necessary for effective retrieval that the user know not only what fields are
indexed but also how they are indexed, that is, just how the extracted data
element is "written" and formatted into the index record.

Figure 13 lists the major approaches to indexing for online retrieval.
Traditionally, controlled vocabulary indexing and uncontrolled or "free text"
indexing have been viewed as two independent approaches to indexing document
records. WESSEL (1975) has stated that they represent "two distinct
conceptual approaches to indexing."

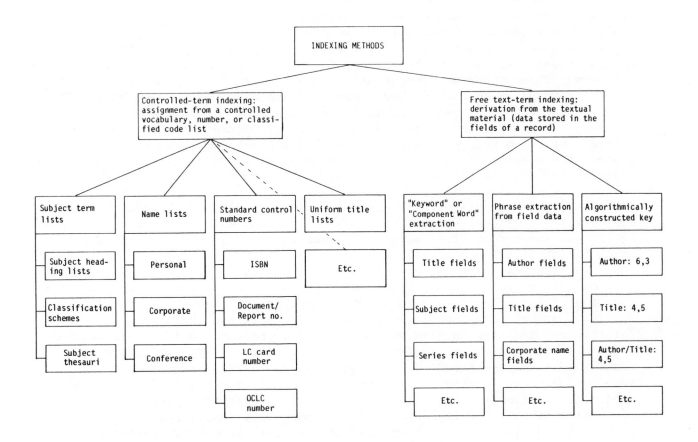

Figure 13. Indexing for Online Access to Bibliographic Records

In controlled vocabulary systems, human indexers assign terms from a
controlled list or thesaurus to documents or document representations stored
in the database. This process may also be accomplished automatically through
the use of standard subject-indexing software, as explained by DILLON, et al.
(1981):

> *In the indexing environment, document text [e.g., a MARC record]*
> *is examined for certain terms; these "free text" (uncontrolled*
> *vocabulary) terms are tied to equivalent (controlled vocabulary)*
> *terms in a thesaurus. When an uncontrolled vocabulary term is*
> *encountered in a document, its associated controlled vocabulary*
> *term is posted to the document as a descriptor.*

Controlled vocabulary indexes are usually supplied with the database by the
database producer.

As explained by MEADOW and COCHRANE (1981), "Descriptors assigned from a
controlled vocabulary represent an intellectual effort to describe what an
item is about using only a predetermined set of words or terms or codes.
Descriptors can be any of a combination of traditional classification codes
(as in the Library of Congress or Dewey Decimal systems), subject headings, or
key words and phrases."

As computer memory became cheaper and the professional searchers of the 70s became interested in searching for individual words within a title or abstract, the major database vendors developed techniques for searching within fields of a record. To make this "free text" searching possible, the database indexes had to be expanded to include words extracted from the natural language (uncontrolled) of the record, as well as the descriptors assigned by indexers. These indexing methods are commonly known by the names, "free text," "natural language," or "uncontrolled language." According to WESSEL (1975), what distinguishes "free text" indexing from controlled language indexing is that the indexing terms are "uncontrolled single words occurring in the text." On the other hand, controlled language or thesaurus indexing employs "descriptor constructs which form a language distinct from the languages of the textual material to which they are to be attached."

LANCASTER (1979) points out that most database vendors now utilize "hybrid" indexing and retrieval systems (both controlled and natural language systems). Controlled and uncontrolled terms are often included in the same inverted index file, but are distinguished by one major difference: controlled terms usually point only to bibliographic records, typically by including one or more unique record numbers. Free text index words usually point to the exact location of the word in each record it references, including the field or subfield, and the exact position of the word within the field. This "positional" indexing permits searching with a precision and flexibility not possible with traditional controlled language systems. In the latter, the controlled term itself must be entered with precision on the part of the searcher, and <u>all</u> records are retrieved that have been assigned that term. Free text indexing may include, of course, the extraction of words from controlled terms, when fields containing controlled descriptors (e.g., Library of Congress Subject Headings) are included in the automatic indexing routines. This permits keyword searching over multi-word descriptors and subject headings.

When we consider the automatic indexing of library catalog records, the traditional distinction between controlled vocabulary and free text or natural language indexing loses much of its importance. The distinction represented by the two original branches of the tree in Figure 13 is no longer relevant to the indexing of <u>cataloged</u> records for online access. There are two explanations for this:

1.   The data in the cataloged record is, for the most part, already controlled. That is, the catalog record is formalized and structured in a standardized manner, according to the Anglo-American Cataloging Rules (AACR1 or AACR2). As NEVILLE (1981) has said, the language of AACR is a "specialized language... it has features of controlled vocabulary, syntax, punctuation, format, and typography, which are not normal English."

     This standardized catalog record is formalized further, and its elements are additionally defined and identified, by the MARC format. The MARC formats, developed by the Library of Congress for the communication of bibliographic information in machine-readable form, identify fields and subfields for computer recognition and manipulation, including automatic extraction and indexing.

2.   Online catalog indexing consists primarily of extracting
      (algorithmically) data from one or more fields of the catalog record
      stored in a MARC or MARC-compatible format.

In the context of online catalog records, free text indexing, according to the
traditional definitions, is the predominant method used. The rightmost branch
in Figure 13 depicts the three most common options employed for indexing from
the "natural" text of the catalog record. The indexing routines operate on
data entered into the fields and subfields of the record when it was created
to catalog a bibliographic item. The differences between the three techniques
(keyword, phrase, and derived truncated key) can be explained by how much data
is extracted from a field or fields and how that data is manipulated to create
an entry in the index.

Keyword, phrase, and derived key indexing techniques provide three different
modes of access to library catalog records. Keyword indexing involves the
extraction of single words from designated fields of the record. These words
are inverted in the appropriate index file with pointers or links to the
records in which they occur. Thus, keyword searching permits access through
component words of a title phrase or subject heading. The user is not
required to remember and enter all or most of the title or subject heading as
it was entered into the record by the cataloger. However, few online catalogs
include word positional data (within the field) in these keyword index
entries. This exclusion eliminates the possibility of word proximity (e.g.,
adjacency) search capabilities in these systems. It may be possible to
specify the field or related fields in which two or more words occur, but it
is not possible to specify the order of these words, or their precise
proximity to each other within a field.

Phrase indexing takes the cataloging data essentially as it was entered into
the field being indexed (e.g., personal author, corporate name, title, subject
heading). Many variations of phrase extractions are practiced, but the phrase
order as entered is usually maintained. Initial articles are commonly
excluded from the phrase index record, as well as certain words considered
nonsignificant. With these "stoplist" word exceptions, and the exclusion of
punctuation and some special characters, the phrase index record is created
from the data in the field "exactly" as it was entered by the cataloger.

Phrase searching is sometimes referred to as the "direct entry" approach to
the catalog, and most closely simulates searching of the card catalog. The
user must know the exact title or subject heading, or at least the leading
words in the phrase. FURLONG (1978) explains this approach as it is used at
Northwestern: "access to a record in the file is by a 'search term' which is
in fact the entry wanted, so that there is no need to devise a search key...
It is not words per se which are indexed; it is the bibliographic entry as a
whole that is indexed under the first word or words, exactly as it would be
found in a card catalog."

However, with systems that employ the "direct entry" (phrase searching)
approach, the dangers of nonstandardization lie in the path of the catalog
user. As FURLONG points out, the searcher must not only be familiar with the
rules of entry (AACR1 or AACR2!), but, "In order to work efficiently, the user
of the index should also know the characteristics of the entry field after its
translation into an index term." This hurdle encountered along the access
path has been raised even higher!

The translation of the phrase as entered by the cataloger into the phrase as indexed for online access varies from OPAC to OPAC. The following are some of the variables affecting this translation:

1. The total number of characters of the data element (e.g., title, corporate name, subject heading) and the subfields that are indexed varies from OPAC to OPAC.

2. The words placed on the exclusion list ("stoplist") not to be included in the indexed phrase varies from system to system, and from index to index in some systems. Some stoplists include more than 100 words, others include only initial articles.

3. The exclusion of punctuation and special characters from the index phrase varies from system to system.

4. The filing arrangement of entries in the phrase indexes (e.g., subject headings) varies frequently from one system to another.

5. Index records often include abbreviated data from other fields. The kind, length, and positional order of this additional data varies from system to system.

Some of the potential problems a user faces with the direct entry, phrase searching approach can be avoided if provision is made for truncated phrase searching. This increases the retrieval set of records, but the user does not have to remember the entire title or subject heading. An indexing variation which aids the phrase searcher involves the permutation of entries which provides second and third word access, etc. For example, the title, "A Study of Renaissance Choral Works," could be entered additionally in the title index as:

        Renaissance Choral Works, Study of
        Choral Works, Study of Renaissance

Unfortunately, many OPACs do not yet forgive a user's ignorance of the local stoplist, or the correct way to enter punctuation. The searcher who enters "The" at the beginning of a title phrase term, or fails to enter a comma after the personal author's last name (entered first), often finds himself dumped into the database far from where he hoped to find an entry. Entering the initial article "The" commonly returns records whose titles begin with "theater." Seldom is there a warning or explanation displayed online.

The third major indexing technique employed in online catalogs requires the construction of derived, abbreviated index keys. A set of formulas determines the maximum and minimum number of characters to be extracted from certain words in one or more fields (e.g., name, name/title, subject). These characters are then combined into constructed or "derived" index keys. For example, "MANC,AMER," might be the derived key for William Manchester's book, American Caesar. As we saw in the preceding chapter, the search key structures and syntax necessary to match these derived index keys vary from one system to another. Derived search keys used over a single field seldom yield a single retrieval, and the multiple records retrieved are related only by the circumstance that the initial characters of the first, second, or third

word of the searched field are the same. The user must remember the match
code for each type of search, usually without prompting or formatting aids
displayed by the system. Like "exact entry" phrase searching, the user must
remember the order of the words in a title or subject phrase to properly
construct the derived search key.

8.5 Search Term Processing Methods

Table 9 illustrates the access methods discovered in the ten OPACs, classified
according to the three indexing techniques explained in the preceding section.
The first level of distinction indicates which system provides keyword,
phrase, or derived key searching.

For example, MELVYL, at the University of California, primarily employs
keyword searching in the current prototype version of the OPAC. Author's
names may be entered with the surname first, followed by a comma and the first
name, or entered straightforwardly (e.g., Joan Didion). Three systems provide
derived key access, but the OPAC at Mankato State offers this method as an
option to the user. That is, an author's name, a title, or a subject phrase
may be entered straightforwardly in its natural form.

The second level distinction illustrates which systems provide either
truncated term searching against the designated index, or permit exact,
character-by-character matches of the term precisely as entered by the user.
In the latter case, the search term, DIDION,J, would not return references to
works written by Joan Didion.

The third level distinction illustrated in Table 9 simply indicates whether
the user must enter an explicit command instructing the system to process a
truncated search against the index, or to process an exact search on the
search term precisely as it was entered by the user.

The table shows that designers are making truncation the default choice more
often than not when phrase searching is employed. On the other hand, if
truncation is desired on a keyword, more systems than not require the explicit
entry of a truncation command. Only Mission College's OPAC requires the entry
of an explicit command to invoke an exact match on a phrase search (the user
appends a "/E" to the search term).

The rules for searching on personal names vary from system to system, and
sometimes, within the same system. For example, if the author's last name and
first initial are entered on MELVYL, the system will process an implicit
truncated search. That is, FIND PA DIDION,J, will retrieve records by Joan
Didion in the University of California database. However, if more than the
first initial of the first name is entered, the system processes an exact
match search. For example, FIND PA DIDION,JO will not retrieve Joan Didion's
works.

Good common sense design explanations can be offered for many of these search
processing variations. However, there is a need to inform the user, in terms
he can understand, just what the system is doing with the search as entered,
and what options, if any, are available. In addition to facing different

command-entry requirements, the user searching on various OPACs cannot assume that the actual processing of a search term will be consistent from OPAC to OPAC.

Table 9. How Indexed Fields Are Searched

SEARCH TERM PROCESSING VARIATIONS	California, University of	Claremont Colleges	Dartmouth College	Mankato State University	Mission College	Northwestern University	OCLC	Ohio State University	Pikes Peak Library District	RLG/RLIN
KEYWORD										
Exact match										
- explicit user command ,or										
- implicit (system default)	X		X	X						X
Truncated match										
- explicit user command ,or	X		X	X						X
- implicit (system default)		X			X					
PHRASE (leading)										
Exact match										
- Explicit user command ,or				X						
- implicit (system default)		X	X							X
Truncated match										
- explicit user command ,or			X	X						X
- implicit (system default)		X			X	X		X	X	
DERIVED SEARCH KEY			X[1]				X	X[2]		

1. User has option to construct the search key (e.g., the 8,3,3,2 format for the entry of the first four subject term words) or to enter the term in its natural language form.

2. For a subject search, the user must enter a Library of Congress Subject Heading in its natural form. For an author search, the author's name may be entered (last name first) as it normally appears, or as a derived key (e.g., AUT/TOFFLER ALVIN or AUT/TOFFLEALV).

8.6 Subject Access Variations

The principal subject vocabulary used for constructing online indexes for subject access is the Library of Congress Subject Headings (LCSH). The subject data element extraction techniques may operate on all 6XX fields of the MARC record, or the extraction of index terms may be limited to selected subject fields, such as 650 and 651. However, for the most part, a user conducting a subject search in one of today's OPACs is limited to the LCSH vocabulary when entering a search term. Effective retrieval of records resulting from a match of the LCSH search term with an index record is further diminished by the fact that, on average, less than two subject headings are assigned by the Library of Congress to each item cataloged . (O'NEILL and ALURI, 1979, report an average of 1.4 subject headings per monograph in a sample of the OCLC database.)

Table 9, reviewed in the preceding section, may be used to ascertain which OPACs offer keyword or phrase searching on index terms. However, exceptions often apply to subject searching. For example, RLIN no longer permits keyword access to subject headings, and keyword access at Mission College is limited to title in the combined author/title search only. It is interesting to note that of the three systems which offer derived key access, one does not permit subject searching (OCLC), one requires the user to enter the LC subject heading in its natural (cataloged) form and word order (OSU), and one offers the option of entering the heading in its natural form (Mankato State). The assumption seems to be that users are familiar with LC Subject Headings (or know where and how to discover them), and have little difficulty in entering the LC phrases correctly.

Another perspective on the diversity of subject access approaches in OPACs is presented by Table 10. This table groups systems into (1) those which provide keyword searching over LC Subject Headings, and (2) those which require character-by-character, word-by-word, phrase matching of LC Subject Headings. The truncation capabilities illustrated on Table 9 may be applied to the OPACs which offer subject searching. Access to the LCSH subdivisions, independent of the entire subject heading, represents a third and special case of subject access. Keyword access to LCSH subdivisions depends, of course, on whether or not the subfields are indexed.

Table 10. Subject Access and Response

SUBJECT ACCESS VARIATIONS	California, University of	Claremont Colleges	Dartmouth College	Mankato State University	Mission College	Northwestern University	OCLC	Ohio State University	Pikes Peak Library District	RLG/RLIN
LCSH* phrase match searching followed by display of bibliographic record(s)	X	X	X					X	X	
LCSH phrase match searching followed by automatic display of subject index records				X	X		X[1]			
LCSH phrase match searching with option to browse subject index records				X						
LCSH subdivision searching followed by display of bibliographic records(s)									X	
LCSH keyword searching followed by display of bibliographic record(s)	X	X	X							
LCSH keyword searching followed by automatic display of subject index records										
LCSH keyword searching with option to browse subject index records	X[1]	X								
Title keyword searching	X	X	X						X	

*LCSH = Library of Congress Subject Headings

1. Displays cross-references associated with a subject heading

The three approaches to subject access represented on Table 10 are further categorized into those systems which display bibliographic records immediately following the subject search, and those which immediately display a list of subject index records containing alphabetically arranged or logically related terms. An optional index browsing feature is available in the OPACs at Dartmouth College (BRS command capabilities) and the University of California. This browsing feature requires the use of a separate command. Ironically, many systems which require or offer phrase-match searching of LC Subject Headings do not provide the user the opportunity to peruse those headings online.

Title keyword searching may be considered a fourth approach to subject access (call number searching is another). Keyword access to both titles and subject headings is a required feature of online catalogs as specified in the CONDOC guidelines (MATTHEWS, 1981).

The shortcomings of LCSH for subject indexing of bibliographic works (e.g., lack of specificity and currentness, awkward phrase construction) have been discussed frequently in the literature. For two recent reviews of these problems, see MANDEL (1981) and MISCHO (1982). In a recent bibliographic essay, COCHRANE and KIRTLAND (1981) identify and review critiques of LCSH in eight categories (e.g., specificity, syndetic structure, ease of use, etc.). The further limitations on subject access imposed by today's OPACs include the following:

1. Many OPACs do not permit the searcher to view a portion of the subject headings index.

2. Most OPACs do not display "see also" references to related subject headings.

3. In many systems, the user must enter the LCSH phrase in the exact word order, character by character. (Stoplists and acceptable punctuation varies.)

4. Few OPACs provide title keyword access.

5. Few OPACs provide a call number or shelf list browsing capability (Notable exceptions are the OPACs at Claremont, Ohio State, and Pikes Peak). This feature requires not only call number searching, but the ability to move among records in the shelf list file without entering additional searches.

6. Keyword access to titles and subject headings is not always accompanied by limiting/refining features such as field specification, or word position or proximity operators. These features diminish the possibility of false term coordinations when Boolean operations are carried out on keywords.

7. Because of the processing overhead required for Boolean searches on keywords, many systems are placing artificial limits on the number of "hits" allowed, or the time allocated to process these requests. Suggestions for reducing the results are seldom provided online.

COCHRANE (1982) has recently reviewed subject access developments in online catalogs. While reporting major improvements in subject access in online catalogs, she also discusses "unfortunate consequences already evident in the newest online forms of a library's catalog." COCHRANE concludes from her examination of more than twelve operational OPACs that "we are not necessarily making improvements when we make changes for increased subject access." Her list of "Unfortunate Consequences of Present-Day Online Subject Access Procedures" overlaps with our "limitations" list, presented above, but warrants repeating here:

1. In those OPACs in which content of the catalog record (i.e., unit record) is more accessible, this access is less controlled. All words in the title field(s) are now accessible except for those words on a "stop list." The fields used to build "title" keyword searches may not be uniform across online catalogs.

2. In those OPACs which require letter-for-letter matches with LCSH and titles, punctuation (especially hyphens), word order, and abbreviations may cause problems in searching unless treatment before indexes is explained to user.

3. The controlled vocabularies (e.g., LCSH, LCC, DDC) exist in the online index (created from the catalog records) only as a subset of used headings or class numbers. These indexes include "uncontrolled" or unrecorded use of subdivisions and Cutter numbers. There are no lead-in terms (see references) and no see also references online in these lists usually. The call numbers appear as unexplained codes.

4. Common words in titles or subject headings (e.g., history, basic, education, literature, America, etc.) which cannot be placed on a stop word list, slow transaction throughput and may be prohibited or placed in background processing for Boolean searches or proximity checks.

5. Allowing keyword searches in a combination of fields (e.g., title and subject heading, or both subject headings in a record) may cause false drops. The retrieval techniques needed to prevent this, such as proximity operators, may not be present.

6. The filing order of the subject heading entries in the index lists (e.g., main LCSH and all subdivisions) may cause confusion by not following the LCSH printed order or the order of headings in the card catalog. Main heading and subdivisions may be interspersed with inverted or compound headings.

7. The number and kind of heading indexes in which the user may browse vary from OPAC to OPAC.

8. Entry of Boolean operators exists as explicit or implicit procedures from OPAC to OPAC, or within a single OPAC.

Despite these limitations and questionable consequences of new access features, the immediate future for online subject access is promising. Opportunities exist for enhancing subject access not possible in earlier forms of the catalog. The prospect of combining the best subject access features discovered among the ten OPACs in this study is exciting, indeed. These features include (1) current terminology access through title keyword searching, (2) refining results by limiting search parameters to field, word position, publication date, language, or type of material, and (3) browsing headings files (with cross-references), keywords in titles, and the shelves themselves (represented by records in the shelf list file). Online catalogs offer almost unlimited possibilities for quickly bringing together, for easy review, related records of interest to the searcher, whether that interest centers on a particular author, organization, or topical subject.

8.7 Specialized Search Mechanics

With regard to the number and kind of search and retrieval features they offer
the user, today's OPACs range from the simple, easy-to-learn, computer-guided
model which provides only author and title or subject phrase searching, to the
powerful, often complex, command language systems which incorporate most of
the special features developed for the major commercial retrieval systems
(e.g., DIALOG, ORBIT, and BRS). In addition to the number and kind of access
points provided, and the quality of indexing, a major factor affecting the
quality of access in an online catalog is the number and kind of specialized
search features it provides to permit more flexible and precise retrieval by
name, title, or subject. One challenge to designers of online catalogs is to
serve the needs of the occasional, naive user well; another is to provide
features that can be used advantageously by the skilled, experienced searcher.
Before reviewing the provision of these advanced, specialized capabilities in
various OPACs, a few definitions may uncloud the territory to be covered.

In her review article, "Search Techniques," in the 1981 Annual Review of
Information Science and Technology, BATES defines search techniques as
"methods, heuristics, tactics, strategies, or plans that can be used by people
in searching in manual or automated information systems." Because of the
vague terminology and the overlapping and inconsistent usage of terms in this
conceptual area, BATES further proposes these useful distinctions:

1. Search mechanics--"the methods or operations by which a database or
    service is accessed and a search is performed--i.e., the 'how to'.
    This term includes the means of logging on and off a database,
    explanation of commands, and the mechanics of Boolean logic."

2. Search formulation--"a search statement or series of statements
    expressing the search topic of a request." The search formulation
    describes a specific search query in the language acceptable to the
    retrieval system.

3. Search strategy--"an approach to or plan for a whole search. A
    search strategy is used to inform or to determine specific search
    formulation decisions; it operates at a level above term choice and
    command use." Strategies can be developed and used independently of
    particular search topics. However, they are confined in reality to
    the possibilities for formulating a search given the command
    capabilities provided by a particular retrieval system.

Figure 14 is a representation of the search and retrieval universe delineated
above. Search strategies appropriate to various information retrieval needs
addressed to online library catalogs have yet to be developed and tested.
Given the structure and content of records in the catalog database, not all of
the traditional search strategies may be relevant (e.g., the "building-block"
approach, or "citation pearl-growing"). A useful review of these traditional
strategies may be found in HAWKINS and WAGERS (1982).

In general, search formulations are made up of search mechanics and terms in the vocabulary of the system. In practice, the command capabilities provided by the system being used set the limits on the searcher's efforts at successful retrieval. A wide range in the number and kind of search formulation capabilities ("mechanics") offered the user is represented by the online catalogs participating in this study.

Figure 14. The Structure of Search Methods

In chapter 3, Table 3 illustrated many of the search capabilities available in the ten online catalogs. Table 11, presented here, pulls together several related features to allow comparisons to be made with greater specificity. Two groupings of systems are immediately apparent after viewing Table 11. Four of the systems have features comparable to those available on Lockheed's DIALOG or BRS. In fact, the OPAC at Dartmouth College employs the BRS retrieval software, which explains the availability of that OPAC's many advanced features.

Table 11. Special Search Formulation Capabilities

USER ACTION	California, University of	Claremont Colleges	Dartmouth College	Mankato State University	Mission College	Northwestern University	OCLC	Ohio State University	Pikes Peak Library District	RLG/RLIN
Controlled subject term searching*	X	X	X	X	X	X		X	X	X
Free-text term search of entire record			X							
Free-text term search in a user-selected field	X		X	X	X[6]					X
Free-text term search in user-combined fields	X		X	X						X
Free-text term search in system default field(s)		X	X[2]	X						
Word truncation for a free-text search	X		X	X						X
Explicit use of Boolean operators with search terms	X		X	X	[3]					X
Explicit use of Boolean operators on previous search set(s)	X		X	X						X
Explicit use of word adjacency/ proximity operators	[1]		X							
Restrict (limit) search results by date, language, etc.	X	X	X	X			X	X		
Explicit use of relational operators	X	X	X	X			X	X		
User can view index or thesaurus terms	X		X		X[5]	X[4,5]		X[5]		
User can view search history	X		X	X					X	
User can save search statements for later execution	[1]		X	X						

X = Search capability available for user when formulating a search

* A search term may consist of a truncated word, a single word, or a multiple-word phrase.

NOTES: 1. To be implemented
        2. The default includes all fields (default = user does not have to specify value or option during search).
        3. Author/title and course/instructor (reserved materials) searches are implemented with Boolean "and", but user does not select and enter the Boolean operator.
        4. An index display results automatically in the display of author or title multiple search results. No distinct command is available.
        5. Index display results automatically in the display of subject search results. No distinct command is available.
        6. Possible only in the title field when combined author/title search is utilized.

The dividing line between two groups of systems is clearly represented by those OPACs which offer keyword access ("free text") to user-selected fields, combined with Boolean search capabilities and commands to precisely define the parameters of a search by date, language, and type of material. Noticeably missing at this time is the provision for specifying word position within a field or word-to-word proximity (except Dartmouth/BRS).

Boolean "AND" operations on keywords are simulated in two systems, Claremont's TLS and the ULISYS system at Mission College. This is made possible by the inclusion of multiple-field data within a single index record. For example, at Mission, the author index records include a portion of the title phrase up to a maximum number of characters. When entering an author/title search, the user may choose any single word from the title: for example, AT=HEMINGWAY/BELL. When processing this search, the system gathers all records in the author index that match "Hemingway," then a character-by-character string search of the title portion of the index record is conducted to locate the word "Bell." The "Hemingway" records that also have "Bell" in the title are then retrieved. In traditional Boolean operations, all titles having the word "Bell" would be retrieved (including Sylvia Plath's Bell Jar) and intersected with all the records retrieved from the author (or personal name) index which matched "Hemingway." Claremont's TLS processes the combined subject and author or title search in a similar manner. The matching subject records are retrieved first from the subject index, then each is scanned for the presence of the author or title term entered by the user.

Nothing suffices for making judgments about the quality of access in these OPACs short of actual "hands-on" use. The reader is especially discouraged from making evaluations based on the review of a single table presented in this report. In one sense, an OPAC is the sum of its functional parts; however, its "personality" and retrieval effectiveness cannot be captured by adding up its features as registered on these tables.

A detailed overview of each system can be obtained by a careful examination of all the comparative tables in this report. The "picture" of a system will change when, for example, the information provided on Table 11 is joined by the descriptions of the system's access points and results manipulation (output) capabilities (discussed in the next chapter). We have attempted to provide an analytic framework that identifies the vital issues at stake in the design of online catalogs. The checklists (tables) suggest questions that catalog planners may ask of those responsible for designing and marketing the new online systems.

9

9.1 Design Issues/User Options
9.2 Results Manipulation Capabilities
9.3 Optimal Bibliographic Display Formats: Fact and Opinion
9.4 Display Formats in Ten Online Catalogs

Results Manipulation and the Display of Bibliographic Information

9.1 Design Issues/User Options

In the simplest terms, considerations of output control design features may be grouped into two categories: (1) those features which enable the user to manipulate the results of a search according to his needs or preferences, and (2) the characteristics of the displays themselves, or rather, guidelines for the visual presentation of bibliographic information.

In chapter 3, we discussed output control capabilities in the form of brief notes which accompanied Table 5. That discussion will be recapitulated in the following section along with a more in-depth look at display/print capabilities available to the users of these ten OPACs. The third and last sections of this chapter will include a discussion of display format options and an analytical review of displays discovered in our use of the ten OPACs.

The common themes that have emerged from this analysis of operational online catalogs are diversity and nonstandardization at every dimension of the user interface. This diversity is more evident in the many output control and display options available than at any other dimension of the user interface. For example, thirty-seven different display formats for the same record were discovered among the ten OPACs included in this study.

To some, the control and display of retrieved bibliographic records may seem a simple matter. If only a single record is retrieved, should not the system display it automatically? Of course, if multiple records are retrieved, the user should be able to choose one or more from among them for display. And should not the display of a single record look like the standardized, traditional presentation of bibliographic information on the familiar 3x5 catalog card?

If matters of output and display are this simple, the designers of today's online catalogs have needlessly embraced complexity. However, given the variety of human needs and preferences, and the vast capabilities present in computer catalogs, our analysis has revealed that the design issues are both many and complex. Little research has been conducted to determine user needs and preferences in this area, but some recent studies are suggesting that the conventional wisdom regarding display formats is in need of revision. The following is a bipartite list of <u>design issues</u> facing online catalog planners and designers today:

System Display Provisions

1. Accept, store, and manipulate for display full MARC records in the database

2. Provide several levels of display formats from brief to full record displays

3. Among formats, provide one which replicates the layout of the 3x5 catalog card

4. Among formats, provide a complete record display that includes MARC content designators

5. Provide a one-line format for multiple listings

6. Automatically display a single-record "hit" or retrieval

7. Automatically display several records of a multiple-record retrieval set

8. Automatically display some record (e.g., next in the file) when no match or "hit" occurs

9. Provide location and/or item availability status on one or more display formats

10. Include search formulation and summary of results (postings) on each display

11. Provide suggestive prompts with each display to indicate additional formats, records, or "pages" and valid commands

User Control Options

1. Choose a "prepackaged" (system-supplied) format in a particular situation

2. Choose a system-supplied format for the display default value

3. Design a format from one or more fields for a single display

4. Set the display default value to the user-designed format

5. Move discretely forward or backward among multiple records or pages (screens)

6. Scroll multiple records forward or backward

7. Select a single record from among multiple "hits" to display in the chosen format

8. Select more than one record, or a range of records, to display from a multiple listing

9. Sort and/or merge retrieved records by user-supplied criteria for inclusion and order

10. Request hardcopy print of selected records

No claim is made for exhaustivity in the above list, and some of the design issues implicitly contain multiple questions. The list is offered as an indication of the many complex decisions facing today's planners and designers of online catalogs. There is no better time for users to express their needs and preferences, and we hope that research projects aimed at obtaining knowledge of user needs and preferences continue to increase in the near future.

9.2 Results Manipulation Capabilities

Table 12 presents descriptive information regarding the display and print capabilities available to the users of the ten OPACs.

Table 12. Display/Print Capabilities

DISPLAY/PRINT CAPABILITIES	California, University of	Claremont Colleges	Dartmouth College	Mankato State University	Mission College	Northwestern University	OCLC	Ohio State University	Pikes Peak Library District	RLG/RLIN
Does a single-record search result display automatically?	Yes	Yes	Yes	No	Yes	Yes	Yes	Yes	Yes	Yes
Does a multiple-record search result display automatically?	No	Yes[k]	Yes[l]	No	Yes	Yes	Yes	Yes	Yes[l]	No
General command for record display in a standard (default) format?	Yes	Yes	Yes	Yes	Yes	Yes	Yes	Yes	Yes	Yes
No. of predefined record display formats utilized by the system	4	4	4	7	3	2	2	3	2	5
No. of predefined display formats user can explicitly choose to display a single record by itself	4	3	4	6	3[e]	1[b]	1[b]	3d,[e]	1[f]	5[c]
Can user select a single record from multiple search results for display?	Yes	Yes	Yes	Yes	Yes	Yes	Yes	Yes	Yes[j]	Yes
Using a single command can user specify more than one record from multiple search results for display?	Yes	No	Yes	Yes[h]	No	No	No	Yes[g]	No	Yes
Can user select one or more individual fields to create a single display?	Yes	No	Yes	No	No	No	No	No	No	Yes
Can user sort results by a field, or request a merge of various results for display?	Sort[a]	No	Yes[m]	No	No	No	No	No	No	No
Online capability to request an offline printout of results?	[a]	No	Yes	Yes	Yes	No	No	No	No	No
Is a hardcopy terminal or printer available to the user when searching?	Yes[i]	No	Yes	Yes[i]	Yes	No	Yes[i]	Yes	Yes	Yes[i]

NOTES: a. To be implemented
   b. If single record retrieved, it is displayed in a standard format. No other format can be chosen for this record.
   c. RLIN's "Multiple" format can be chosen only for last record in set of multiple results.
   d. Full bibliographic record ("FBR") format available only for materials published since 1975.
   e. User can choose the brief one-line format only for a single record result.
   f. A partial MARC format (with tags) is available for about half the database, mostly recent publications.
   g. Accomplished with a single command by chaining the desired record numbers to one of two display commands.
   h. Only in brief one-line format
   i. Some member institutions provide hardcopy terminals or attached printers.
   j. User can select the next record entered in the file under the heading for the record retrieved.
   k. Only if "E" command (a Boolean search) used
   l. Only the first record of retrieved set displays
   m. Offline output only

A few of these capabilities were discussed in chapter 3 along with the
checklist for output control capabilities (Table 5). The first item on Table
5, "general command to display results," was "checked" for each of the ten
OPACs. However, as Table 12 indicates, most systems do not require the use of
a display command for the <u>initial</u> display. Eight of ten display a single
"hit" automatically. Six of the ten OPACs display a multiple-record retrieval
automatically, usually in a one-line review format. For example, the
following is a review display of a multiple-record retrieval on the ULISYS
OPAC at Mission College:


```
H?A=COMMONER BARRY
HJH?                                                    A=COMMONER BARRY
Line# Call #        Author               Title

1    HD9502.U52 H                        Human welfare : the end use for power :
2    HD 9502 .U52                        Human welfare : the end use for power /
3    TD195.E4S6                          The Social costs of power production /
4    TP319.A56                           Alternative technologies for power prod
5    VIDEO 75-14   Buckley, William Fr   Is there an ecological crisis? [videore
6    MANUAL 75-48  Buckley, William Fr   Is there an ecological crisis? [manual]
7    GF75.C65      Commoner, Barry, 19   The closing circle; nature, man, and te
8    GF75.C65 197  Commoner, Barry, 19   The closing circle; nature, man & techn
9    HD9502.A2C64  Commoner, Barry, 19   The poverty of power : energy and the e
10   HD9502.A2 C6  Commoner, Barry, 19   The poverty of power : energy and the e
11   Q 125 .C56    Commoner, Barry, 19   Science and survival
```


Two systems display a single-record retrieval automatically, but require the
user to enter an explicit command to view a multiple-record retrieval list.
Only two systems, Dartmouth (BRS mode) and Mankato State, do not automatically
display either a single-record retrieval or a multiple-record retrieval set.
At Mankato State, a multiple-record retrieval is displayed in this manner:


```
>AU COMMONER, BARRY
    6 RECORDS MATCHED THE SEARCH
TYPE DI 1-6  TO DISPLAY THE RECORDS
>DI 1-6
Screen 001 of 001
NMBR DATE --------------------TITLE-------------------- -------AUTHOR----
0001 1971  The closing circle;  nature, man, and technol  Commoner, Barry,
0002 1975  Human welfare :  the end use for power : prep
0003 1979  The politics of energy /                       Commoner, Barry,
0004 1976  The poverty of power :  energy and the econom   Commoner, Barry,
0005 1966  Science and survival.                           Commoner, Barry,
0006 1970  Science and survival.                           Commoner, Barry,
----Type DI NMBR(s) to display specific records
>
```


All ten of the systems provide a command for displaying a record in a
system-supplied standard format. In those systems which display the results
automatically, this command may be used to redisplay a previously displayed
record, or to select a standard format for a record that has been displayed
within a multiple listing.

The number of predefined display formats provided by the ten systems ranges
from two to seven. Six of the ten systems include a MARC-like display with
tags. In some systems, not all of the system-supplied formats can be selected
freely by the user. Thus, there are some discrepancies in Table 12 between
the numbers for predefined display formats utilized by the system and those
formats a user can choose to display a single record. In some cases, the
"automatic" display format cannot be selected subsequently by the user. In
other cases, not all of the records in the database have been loaded in a
manner that would permit display in all formats.

All ten systems permit a user to display a single record from multiple search
results, although the mechanics for doing this differ. These mechanics
include a simple line number selection, sometimes with the "display" command
implicit, and a command which permits displaying single records, one at a
time, in the order they were sorted in the multiple-record retrieval set.

A suggestive prompt is frequently supplied at the end of a multiple listing,
informing the user of available display options, and how to request them. The
following is an example from Mission's OPAC:

> To determine the location and availability of a specific title, type ST=
> followed by the line number. EXAMPLE: ST=2 and RETURN
> For more detailed information on a specific title, type BI= followed by the
> line number. EXAMPLE: BI=5 and RETURN

Specifying a series or range of records from a multiple-record retrieval set
for display is not permitted in five OPACs, and encounters format restrictions
in others. For example, when browsing, the user may want to see every other
record in a multiple-record retrieval set in a brief format. If the multiple
records are sorted by date of publication, the user may want to specify a
range of records at either the beginning or end of the list. A recent
enhancement has added this capability to the OPAC at Mankato State University,
as explained by this online message:

> Screen 001 of 001
> ONLINE CATALOG NEWS
> ---
> The display command has been enhanced to allow multiple records to be
> displayed on 1 command.
>   *EXAMPLE: DI 1 3 8-11 15
>   DI 3 4 9-13 17 SHORT
>   This command will cause the first record of the display list to be
>   displayed in the specified format. The remaining records will be
>   placed on a display queue. The system will prompt the user to
>   type NR (Next Record Command) to proceed thru the display list.
>   The format may be changed on succeeding NR/PR commands.
> A maximum of 20 records may be displayed on 1 display command.
> The NR and PR commands will continue to work as before when only 1 record
> has been displayed on a display command.

The opportunity to design a single display format during a search session is
provided by only three of the ten OPACs. This capability is limited to

selecting one or more of the available fields for display. The user may wish
to browse only among titles or subjects, or may wish to view subjects and call
numbers together, as a convenient way to identify desirable shelf locations.
In the California and RLIN OPACs, the user may specify the fields chosen for
display either by entering the field group name (e.g., SUBJECT) or the MARC
tag (e.g., 245). The following example illustrates this capability on
California's MELVYL OPAC:

->dis sub 1-2

Search request: F SU ORGANIC CHEMISTRY AND DATE 1979-
Search result: 97 records at UC libraries

1.
Subjects: Nuclear magnetic resonance spectroscopy.
             Chemistry, Organic.

2.
Subjects: Isomerism -- Congresses.
             Carbohydrates -- Congresses.
             Carbohydrates -- Chemical synthesis -- Congresses.
             Heterocyclic compounds -- Congresses.
             Chemistry, Organic -- Congresses.
             Carbohydrates -- chemical synthesis -- congresses
             Molecular Conformation -- congresses
             Stereoisomers -- congresses
             Carbohdrates -- Congresses. SC

Another example of selecting individual fields for display is provided by
Dartmouth's OPAC (using BRS commands, the location and title are selected):

                    ..PRINT 2 LO,TI/DOC=1

         1
LO DRBU.
     GF75-C65-1974.
TI The closing circle: nature, man, & technology / Barry Commoner.

RØ6Ø1 * END OF DOCUMENTS IN LIST

Another way to tailor output to the user's needs may be provided by a
capability to sort and/or merge the results of one or more retrieval sets.
However, only one system (Dartmouth/BRS) currently provides this feature.
Typical uses of a sort capability would be to arrange results alphabetically
by title, or to sort all the records in chronological order by date of
publication. These features are especially useful when a hardcopy print of
results is desired. However, selecting the arrangement of multiple records is
also useful for online browsing. Currently, some systems display multiple
listings in random order, others by date, others alphabetically by author or
title, and still others sequentially by some numeric value.

Browsing is an activity of information retrieval which has many applications, both in manual systems and online systems. The purpose, generally speaking, is to bring related records of interest together for convenient perusal and consideration. Many online mechanics can facilitate the browsing process, including display capabilities already discussed. The ability to move forward or backward among the records in a retrieved set is fundamental to browsing online, due to the limited display area of a typical visual display unit such as a CRT. Paging between the screens of a single record is common, but complete freedom of movement among all records of a retrieved set is less common. A special feature provided by some OPACs is the ability to move forward or backward through an entire file (or a portion of it) from whatever point the user enters the file. This feature is especially useful for scanning the shelf list file, accessed by a call number search. Continuous shelf list review, without the necessity of entering additional searches, is available on the OPACs at Claremont, Mission, Ohio State, and Pikes Peak. The LCS OPAC at Ohio State implements a "shelf position search" by retrieving thirty records surrounding the truncated call number entered by the user. Ten records are allocated to each of three screens, the second of which is displayed first to the user. For example:

SPS/BF159

11 BF151C97 / CUNNINGHAM / FIVE LECTURES ON THE PROBLEM OF MIND/1925
12 BF152C31844 / CABANIS, P / RAPPORTS DU PHYSIQUE ET DU MORAL DE L'HOMME/1844
13 BF152C31805 / CABANIS, P / RAPPORTS DU PHYSIQUE ET DUMORAL DE L'HOMME/1805
14 BF153R36 / Rappard, H / Psychology as self-knowledge :/1979
15 BF1581542 / SETH, RONA / IN THE NAME OF THE DEVIL: GREAT SCOTTISH WITCH/1969
16 BF159
17 BF161A371974 / Alexander, / The resurrection of the body :/1974
18 BF161A7 / ARMSTRONG, / A MATERIALIST THEORY OF THE MIND/1968
19 BF161A74 / Armstrong, / The nature of mind, and other essays //1981
1A BF161A741981 / Armstrong, / The nature of mind //1981
1B BF161A91959A / AYER, SIR / PRIVACY/1959
   PAGE 2. FOR PRECEDING PAGE, ENTER PG1; FOR FOLLOWING PAGE, ENTER PG3.

After viewing the third screen, the user may retrieve thirty more records, in sequence, simply by entering the PG+ command. Individual record displays containing more information may be retrieved by entering the appropriate command and a line number.

In traditional online retrieval systems, commands which permit the user to view a portion of an index or thesaurus are a common feature of the command repertoire. Many OPACs do not provide special commands for this purpose, and only a few display a portion of the index when a routine search is conducted (see Table 10 in chapter 8). One notable exception is the BROWSE command available on California's MELVYL OPAC. This command permits the user to browse through the entries in six primary indexes (e.g., personal author, title, series). Matches on the keywords entered with a BROWSE command result in the display of records from the index specified. If the index selected is the title index, MELVYL displays the full title for each entry which contains the keyword(s) entered by the user. The following is an example of this capability:

```
-> browse ti mendel genetics
```

Browse request: BROWSE TI MENDEL GENETICS
Browse result: 4 titles found in the title index

1. Commemoration of the publication of Gregor Mendel's pioneer experiments in
      genetics
2. History of genetics, from prehistoric times to the rediscovery of Mendel's
      laws
3. Mendel centenary: genetics, development and evolution; proceedings of a
      symposium held at the Catholic University of America, November 3, 1965
4. The origin of genetics; a Mendel source book

Space does not permit us to illustrate all the output control and display
features we discovered in our use of these OPACs. Problems were encountered
that can only be understood by actually using the systems. Our aim has been
to provide information, in Tables 5 and 12 and through samples of online
displays, sufficient to indicate the range and complexity of design issues and
user needs in this functional area of the user interface.

9.3 Optimal Bibliographic Display Formats: Fact and Opinion

The predominant model for the display of library catalog records has been the
traditional, standardized, 3x5 main entry card found in most library card
catalogs. The layout, spacing, punctuation, content, and arrangement of data
elements on catalog cards is generally uniform from catalog to catalog, and
represents a display format familiar to all users of the card catalog.
Alternatives to the traditional card format may be found in some COM catalogs,
but most of the COM formats we have seen do not vary radically from the
traditional format. Many book catalogs replicate the 3x5 card format. Even
when the entries vary in size from the 3x5 dimensions, the outline of the card
and even the hole in the bottom center of the card are frequently depicted in
the book catalog. The following is an example of a traditional (Library of
Congress) main entry catalog card:

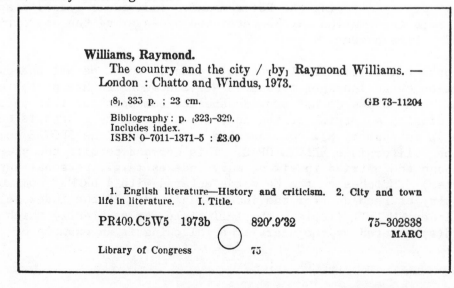

As mentioned previously, thirty-seven different system-supplied display
formats were discovered among the OPACs included in this study. Additionally,
the wide variety of display manipulation capabilities available across these
systems clearly indicates that online catalog designers have "strayed"
considerably from the traditional, LC-sanctioned path. Despite the
variations, the 3x5 card format has not disappeared from the online scene.
Five of the ten OPACs offer a format that closely resembles the catalog card,
although two of these include only part of the data usually recorded on a main
entry card. In the other five, no format resembling the card catalog in
layout could be found.

As the development of new forms of the library catalog has increased in recent
years, many librarians have urged catalog planners and designers to retain the
traditional main entry card format. These librarians feel this format should
at least be included among the alternatives available to the user, if not the
"standard" format in an online catalog. In their list of important "Elements
in the Design of On-line Catalogs," BOSS and MARCUM (1980) state that "It
should be possible to specify a format that resembles that of a card catalog."
The CONDOC requirements (MATTHEWS, 1981) specify four levels of bibliographic
displays, two of which ("brief" and "full") "shall closely resemble or
replicate the information display on existing 3x5 cards in the card catalog."

The opinion that the traditional card format be retained as the standard or
quasi-standard for displays in the online catalog, though popular, is not
universally shared. Suggesting that data presented according to the
traditional format is repetitive, confusing, and generally incomprehensible to
the general public, DWYER (1980) asks "Why tie COM and online catalogs to the
format and jargon that have worked so poorly on cards?" SCILKEN (1979) has
questioned the usefulness to public library patrons of the traditional format
for any form of the catalog:

> *Our entry format should delete, or at least separate, items*
> *that are not of use to most users. The format of every*
> *item in the entry should be tagged to be not only machine*
> *readable, but tagged so that people can read it too....*
> *Public library cards should be simple--have no*
> *abbreviations, no unusual punctuation or symbols, and be*
> *written in English.*

Presumably, the language of AACR2/ISBD is not ordinary English. Many would
agree with NEVILLE's (1981) characterization of this "specialized language":

> *In an English-speaking environment this language appears*
> *superficially to be English, but it has features of*
> *controlled vocabulary, syntax, punctuation, format, and*
> *typography, which are not normal English.*

With "tongue-in-cheek" NEVILLE re-christens this language with the name,
"Biblish."

The opinions of concerned librarians are clearly not in agreement and many
preferences can be observed at this time of developmental fervor. It will
serve us well to keep the issues clear and distinct. Two related but
different questions are before us: (1) How many or what levels of display
formats are desirable in an online catalog? and (2) What is the most useful
layout, typography, vocabulary, data sequence, etc., for those formats?

We are not aware of research findings which may help answer the first
question, but recent research projects have addressed the second question.
Perhaps the most important finding at this time is the significant impact of
alternative display formats on user performance or preference. In short,
researchers have discovered that the format makes a difference.

Two recent studies which demonstrate this fact present compatible findings
regarding the most effective and preferred formats for the display of
information on a VDU (visual display unit). TULLIS (1981) tested the
subject's response to four different types of display formats in a controlled
environment. The formats ranged from a narrative form using ordinary English,
to a structured, tabular format, to one which used color graphics. The
evaluation measured the speed and accuracy of the subject's interpretation of
data contained on the displays. TULLIS found that "the format in which test
results were presented had a clear effect on subjects' performance as well as
their preference." The two graphic formats were found superior to the
narrative format, and after the subjects had gained experience from the first
session at the terminal, "the structured format was clearly grouped with the
graphic formats in yielding significantly shorter response times than the
narrative format." TULLIS recommends the structured format as providing the
best combination of human performance benefits and low cost of implementation.
He recommends that these techniques be applied to the design of alphanumeric
displays:

    (a) key information should be presented in a prominent location;

    (b) logically related data should be clearly chunked and separated from
         other categories of data;

    (c) information should be presented in a fixed, tabular format so that
         users can develop spatial expectancies; and

    (d) information should be presented as concisely as possible.

FRYSER (1981) conducted a study which evaluated the responses of 347 library
patrons (college students at an academic library) to two versions of a single,
bibliographic record displayed at a VDU terminal. In each case, one format
replicated the traditional Library of Congress main entry card, the other
included one of several different formats for the same title. These formats
were displayed in a random manner to the subjects, one being paired with the
traditional format. The nontraditional formats could be grouped into two
categories: (1) those which resembled a "table of contents" and (2) those
which arranged their data elements vertically, including underlined field
labels.

FRYSER reports that the study "examined the effects of selected format,
typography and letter-background contrast combinations of a single
bibliographic record on (1) the ability of the library patron to locate
information quickly, and (2) his subjective reaction to the aesthetic appeal,
logical arrangement and readability of the record."

The data analysis revealed that, independent of variations in typography
and/or special video effects, "for aesthetic appeal, readability and overall
preferences, proportionately more LPs (library patrons) preferred the 'table

of contents' and the 'labeled, underlined' formats than they did the 'traditional' one." FRYSER adds these "conclusions" to his list of findings:

1. Significantly more library patrons preferred the experimental format designs over the standard, traditional format design.

2. The format which resembled a table of contents page, and which utilized upper-lower case typographic cues, emerged as the most readable, most logically arranged, and most pleasing to the eye relative to all other displays.

3. More patrons preferred information displayed in black characters against a grey background than white characters against a black background.

4. Information displayed in a grammatically correct upper-lower case typographic mode was ranked higher in appeal than either upper case or lower case alone. (Not all traditions are being rejected.)

5. Format preferences were highly correlated with user response time. The most preferred displays were associated with shorter reaction times.

These findings indicate, at the very least, that a fresh approach to the design of display formats for online catalogs is warranted. However, the stakes are high if user performance and satisfaction are highly correlated with some formats but not others. In his review of recent contributions to the principles of interface design from the discipline of graphic design, MARCUS (1982) urges system designers to redirect their efforts to improving the basic legibility and attractiveness of information displayed to users of computer systems:

> *The greatest need for guidelines is in matters of readability. What aspects of interfaces encourage people -- who might have limited abilities, failing interest, antipathy towards computers -- to use the systems? As computer systems reach ever wider audiences, the notion of attracting and holding a user's interest and attention will not seem so foreign a goal.*

The issue of effective, desirable display formats cannot be passed off to the designers or keepers of our catalog traditions for resolution. Studies of user preferences must continue, in all types of library environments, and additional, controlled experiments at the user interface are needed to validate the findings of TULLIS and FRYSER. Such experiments could manipulate the many component variables of display formats, including spacing, layout, typography, vocabulary and punctuation, data content and arrangement (sequence). A recent British Library Research and Development Report (REYNOLDS, 1980), which made recommendations for the display of bibliographic information on Prestel, begins with this statement of principle:

> *It is important that the visual presentation of bibliographic information should both reflect its logical structure and facilitate its use.*

We now have the means to exhaustively test and evaluate user performance and
preferences across a variety of display formats in controlled environments.
Compared to the millions of dollars being expended for the uncoordinated
development of diverse systems, support for such research seems easily
justified. We would hope that the objective findings of such research would
be utilized by the library community in the adoption of any new standards for
the presentation of bibliographic information.

9.4 Display Formats in Ten Online Catalogs

Figures 15a-j, included at the end of this chapter, represent online displays
of the same or a similar bibliographic record in each of the ten OPACs.
Selecting these formats from among the 2-7 display formats available in each
system was largely a subjective process, but these criteria were applied: (1)
when only a brief and "standard" format was provided, the latter was chosen;
(2) when three formats were provided representing different levels of display,
the middle level was chosen if it contained a significant amount of data; (3)
if more than three formats were provided, with each having different amounts
of data, one with less data than the "fullest" format, with or without MARC
tags, was chosen. An exception was made in the case of OCLC whose only full
bibliographic format is displayed in a MARC format, including the fixed field
and content designators for the variable fields. In all other cases, the aim
was to avoid the briefest format (usually a one line entry) and a long format,
especially if it displayed with MARC tags.

The attempt to discover a de facto standard proved fruitless. The OPAC
displays vary across most descriptive dimensions, including the terms assigned
to the various formats which were named. The following is a grouping of names
applied to similar formats used by these systems:

I.	II.	III.	IV.
Review	Brief	Standard	Long
Multiple	Short	Medium	Full
Title	Partial	Detailed	Expanded
Index display			Total
Truncated entry			Base
			MARC

Six of the ten OPACs provide a MARC format for display, but no two look
exactly alike. Some include the fixed field, for example, others display only
the variable fields. As stated previously, five offer a display format which
resembles the catalog card, but two of these include fewer data elements than
the traditional main entry card.

The descriptive categories in terms of which the ten displays represented in
Figures 15a-j will be reviewed are vocabulary, spacing, layout, typography,
punctuation, content, and sequence of data elements. Variations may be
observed in each of these categories. While the user of the card catalog can
be sure of seeing fairly similar card formats from one library to the next,
the OPAC user cannot.

The OPACs do share one tie to tradition and conventional practice, namely, the
language of bibliographic description ("Biblish"). Most of the OPACs present

their bibliographic information (if not in one format, then another) in the traditional language. For example, main entry is presented surname first, first name or initial, middle name or initial, and then birth date. The "title" statement often includes a statement of responsibility, and the collation usually appears as it does on the library card, using the same jargon and abbreviations.

Before we compare the "standard" displays in Figures 15a-j, several short formats from different OPACs are provided to indicate the variety at this level. Each is identified by OPAC institution, and the assigned format name, if any, is given in parentheses.

University of California ("Brief" format)

Search request: FIND TI POVERTY POWER AND PA COMMONER
Search result: 1 record at UC libraries

1.   Commoner, Barry, 1917-
        The poverty of power : energy and the economic crisis / Barry Commoner.
     1st ed.
        New York : Knopf : distributed by Random House, 1976.
            UCB   Physics   HD9502.A2C6431 1976
            UCB   Soc Sci   HD9502.A2C6431 1976
            UCB   Trans   HD9502.A2 C643 1976
            UCD   Law Lib   HD9502.A2.C643
            UCI   Main Lib   HD9502.A2 C643 1976
            UCLA Arch/Urb   HD9502.A2 C74
            UCLA College   HD9502.A2 C74
            UCLA GSMgmt   HD9502.A2 C74
            UCLA URL   HD 9502 A2C74
            UCLA URL   HD9502.A2 C74
            UCSC McHenry   HD9502.A2C643
            UCSD Cluster   HD9502.A2 C643 1976

Claremont Colleges

****INQ: A   COMMONER
      Geology   333.7   C737
    COMMONER , BARRY, 1917- .
    THE POVERTY OF POWER :/ENERGY AND THE ECONOMIC CRISIS -

Dartmouth College ("Brief" format in user-prompted mode)

      1
LO DRBU.
    GF75-C65-1974.
ME Commoner, Barry, 1917-.
TI The closing circle: nature, man, & technology / Barry Commoner.
IM New York: Bantam Books c1974.
SU Pollution.

R0601 * END OF DOCUMENTS IN LIST

Mankato State University ("Short" format)

Screen 001 of 001   Record 0004 of 0006 MSU
LOCTN: HD9502.A2 C643 1976
AUTHR: Commoner, Barry, 1917-
TITLE: The poverty of power : energy and the economic crisis / Barry
        Commoner.

Pikes Peak Library District

Call Number   Author / Title   LCCN:75-036798
               COMMONER,B
333.7   POVERTY OF POWER: ENERGY AND THE ECONOMIC CRISIS
C734P   BC:102262136   Old Colo City
Subjects: United States - Economic policy - 1971-
          Economic history.
          Power resources.
          Energy policy - United States.
          Power (Mechanics)

Mission College ("ST=" format)

H?ST=9
HJH?   ST=9
HD   Commoner, Barry, 1917-
9502
.A2C643   The poverty of power : energy and the economic crisis.
1977
          New York : Bantam Books, 1977, c1976

J
LOCATION   VOL MED AVAILABILITY DATE--DUE--TIME

MISSION MIS LRN RES   ON SHELF

The Ohio State University ("DSL/" format)

DSL/1

S.574.5C737C Commoner, Barry, 1917- The closing circle;   :1st ed.:
76-127092   2311955 1971   2 ADDED: 781229   FBR
01   001   OHI
02   002   OHI
PAGE 1 END

The balance of this chapter will be devoted to analysis of sample screen display formats from the ten OPACs. References to the formats will be by figure number only. Following is a list of those figure numbers and their corresponding institutions. The figures, themselves, are presented after the discussion.

15a. University of California
15b. Claremont Colleges
15c. Dartmouth College
15d. Mankato State University
15e. Mission College
15f. Northwestern University
15g. OCLC
15h. Ohio State University
15i. Pikes Peak Library District
15j. RLG/RLIN

Vocabulary

As seen in Figures 15a-j, six OPACs use labels to help identify the component elements of the bibliographic information (15a, 15c, 15e, 15g, 15h, 15j). Of these six, only the University of California and Dartmouth OPACs label elements in the body of the entry. The University of California OPAC uses complete English language words, but its labels are misleading. "Title" actually means title statement, imprint, and collation; "call numbers" means campus, library, and call number. Dartmouth uses two letter mnemonic abbreviations for bibliographic jargon: ME for main entry; TI for title statement; IM for imprint; CO for collation, etc. OSU identifies subjects by the abbreviation, SUB. Some of the systems label the LC card number (OSU, Mission, RLIN, Pikes Peak), OCLC number (OSU, OCLC), or MARC fields (OCLC, RLIN). Four of the ten systems use the title alone (instead of the title statement) in their displays (15d, 15e, 15h, 15i). Two of these systems use common English language labels for the body of the entry. Pikes Peak's display (15i) labels call number, author/title, and subjects. Mankato State (15d) uses abbreviated English: AUTHR for author; PUBLR for publisher; DESCR for description; SUBJT for subject, etc. LOCTN means location, but it also provides the call number. Pikes Peak and Mankato State, along with the University of California, provide the user with the most help in interpreting the bibliographic display.

Spacing

Six systems favor a vertical approach to the spatial arrangement of bibliographic information on their displays (15a, 15c, 15d, 15e, 15g, 15i). A horizontal approach is shown in the other four systems (15b, 15f, 15h, 15j). However, most systems combine the two approaches to some degree. Six systems use single spacing between lines (15b, 15c, 15d, 15g, 15h, 15i). One OPAC uses double spacing (15f). Three combine both single and double spacing (15a, 15e, 15j).

Layout

Record layout varies widely from left justified bibliographic information in
one system (15e), left justified labels followed by left justified
bibliographic information in two systems (15c, 15d), left and right justified
information in one system (15b), indented information in three systems (15f,
15h, 15j), and various combinations of the above in three systems (15a, 15g,
15i).

Typography

Typography also varies greatly from OPAC to OPAC. With the exception of
Claremont's OPAC which displays entirely in upper case, all of the OPACs
combine lower and upper case letters. However, none of them do it in a
consistent way. Mankato State uses upper case letters for labels, while Pikes
Peak uses upper case letters for emphasizing information within a record. Two
systems use upper case letters for search request/instructions (15a, 15g) and
five OPACs use combinations of the above (15c, 15e, 15f, 15h, 15j).

Punctuation

Most of the OPACs' machine-readable records include ISBD punctuation, but
these OPACs do not display exactly the same punctuation. Of the six systems
with a title statement, four set off the statement of responsibility with a
slash (15a, 15c, 15f, 15j). One system uses a slash and a letter code (15g).
One system employs a hyphen for this purpose (15b). Six of the OPACs have a
colon between the place of publication and the name of the publisher (15a,
15b, 15c, 15e, 15f, 15j); one has a colon plus a letter code (15g). Two
systems substitute a comma for the colon (15d, 15h). In the subject headings,
seven end the heading with a final mark of punctuation (15a, 15b, 15c, 15d,
15g, 15i, 15j) while two do not (15e, 15h).

Content and Sequence

None of the ten formats depicted in Figures 15a-j contain exactly the same
bibliographic information. It is not possible to select a group of displays
from the OPACs, each having the same data elements as the others. The only
two elements common to all ten records are the author and the title proper.
Of the displays which contain additional common elements (e.g., call number,
imprint, collation, notes, subjects) none of the records display the
information in same sequence.

Conclusion

Most of the records loaded into the databases of these systems are either LC,
OCLC, or RLIN MARC records. At this level then, there is a linking
commonality of standard bibliographic description, using a formal language
system created solely for that purpose. However, the variations in display
languages which confront the user of different OPACs seem almost unlimited.
It should be clear by now that many dialects of "Biblish" exist. The language
roots of the OPACs' displays may be discernible to the librarian, but the

systems "speak" in different dialects to the user. Perhaps we are merely
compounding the confusions inherent in the "Biblish" recorded on the
traditional 3x5 main entry cards.

Studies such as FRYSER's indicate that when given a choice, catalog users do
not prefer the traditional card format, nor can they interpret its contents
very easily. Mankato State's OPAC display formats most closely resemble the
"table of contents" model employed in FRYSER's experiment. For logical
arrangement, 85% of FRYSER'S interviewees preferred the "table of contents"
model. In addition, the students more quickly identified data elements within
these formats when requested to do so by the monitor.

The variations in the OPAC displays illuminate the necessity for more research
in this area. The end users should provide the principal input for design
decisions affecting the display of bibliographic information. As the FRYSER
study shows, users do have strong ideas about bibliographic displays when
given the opportunity to voice them. Investigation into the information
display needs and preferences of catalog users could result in a sound,
"standard" online bibliographic record. Variations on this standard display
could then be offered as enhancements by the individual systems. Since no
de facto standard exists at this time, the current display variations are a
source of confusion to anyone who uses more than one online catalog.

```
Search request: FIND TI POVERTY POWER AND PA COMMONER
Search result:  1 record at UC libraries

1.
Author:      Commoner, Barry, 1917-
Title:       The poverty of power : energy and the economic crisis / Barry
               Commoner. 1st ed. New York : Knopf : distributed by Random
               House, 1976.
             314 p. ; 22 cm.

Notes:       Includes bibliographical references and index.

Subjects:    Power resources.
             Power (Mechanics)
             Energy policy -- United States.
             Economic history.
             United States -- Economic policy -- 1971-

Call numbers: UCB  Physics    HD9502.A2C6431 1976  (CU-PHYS)
              UCB  Soc Sci     HD9502.A2C6431 1976  (CU-SOCS)
              UCB  Trans       HD9502.A2 C643 1976  (CU-IT)
                                      (Record 1 continues on the next screen.)
Press RETURN (or type NS) to see the next screen.
->
```

```
Search request: FIND TI POVERTY POWER AND PA COMMONER
Search result:  1 record at UC libraries

1. (continued)
             UCD  Law Lib    HD9502.A2.C643  (CU-AL)
             UCI  Main Lib   HD9502.A2 C643 1976  (CU-I)
             UCLA Arch/Urb   HD9502.A2 C74  (CLU-AUF)
             UCLA College    HD9502.A2 C74  (CLU-COL)
             UCLA GSMgmt     HD9502.A2 C74  (CLU-MGT)
             UCLA URL        HD 9502 A2C74  (CLU-URL)
             UCLA URL        HD9502.A2 C74  (CLU-URL)
             UCSC McHenry    HD9502.A2C643  (CU-SC)
             UCSD Cluster    HD9502.A2 C643 1976  (CU-SCL)
```

Figure 15a. University of California ("Long" Format)

```
@
COMMONER , BARRY, 1917-  ./THE POVERTY OF POWER :/ENERGY AND THE ECONO
MIC CRISIS - BARRY COMMONER. 1ST ED. <NEW YORK : KNOPF : DISTRIBUTED B
Y RANDOM HOUSE, 1976.> 314 P. ; 22 CM./# POWER RESOURCES./# POWER (MEC
HANICS)/# ENERGY POLICY-- UNITED STATES./# UNITED STATES--ECONOMIC POL
ICY--1971-  ./
```

Figure 15b. Claremont Colleges (Full Format)

```
LO DRBU.
   GF75-C65-1974.
ME Commoner, Barry, 1917-.
TI The closing circle: nature, man, & technology / Barry Commoner.
IM New York: Bantam Books c1974.
CO viii, 343 p. 19 cm.
SU Pollution.
NT Includes bibliographical references and index.

R0601 * END OF DOCUMENTS IN LIST
```

Figure 15c.   Dartmouth College ("Standard" Format)

```
 DI 4 MEDIUM
 Screen 001 of 001    Record 0004 of 0006 MSU
 LOCTN: HD9502.A2 C643 1976
 AUTHR: Commoner, Barry, 1917-
 TITLE: The poverty of power : energy and the economic crisis / Barry
         Commoner.
 EDITN: 1st ed.
 PUBLR: New York ; Knopf : distributed by Random House, 1976.
 DESCR: 314 p. ; 22 cm.
 SUBJT: Economic history.
 SUBJT: Energy policy--United States.
 SUBJT: Power (Mechanics)
 SUBJT: Power resources.
 SUBJT: United States--Economic policy--1971-
 >
```

Figure 15d.   Mankato State University ("Medium" Format)

```
H?BI=9
HJH?                                                                    BI=9
HD          Commoner, Barry, 1917-
9502
.A2C643     The poverty of power : energy and the economic crisis .
1977
            New York : Bantam Books, 1977, c1976

            297 p. ; 18 cm

            1. Power resources
            2. Power (Mechanics)
            3. Energy policy--United States
            4. United States--Economic policy--1971-
            5. Economic history
            ISBN/ISSN  0553108565     L.C.CARD NUMBER  75-36798



To repeat previous screen type PS and RETURN
7mTo determine the location and availability of a specific title, type ST=
followed by the line number. EXAMPLE:  ST=2 and RETURNOm
```

Figure 15e. Mission College (Standard Format)

```
LUIS SEARCH REQUEST:  A=COMMONER

BASIC BIBLIOGRAPHIC RECORD -- NO. 6 OF 7 ENTRIES FOUND

Commoner, Barry, 1917-

  The poverty of power : energy and the economic crisis / Barry Commoner. -- 1st

ed. -- New York : Knopf : distributed by Random House, 1976.

HOLDINGS IN NORTHWESTERN UNIVERSITY LIBRARY

LOCATION:  main

CALL NUMBER:  333.7;C734p

LOCATION:  core (copy 2)

CALL NUMBER:  333.7;C734p

LOCATION:  main (copy 3)

CALL NUMBER:  333.7;C734p

TYPE m FOR NEXT RECORD, d FOR CIRCULATION STATUS (FIRST WRITE DOWN CALL NO.)

TYPE i TO RETURN TO INDEX.  TYPE e TO START OVER.  TYPE h FOR HELP.

TYPE COMMAND AND PRESS ENTER
```

Figure 15f. Northwestern University (Standard Format)

```
Screen 1 of 2
¬NO HOLDINGS IN OCC -  FOR HOLDINGS ENTER dh DEPRESS  DISPLAY RECD SEND
OCLC: 2020127        Rec stat: c Entrd: 760127        Used: 810610
¬Type: a Bib lvl: m Govt pub:    Lang:  eng Source:    Illus:
Repr:    Enc lvl:    Conf pub: 0 Ctry:  nyu Dat tp: s M/F/B: 10
Indx: 1 Mod rec:    Festschr: 0 Cont: b
Desc: i Int lvl:    Dates: 1976,
¬ 1 010        75-36798
¬ 2 040        DLC c DLC d WQM d m.c.
¬ 3 020        0394403711 : c $10.00
¬ 4 043        n-us---
¬ 5 050 0      HD9502.A2 b C643 1976
¬ 6 082        333.7
¬ 7 049        OCCL
¬ 8 100 10     Commoner, Barry, d 1917- w cn
¬ 9 245 14     The poverty of power : b energy and the economic crisis / c
Barry Commoner.
¬10 250        1st ed.
¬11 260 0      New York : b Knopf : distributed by Random House, c 1976.
¬12 300        314 p. ; c 22 cm.
¬13 504        Includes bibliographical references and index.
¬14 650  0     Power resources.
¬15 650  0     Power (Mechanics)
¬16 650  0     Energy policy z United States.
```

```
Screen 2 of 2
¬17 651  0   United States x Economic policy y 1971-
¬18 650  0   Economic history.
¬19 650  2   Conservation of Energy Resources x economics.
¬20 650  2   Power Sources x economics.
```

Figure 15g.   OCLC (Full Format)

```
FBL/1

S.574.5C737C
Commoner, Barry, 1917-
   The closing circle; nature, man, and technology.  :1st ed.:  New York,
Knopf, 1971.  326, x p.  22 cm. $6.95
   Includes bibliographical references.
SUB: 1. POLLUTION  2. MAN--INFLUENCE ON NATURE
LC CARD #:76-127092  TITLE #:2311955  OCLC #:0180245     &ZZ770701
PAGE 1  END
```

Figure 15h. Ohio State University ("Full" Format)

```
Call Number    Author / Title    LCCN:75-036798
               COMMONER,B
333.7          POVERTY OF POWER
C734P             BC:100909167      Calhan Branch
Subjects: United States - Economic policy - 1971-
          Economic history.
          Power resources.
          Energy policy - United States.
          Power (Mechanics)
```

Figure 15i. Pikes Peak Library District (Short Format)

```
:? LONG

Cluster 1 of 1

Commoner, Barry, 1917-
  The poverty of power : energy and the economic crisis / Barry Commoner. 1st
ed. New York : Knopf : distributed by Random House, 1976.
  314 p. ; 22 cm.

  Includes bibliographical references and index.
  ISBN 0394403711 : $10.00

  1. Power resources. 2. Power (Mechanics) 3. Energy policy—United States. 4.
Economic history. 5. United States—Economic policy—1971-  I. Title.

  LCCN: 7536798
  035: NN764414909
  050: HD9502.A2 C643 1976
  ID: NYPG764414909-B              CC: 1665       DCF:
:?
```

Figure 15j. RLIN ("Long" Format)

10

10.1 The Clear and Present Need for Online Guidance and Instruction
10.2 Types and Levels of Help Information
10.3 Selected OPAC Help Features Illustrated

Online User Assistance and "Help" Facilities

10.1 The Clear and Present Need for Online Guidance and Instruction

The need for guidance in the use of an online catalog is relative to both the actual or perceived complexity of the system and the acquired skills of the end user of the system. A simple system having few commands and few options for using them will appear unfamiliar and complex to the first-time user of the system. However, an introductory display listing the commands with simple instructions for using them (or examples) may provide the guidance the novice needs to successfully use the system.

A complex system featuring a variety of special capabilities and options for their use may present problems for the experienced, but moderately skilled user who may not remember all of the search mechanics and options from session to session. Such a system may require a number of user assistance features, each addressed to a specific informational or instructional need. A convenient way of requesting specific assistance at the point of need should be provided in any online catalog system.

Because the interface technology and communications protocols of this form of the catalog are new and not yet standardized, for some time to come the basic operation of any online catalog will not be intuitively obvious to (or manageable by) most OPAC users. We have only begun to develop effective, easy-to-use interfaces for the end user who is unassisted by a professional intermediary.

On the frequency of use continuum (see section 5.7), most OPAC users will range from first-time use to occasional, infrequent use. We cannot imagine a scenario where a particular OPAC will be used repeatedly, day after day, by most of the library's patrons. In both public and academic libraries, end users with a variety of skills and levels of usage will have to be assisted in the understanding and use of these new online catalogs. The first-time user may need to use the OPAC when staff assistance is not available. The occasional user may need a "how to" reminder to perform a particular activity during a search session. After initial training and use, the infrequent user may need to relearn how to use the system, quickly, conveniently, and on demand, while at the terminal. Online assistance features can be provided to meet these informational and instructional needs. User acceptance of this new catalog may depend on the availability of such assistance.

Studies have shown that the most critical time for a novice user is his first encounter with the online system. With OPACs placed in public access areas, the novice may frequently find himself alone with the system. Written instructions may not be available or adequate to the user's needs. Usage analysis studies have indicated that it is critical that users be successful in their first use of the system. HELANDER (1981) reports that after the introduction of a new text processing and report generation system in a business office environment, "Users who received early guidance and answers to questions continued to use the system; others stopped almost immediately. Those who were able to achieve their application objectives... were much more likely to continue with the system than those who did not."

Occasional and frequent users may experience difficulties when using online catalogs. Immediate and specific assistance from the system is highly desirable for resolving these difficulties. These difficulties may be grouped into three problem categories (these categories are not exhaustive):

1.   Command semantics (Which command must I use to do this or that?)

2.   Command syntax (How do I correctly enter this command?)

3.   The logic of command selection (May I use this command now?)

After a mistake is made by the user in one of these categories, an error message may provide corrective information for curing the problem. However, the user may prefer the "preventive medicine" approach and seek guidance before an unlearned or forgotten rule of practice is misapplied. Preliminary research findings indicate that OPAC users prefer to request and receive online instruction when they encounter difficulties and when they are unsure how to proceed.

In 1979, a survey was administered to a sample population of users of the Library of Congress SCORPIO online catalog. The survey was distributed at LC's Computer Catalog Center adjacent to the Main Reading Room. Users were asked to rate various interaction mechanics (e.g., which command to use, correct entry format and punctuation) as easy, medium, or hard to learn. Analysis revealed that the semantics and syntax of command usage was not particularly troublesome. But PRITCHARD (1981) reports that "By far the most difficult factor was 'figuring out what to do when problems occur'; only 17% rated this easy, 37% medium, and 41% hard." PRITCHARD attributes this frustration to "gaps in instructional materials and ambiguous system messages." At the time the survey was conducted, SCORPIO did not provide a "help" facility to aid in the use of the system.

Another question in the survey of SCORPIO users listed options for improving instruction in the use of the system. PRITCHARD reports that "The strongest preference (64%) was for computer-assisted or online instruction." In addition, 57% responded that more complete instructions and messages displayed by SCORPIO would have made it easier to use the system.

Few institutions where online catalogs have been installed rely solely on online guidance or instruction to train and otherwise assist the user. One-to-one or group training, flip charts, and written manuals are frequently provided for new and occasional users. However, the belief shared by many designers of online systems intended for novice and casual users may prove to be very sound:

*...in interactive use, if the user can get all the help he
needs from a system and if he knows how to get it, the use
of manuals can largely be avoided. This makes the
interface more attractive to users by creating a good
initial impression of friendliness. (RAYNER, 1980)*

Directing their attention to how a system presents itself through dialogue to
the user, NIEVERGELT and WEYDERT (1980) report that observation of hundreds of
casual users of interactive systems suggests that the following questions
characterize the difficulties most commonly experienced by these users:

> Where am I?
> What can I do here?
> How did I get here?
> Where can I go, and how do I get there?

NIEVERGELT and WEYDERT offer the opinion that "A well designed system allows
the user at all times to obtain conveniently a clear answer to the above
questions."

In chapter 3 (section 3.2.5), user assistance features provided by one or more
OPACs were identified as belonging to one of three categories:

1. General information about a system's files, commands, or operational
    status

2. Specific search/session status information

3. Instructional facilities, including prompts, discrete, retrievable
    "help" displays, and online tutorial packages.

The comparison matrix represented by Table 6 in chapter 3 illustrated the
variety of user assistance features provided by the different OPACs. More
OPACs answer questions about the system's general features (e.g., searchable
fields, available commands) than about the status of a particular search or
session. Only four OPACs provide retrospective information about a search or
session in progress.

Three techniques are commonly employed in online systems to provide guidance
or instruction to the user. Suggestive prompts are frequently embedded in the
system-to-user dialogue at key decision points to indicate likely options to
pursue (e.g., NO SUCH TERM FOUND. WOULD YOU LIKE TO SEE THIS PORTION OF THE
INDEX?), or to list commands that are valid at each transition point of the
dialogue. In today's OPACs, suggestive prompts are limited to guiding the
user in the "how to" or mechanics of the search. Assistance with the
formulation of a search or the selection of an appropriate search strategy is
generally absent. In some systems, a general suggestion for an alternative or
modified search approach may be offered if either no matches occur, or too
many matches result from the user-supplied search argument.

OPAC diagnostic facilities also include system-supplied error messages
displayed when a user commits an error in command syntax, semantics, or logic.
Unfortunately, not all error messages qualify as instructional messages. To
satisfy this requirement, error messages must indicate clearly what the error

is, where it occurred, and how to correct it. The user needs to know what is
expected by the system and how to go about it. In addition, SHNEIDERMAN
(1982) encourages designers to provide error messages that are brief, free of
computer jargon, positive in tone, and that "emphasize user control over the
system." SHNEIDERMAN reports that preliminary findings of user studies
indicate that system messages exhibiting these qualities impact significantly
on user performance and satisfaction with the system.

Suggestive prompts and error messages are unrequested forms of guidance or
instruction. Both usually supply assistance specifically relevant to the
user's last action and/or the immediate context of the interaction.

A third technique for providing online instruction consists of what has become
commonly known as a "help" facility or function. A "help" facility consists
of one or more system messages, discrete displays, or tutorials that may be
requested by the user to (1) answer specific questions about "how to" proceed
at any given point in the interaction, (2) explain an error message or brief
instruction in more depth, or (3) provide comprehensive instruction in the use
of the system.

A help facility may be broadly defined by some designers to include the system
of prompts and error messages, but we think it is useful to distinquish these
three online instructional techniques for the purpose of descriptive analysis.
In the narrow sense, a help facility is distinguished from suggestive prompts
and constructive error messages by its optionality. The user decides when to
request assistance, and the help available may extend beyond the immediate
context of the user-system interaction. Help displays usually provide more
detailed information than suggestive prompts and error messages. In practice,
a truly user-friendly system will employ both suggestive prompts and
constructive error messages, and also offer a number of instructional help
displays and/or tutorial lessons which may be requested if the user so
desires.

The focus of the remainder of this chapter will be confined to help facilities
(as defined here) provided by the designers of various OPACs. After a brief
discussion of types and levels of help messages or displays, specific help
features encountered in our use of the OPACs will be illustrated.

10.2 Types and Levels of Help Information

Retrievable help displays (used here to include "messages," "screens," or
"frames") differ from OPAC to OPAC in the way they are retrieved, and in the
scope or level of information they contain. Three common types of help may be
described as (1) general help, (2) explicit specific help, and (3) implicit
specific help.

General help is typically requested by using a command such as HELP or ?,
unaccompanied by a command parameter specifying a particular topic. If a
parameter is required, the command word is usually repeated, for example,
"HELP HELP." General help includes an explanation of the help facility or
function and how to use it, and a list or "glossary" of specific help
displays. When the help command word or symbol is reserved for requesting
specific help, and must be followed by a specific value (e.g., HELP DISPLAY),
a special command (or function key) may be provided for requesting general

help instructions and options (e.g., EXPLAIN or ?). Some OPACs offer general help via an introductory screen which displays after sign on. A BEGIN or START command may be provided to retrieve this display at any point during the session.

When help displays are provided on a variety of topics or instructions, keywords (or codes) may be used to identify and request a specific topic or instruction. These keywords are usually listed in the help directory or glossary. Explicit specific help may be requested by qualifying the help command with one of the keywords (e.g., HELP BOOLEAN). The glossary-based keyword approach to help information offers the user direct and immediate access to the specific help desired, independent of the immediate context of interaction. If the assigned help keyword is forgotten, the user can consult the online glossary and then request a specific display.

Implicit specific help is often referred to as "help-in-context" or "point-of-need" help. This help feature permits the user to request specific help when difficulties occur but the particular instruction or help keyword is not known. The user needs specific help, but is not required to explicitly name that help in the request. When this feature is employed, a simple, unqualified help command is entered, and the system responds with help appropriate to the user's last command and/or the immediate context. Suggestions for more detailed information or related help options may be included in these system-supplied instructional displays.

Some OPACs provide context-specific help unrequested by the user. Criteria useful for identifying various user difficulties, such as "floundering" and the inability to understand routine error messages, can be designed into the system. Predefined user behavior (e.g., making the same error three times in succession) may trigger the system's help response. When this occurs, a more detailed instruction will be displayed. This completely automatic help function should probably be offered as a session option for the experienced user.

Help displays may also be distinguished by the amount of information the user is required to read in a particular display, or by the display's level of detail or comprehensiveness. The user may prefer a brief, "how to" instruction when a search is in progress. More detailed explanations of the system and its use may be confined to a special set of help displays, retrievable at the discretion of the user when he has time to study them. Another technique for providing more than one level of help consists of permitting the user to select either a "terse" or "verbose" mode for help messages at the beginning of the search session, with the option of switching modes at anytime. Combined with the option to choose the automatic help mode, this feature permits the user to tailor the system's help facilities to his own needs.

Designers of OPACs which immediately introduce detailed, comprehensive help services have recently reported that such a facility can confuse most users who simply want to get started and learn the "basics" of the system quickly. Comprehensive, detailed help services have been restructured in some cases to provide quick and convenient access to brief, basic instructions at the initial point of need. Various approaches are then utilized to offer the user the option of selecting more detailed or comprehensive instructions when time permits and such instruction does not impede the progress of the session.

RAYNER (1980) suggests that three levels of help should be included in a help facility to satisfy the needs of all potential users of the system:

1. First-level help

    If the user requests implicit specific help, the system should briefly indicate what is expected of the user in the current context. Valid commands can be listed, with concise instructions (or samples) on how to use them. A menu may be displayed from which the command can be executed.

    If the user specifies a help topic or instruction, the system should present a brief explanation not to exceed five lines on a typical display terminal. The user who needs basic "how to" help during the progress of a search will not want to wade through lines or screens of information to find the answer to his question.

    In either case, the system should retain the context of the interaction at the point the user requested help.

2. Second-level help

    When designing a search formulation, the user may desire a fuller explanation of a particular system function or the action of a specialized command. The mechanics of a command capability may be understood, but assistance may be needed on the appropriate or most effective use of the capability.

    Second-level help information explains in greater detail all the consequences of using a particular feature, and may also suggest various uses of the feature for formulating a search.

    The user may be prompted for second-level help at the end of a first-level display, or independent commands may be provided for obtaining more detailed, second-level information displays. In either case, RAYNER recommends that the system retain the context of interaction and provide a convenient means of returning to the point at which help was requested. This is especially useful when second-level help information requires more than a single screen for display.

3. Third-level help

    In RAYNER's words:
    A third level of help could be an interactive user manual. This information retrieval process could be entered by a specific command that would be given as part of an appropriate menu. Unlike the other two levels, this third level of help should not retain the context for the user. The other two levels give a single response, but long and complex interaction could be involved at this third level. Since the user cannot be expected to remember his previous context, it is better to return him to some default state. The user is likely to view the acquisition of this level of help as a new and separate activity, and so will not be disconcerted by the loss of the previous context.

Several guidelines for the design of help facilities have been encountered in our review of the literature on user-friendly systems for the end user. These guidelines are based on the observations or intuitions of system designers. Detailed research is needed to validate these considered opinions and to provide the data needed to translate user needs and preferences into design specifications. To summarize the information presented in this section, a list of the more important guidelines follows:

1. Provide an easy-to-remember, easy-to-use command for requesting help at any point in the interaction.

2. Provide an "introductory" display whereby the system explains its basic use and how to get additional help.

3. Provide a list or glossary of available help displays.

4. When specific help is not explicitly requested, automatically provide help appropriate to the context of interaction.

5. Retain the context of a search in progress, and provide an easy way for the user to "return" to it if it is no longer displayed on the screen.

6. Provide both brief and detailed levels of help.

7. If unrequested verbose help is displayed, provide the experienced user a means of "switching-off" this automatic feature.

8. Phrase help messages in a positive manner, emphasizing the user's control of the system.

9. Be concise and specific when constructing "how to" instructional statements. Include examples when appropriate.

10. Avoid the use of computer jargon in help messages. Employ language familiar to the user.

10.3 Selected OPAC Help Features Illustrated

Table 13 provides supplementary information to some of the user assistance features listed in Table 6 (presented in chapter 3). Although the information and style of presentation varies considerably from OPAC to OPAC, seven of the ten systems provide some sort of introductory, "how to get started," guidance. Most of these displays either include examples of basic searches or lead the user through prompts to additional help displays. In one way or another, eight of the ten systems offer explanations of how to use their commands.

In the previous section, a distinction was drawn between suggestive prompts, error messages, and retrievable help displays. The former system-to-user messages come with the dialogue in the normal course of using the system. The frequency of occurrence of such messages, and the amount of information they provide, varies from system to system. No attempt was made to systematically evaluate the quality of these messages, but the OPACs were ranked according to the degree or amount of helpful information provided through suggestive prompts and error messages (see Table 13). The rankings assigned (low, moderate, high) are relative, and they are based on a consensus of opinion among our project team members. The "high" rankings assigned to the OPACs at Dartmouth and the University of California apply to their unique and independent computer-guided modes of interaction. With both systems, the user has the option of choosing the computer-guided or the user-guided command language dialogue mode to proceed with a search session.

Table 13. Online User Aids

ONLINE USER AIDS	California, University of	Claremont Colleges	Dartmouth College	Mankato State University	Mission College	Northwestern University	OCLC	Ohio State University	Pikes Peak Library District	RLG/RLIN
Is introductory guidance screen provided?	Yes	Yes	Yes	Yes	Yes	Yes	No	No	Yes	No
Can explanation of available commands be requested?	Yes	Yes	Yes	Yes	Yes	Yes	No	No	Yes	Yes
Degree of guidance/explanatory information embedded in dialogue	H/L	M	H/L	L	L	M	L	L	L	L
Number of discrete "Help/ Explain" screens available	155[a]	10	27	28	2[b]	17[c]	0	0	1	5
Does system provide context-specific help in response to unqualified "Help" request?	Yes	No	No	No	Yes	Yes	No	No	No	No
Are structured tutorials available?	No	No	No	No	No	No	No	No	No	No
Are directions for offline assistance available?	No	No	Yes	No	No	Yes	Yes	No	No	Yes

L = Low
M = Moderate
H = High
H/L = High (prompt mode)/Low (command mode)

NOTES: a. 94 user-specifiable; 61 contextual (system responds to point of need)
        b. 1 general; 1 contextual
        c. 10 user-specifiable; 7 contextual

As Table 13 indicates, the number of available help displays varies considerably across the ten systems. The OPACs at the University of California, Claremont, Dartmouth, Mankato State and Northwestern provide two levels of display for some of their help messages. No OPAC offers a third-level tutorial help facility at this time, but a tutorial mode is under development at the University of California. A tutorial help facility would consist of a series of lessons which the user could take in a self-paced manner. It is not yet clear whether such a facility is needed or would be used by many catalog users. Because these tutorials are time-consuming and self-administered independently of a search session, their use may have to be restricted to terminals reserved for this purpose. Learning while using the system, guided by suggestive prompts, constructive error messages, and first- or second-level help displays, may well become the preferred method of self-training for the new population of OPAC end users.

Illustrations of OPAC help features and displays comprise the remainder of this chapter.

Mankato State University

After signing on with the BEGIN command, the user is welcomed with this introductory display:

```
BEGIN SESSION ON SUS/CAS  12-30-81 13:30:36  ID/WA: 159/056  VSN: 1R1
Have a Happy New Year!
The Online Catalog will go down this evening at 4:30 PM
for database updating. The Online Catalog will be available
Thursday at 7:00 AM.
------------------------------------------------------------
Type HELP at any time to obtain assistance


THE BASIC SEARCH COMMAND FORMS ARE:

AU Last-name First-name Middle-initial      (Author Search)
TI First 4 Title Words                      (Title Search)
CO Author-last-name First-title-word        (Comb Author/Title)
SU First 4 Subject Heading Words            (LC Subject Search)
TE Word1 <BO> Word2 <BO> Word3 ...          (Term/Topic Search)
    *Where <BO> is a boolean operator  (AND NOT OR)

Send messages to the computer by DEPRESSING the (NEW LINE) key
Use the (BACK SPACE) key to BACK UP and type over mistakes

Other search options are available -- type HELP
```

If the user enters the unqualified HELP command, the following general help
display is retrieved:

```
Screen 001 of 001
HELP explanations are available for most of the system commands. Type HELP
followed by the 2 characters corresponding to the type of help needed.
EXAMPLE: for help on author searching enter
    HELP AU

BE -- Beginning and Ending a session     PR -- Offline Printing
AU -- Author Search                      NE -- System News
TI -- Title Search                       SI -- Database Size Statistics
CO -- Combination Author/Title Search    TR -- Truncation, Terms & Statement
TE -- Term/Topic Search                  GE -- General Command Summary
SU -- Subject Search                     SY -- Searching other Libraries
DI -- Displaying Search Results          ST -- System Statistics
DA -- Limiting by Publication Date       DL -- Dial Access to Library Systems
FO -- Limiting by Material Format        DE -- Demand Access to UNIVAC 1100
LA -- Limiting by Language
NA -- Narrowing by additional word(s)
SE -- Sets and Boolean commands
>
```

Specific, first-level help can be obtained for most system commands and
several related catalog topics. The following is an example of a first-level,
specific (explicit) help display. The user has requested help with an author
search by entering the command, HELP AU.

```
Screen 001 of 001
AUTHOR SEARCH

    AU LAST-NAME FIRST-NAME MIDDLE-INITIAL

    *EXAMPLE AUTHOR NAMES
      James William Abert
      William Shakespeare
      John Henry Johnson

    *RESPECTIVE CATALOG COMMANDS
      AU ABERT JAMES WILLIAM
      AU SHAKESPEARE WILLIAM
      AU JOHNSON JOHN HENRY

For more detailed information on author searching type HELP AS.
>HE AS
```

Most of the brief help displays include a prompt explaining how to obtain more
detailed information on the same topic at a second level of explanation.

These detailed explanations range from 1-3 screens in length and include many
samples of command usage and search formulations. The user may consult the
help glossary at any time or directly retrieve a help display by qualifying
the HELP command with a keyword from that glossary (e.g., HELP SU).

Dartmouth College

In response to a user's request for help (unqualified), Dartmouth's "user cordial" interface facility presents this display:

> I'm sorry you are having trouble. I'll try to HELP. If you can tell me what's wrong or what you don't understand, I may be able to give you a better explanation.
>
> To begin, let's review the procedures for telling the computer what you want to do. To issue a command, press the RED key followed by:
> S: To start searching,
> P: To list search results,
> X: To get special list options
> D: To display previously executed search statements
> H: To get Help!,
> E: To get explanations of how the system works,
> L: To logoff and reset the system for the next user,
> Q: To logoff and sign off the system for the day.
>
> Then press the RETURN key.
>
> If you need more information about how the system works, there are lots of topics I can EXPLAIN for you. If you'd like to see some, please give the EXPLAIN command (RED key followed by E) and then press the RETURN key.
>
> Please tell the system what you want to do next by giving one of these commands now. Press the RED key followed by S,P,X,D,H,E,L, or Q and then press the RETURN key.
>
> If you are still in doubt, please call X2574.

If the E (Explain) command is entered at this point, the following brief message is displayed:

> The EXPLAIN feature of the system is available to provide more information about some aspects of the system which may be unfamiliar to you. You can get such an explanation by typing the appropriate topic name when the prompt "Topic?" appears.
>
> For a list of the topics that may be explained, enter the word "topic" when the prompt appears.

Following this last instruction causes a glossary of available help topics to be displayed:

> **The following topics may be EXPLAINed:**
> ADJ AND AUTHOR BEGIN BRS COMBINE DISPLAY EXPLAIN INTERFACE
> LIMIT LOGON NUMBERS OR PARAGRAPH PRINT ROOT QUALIFY
> SAME SEARCH SPECIAL SUBJECT TITLE TOPIC TRUNCATION WITH
>
> **Please type one of these topic names when the prompt appears:**
>
> **Topic?**

A brief explanation of any of these topics can be obtained by entering the correct keyword as listed in this glossary. For example, Topic?ADJ retrieved this display:

> **The ADJACENT feature is used to help you find words that are right next to each other in the citation. Because of the search logic used by the BRS system, each word (bounded by blanks) is considered to be a search entity. Thus, one can search for CINCINNATI directly, just by typing in the word; but to search for LOS ANGELES, one must enter the search phrase LOS ADJ ANGELES. This tells the system to look for the text strings LOS and ANGELES and to retrieve the citation if the terms are adjacent to each other and in the order specified.**
>
> **Some examples of the use of the ADJACENT feature are listed below:**
>
> **NEW ADJ YORK   EQUAL ADJ RIGHTS ADJ AMENDMENT   PHILIP ADJ II**
>
>
> **WITH is a related feature. For more information, please ask the system to explain it.**

University of California

MELVYL automatically retrieves help appropriate to the context of a session when an unqualified HELP command is entered. For example, when help is requested immediately after choosing the COMMAND dialogue mode at the beginning of a session, the following display appears on the screen:

In command mode, every command must begin with a valid command word, or verb. The following verbs are valid:

SET	FIND	DISPLAY
RESET	AND	HELP
SHOW	OR	BROWSE
START	AND NOT	SCAN
	SELECT	LOGOFF
	AT	END
	BACKUP	
	ARRANGE BY	

Any verb may be abbreviated to any length down to 3 letters, and FIND, HELP, and DISPLAY may be abbreviated down to 1 letter.

If you try to type a command beginning with any other word, you will receive an error message.

To learn more about any of these commands, type HELP followed by the verb you are interested in, and press RETURN.

Additional context-specific help displays may be retrieved when a user becomes confused at some point in the search session. For example:

    Search request: FIND SU DRUGS AND VIOLENCE
    Search result: 0 records at UC libraries

  -> DIS ALL

    There are no records to display.

  -> DIS ALL MARC

    There are no records to display.

  -> HELP

You have asked for a display of bibliographic records, but you have not yet retrieved any records which can be displayed. Before you can type a DISPLAY command, you must perform a search which retrieves at least one record.

For further instruction, type
    HELP SEARCH
    HELP DISPLAY

MELVYL maintains an extensive glossary of help topics which may be retrieved by entering, HELP GLOSSARY. A user may request specific help by entering HELP followed by any word listed in the glossary. Many of these specific help displays suggest other glossary requests that may give related or more detailed information. For example, the command, HELP KEYWORD, produced this display:

A keyword is a word or group of words found in the index which you are searching. MELVYL searches for keywords in the index specified in your FIND or BROWSE command, and then returns the books (for a FIND) or access fields (for a BROWSE) containing the specified keywords.

For the personal author index, the keyword is the author's name; for example,
        FIND PA JANE AUSTEN
        FIND PA CUMMINGS, E E

For all other primary indexes, keywords are distinctive words from the access field for which you are searching; for example,
        FIND TI COSMOS LOVE LIFE
        BRO SU ENERGY ATOMIC
These keywords may be combined using conjunctions.

Each of the secondary indexes has its own rules.

For more detailed instruction, type
    HELP PERSONAL AUTHOR   HELP PRIMARY INDEXES   HELP FIND
    HELP BROWSE   HELP CONJUNCTION

Error messages in MELVYL are usually only one or two lines in length. If a more detailed explanation is desired at that point of need, the user can enter HELP after any error message. A unique feature prevents the user from getting stuck in an error situation. If the user makes the same error three times in succession, the system automatically produces the detailed explanation, in this manner:

    -> SELECT 2

        You must perform a BROWSE before you can SELECT any fields.
        To look at your search result, use the DISPLAY command.

    -> SELECT 1

        You must perform a BROWSE before you can SELECT any fields.
        To look at your search result, use the DISPLAY command.

    -> SELECT 2

You have issued a SELECT command, but there were no browsed fields to SELECT. You must issue a BROWSE command before you can SELECT.

If you are trying to display books that you have retrieved, you should use the DISPLAY command.

Remember that typing a FIND command destroys the results of a previous BROWSE.

For further information, type
    HELP DISPLAY

Northwestern University

LUIS's bibliographic display screens include suggestive prompts indicating the most likely commands to be used at any point, including a prompt for obtaining additional help (TYPE h FOR HELP). An introductory display may be retrieved by entering the "e" command (the prompt is, TYPE e TO START OVER):

LUIS: LIBRARY USER INFORMATION SERVICE

LUIS can be used to find BIBLIOGRAPHIC, CALL NUMBER and LOCATION information for materials held by Northwestern University libraries and by the Garrett and Seabury-Western seminary libraries. (Use the card catalog for materials not in the LUIS database.) CIRCULATION information for materials charged out through the computerized system is also available.

TYPES OF SEARCHES:	COMMANDS:
- FOR INTRODUCTORY SCREEN FOR TITLE SEARCHES:	Type t
AUTHOR SEARCHES:	Type a
SUBJECT SEARCHES:	Type s
- FOR USERS ALREADY FAMILIAR WITH LUIS:	Type t=, a=, s=, st=, or sm=,
(To start a search from any screen)	followed by a SEARCH TERM
	(title, author, or subject)
- FOR CIRCULATION INFORMATION SCREEN:	Type d
(Call number must be known)	

TO CORRECT A MISTAKE, type over the error or press CLEAR to start over.

TYPE COMMAND AND PRESS ENTER t=poverty of power

Seven different "help-in-context" displays may be retrieved by entering the command, h. Which display is shown to the user depends on where a user is in his search. For example, when a single bibliographic record is displayed after its selection from an author/title index display, the entry of the command, h, produces this help display:

LUIS SEARCH REQUEST: A=COMMONER

    HELP FOR BASIC BIBLIOGRAPHIC RECORD -- NO. 6 OF 7 ENTRIES FOUND

This display gives brief bibliographic information and holdings (location,

copies, call numbers, volumes, and current issues).

- For BOOKS: Author, title, place of publication, publisher, and publication

               date are usually given.

- For PERIODICALS and other SERIALS: Title, publisher, place, and

               date of the first issue or volume are usually given.

Information on library and call no. locations is available at service desks.

TO RESTORE PREVIOUS BASIC BIBLIOGRAPHIC RECORD SCREEN, press ENTER

TO VIEW BASIC BIBLIOGRAPHIC RECORD OF THE NEXT ENTRY, type m

TO VIEW BASIC BIBLIOGRAPHIC RECORD OF ANY INDEX ENTRY, type line no. of entry.

TO RETURN TO PREVIOUS INDEX SCREEN, type i

FOR INTRODUCTION TO AUTHOR SEARCHES, type a ; TO TITLE SEARCHES, type t

FOR INTRODUCTION TO SUBJECT SEARCHES, type s ; FOR INTRODUCTION TO LUIS, type e

You may start a new title, author, or subject search from any screen.

IF YOU NEED MORE INFORMATION, ask a library staff member.

TYPE COMMAND AND PRESS ENTER

If no matches result from the processing of a user's subject search, the
system responds with the message, NO SUBJECT HEADINGS FOUND.

A request for help at this point retrieves the following help display:

LUIS SEARCH REQUEST: S=ZZZ

Possible reasons for the message NO SUBJECT HEADINGS FOUND:

1. Your request is not in the subject heading form used in one of the three

    subject headings lists used in LUIS. To learn more about subject searching:

    a)   Type s -- for all materials in LUIS except:

    b)   Type st -- for most materials in the Transportation Library

    c)   Type sm -- for most materials in the Medical Library

2. No materials are in the LUIS database under the subject heading you have

    used. Consult the appropriate subject headings list for related subject

    headings, or check the card catalog for materials not in LUIS.

    (Type s or st or sm for information on the subject headings lists.)

3. A typographic or spelling error was made in search term.

4. An inappropriate command code was used (e.g., s= used for searching

    a medical subject).

IMPORTANT: When unsure of spelling or form, try shortening search term.

FOR INTRODUCTION TO LUIS, type e

IF YOU NEED MORE INFORMATION, ask a library staff member.

TYPE COMMAND AND PRESS ENTER

In addition to the seven "implicit specific" help displays, LUIS provides
several help displays which explain how to search by title, author, or
subject. These displays may be explicitly requested by entering one of these
commands: t, a, s, st, or sm. Some of these "first-level" displays prompt the
user to retrieve additional displays containing more detailed information
and/or examples. The following is a response to a request for help with
subject searching (s):

TO SEARCH BY SUBJECT: EXAMPLES:

- TYPE s= followed by a subject term or portion   s=television s=shakesp

  of subject.   s=symbolism in art

To determine the subject headings used in LUIS,

you may wish to consult the Library of Congress

Subject Headings (LCSH) list. This two-volume

red book is available near library terminals.

EXAMPLE: LCSH indicates that materials on the First

          World War will be found under "European

          War, 1914-1918" but not under "First World

          War", "World War One", or "1st World War".

FOR MORE INFORMATION ABOUT USING LCSH, TYPE m

NOTE: Most Transportation Library subjects must   EXAMPLES:

       be searched by st= and Medical Library   st=urban transit

       subjects by sm= ; type st or sm for details.   sm=vestibular nuclei

TYPE t FOR INTRODUCTION TO TITLE SEARCHES, OR a FOR AUTHOR.

TYPE e TO START OVER.

TYPE COMMAND AND PRESS ENTER

<u>Pikes Peak Library District</u>

Once the user has selected the online catalog search function (INVENTORY) from
the initial menu display of information service options, MAGGIE offers the
user this single help display in response to a HELP command:

<pre>
                    Public Dial-Up Access
                         >Menu<
                For HELP enter "?selection"

        AGENCIES   COURSES   CALENDAR   GOODBYE

        INFO   INVENTORY   TERMINAL   CLUBS

            WELCOME
Program: INVENTORY

 "_PPLINV   V7.1   [250,250]   RSTS V7.0-07 Maggie's Place

PPL> HELP

Command choices:
    A/data = author search
    B/data = Barcode search
    C/data = Call number search
    E/   = Expand this record
    F/   = Forward
    L/data = LCCN search
    N/   = Next author/title
    S/data = Subject search
    T/data = Title search
    X/   = Exit program
</pre>

Detailed explanations of each online information service or file can be
obtained by entering "?" followed by the name of the service or file (e.g.,
?AGENCIES).

RLIN

RLIN's online catalog offers the user five help displays. Each must be
retrieved with separate commands. Two of the displays provide RLIN system and
subsystem news (SHOW NEWS and SHOW CHANGES). The SHOW INFORMATION command
(which may be abbreviated to the initial three letters) explains the system's
commands and lists the available help displays in this manner:

 :+? SHOW INFO

 Information display

 Searching
  FINd <index> <value> - initiates search
  AND, &   - restricts search   AND NOT, &~, ~ - restricts search
  OR, | - expands search   RESume - continues search in next file

  SELect FILes <file>,... - Determines which files are to be searched

 Display
  MUL - Multiple record display FUL - Fully tagged display
  LON - Long, card-like display CAT - Cataloged holdings display
  PAR - Partial record display   PRI - Primary cluster member display

  SET DISplay <display name> - sets default local-version record display

 Information
  SHO NEWs - RLIN system news
  SHO CHAnges - Subsystem-specific news
  SHO INFormation - [this display]
  SHO SETtings - User status information
  SHO INDexes - Index information
 :?

The user may review his session and search status by entering SHOW SET, for
example:

 :? SHOW SET

 Settings display

 RLIN Cataloging system - Session date: Ø1/Ø3/82
 Library: CRLG (CStRLIN)   Account: BB.PA2   OID: DKF

 Files: BKS
 No search

 Function: Search   Mode: PROD   Input:
 Display: PAR
 :?

The user, in this case, has not yet entered a search statement, but has
selected the books file. The display format default is set to PARTIAL.

RLIN's index information display is included with the discussion of command
language syntax presented in the last section (7.5) of chapter 7.

Mission College

Mission College's OPAC help facility consists of an introductory general help
display and two additional help displays that are appropriate to different
stages in the search process. The introductory display may be obtained by
entering the command, HI:

Mission / West Valley College - Library Catalog

Hi, when you need information assistance please type the word
HELP then press the RETURN key.

PLEASE NOTE :- The RETURN key must be pressed after you type each message

You can search for material by SUBJECT or AUTHOR or TITLE

Please enter your search

If HELP is entered before a search, the following display explaining search
options and mechanics is presented:

H?HELP
HJ
You can search for material by SUBJECT or AUTHOR or TITLE. Please type your
search in the format shown in the example below.

To search by...

SUBJECT   please type S= followed by the subject term or heading you are
                            interested in. Example: S=REPORT WRITING

AUTHOR   please type A= followed by author's last name, then first name.
                            Example: A=CAMPBELL WILLIAM GILES

TITLE   please type T= followed by title of the material.
                            Example: T=FORM AND STYLE

For Resource Island or Reserve materials you can also search by COURSE or
INSTRUCTOR.

COURSE   please type CO= followed by name of Course. Example: CO=ENGLISH 1A

INSTRUCTOR   "   type IN= followed by the last name of the instructor.
                            EXAMPLE: IN=TAYLOR

If HELP is requested after a search statement has been entered and executed, a display is shown which suggests a method for reducing the results of a search and explains three output options:

    H?HELP
    HJ
    To make your search message retrieve fewer items from the catalog, add /E to
    the end of your search message. This is called an 'Exact Search'.
         Example: S=REPORT WRITING/E or T=THE FRENCH/E or A=CAMPBELL WILLIAM/E

    To print the contents of the screen on the printer nearest the terminal you are
    using, type PR and RETURN.

    To determine the location and availability of a specific title, type ST=
    followed by the line number listed beside it. Example: ST=2 and RETURN .

    For more detailed information on a specific title, type BI= followed by the
    line number listed beside it. Example: BI=5 and RETURN .

Claremont Colleges

The TLS OPAC in use at the Claremont Colleges prompts the user at the beginning of a session to enter a search code or general help command. The latter command (H) will retrieve a listing of nine available specific help displays as shown below:

    ENTER CODE LETTER;D FOR CODE LIST;H FOR HELP:H

    HELPING INFORMATION IS AVAILABLE AS SHOWN HERE:

    Ø   DISPLAY OF WAYS TO SEARCH FOR BOOKS
    1   INTRODUCTORY INFORMATION AND SEARCH STRATEGY HINTS
    2   HOW TO SEARCH BY CALL NUMBER
    3   HOW TO SEARCH BY AUTHOR, ADDED ENTRY (EDITOR, ETC.)
    4   HOW TO SEARCH BY TITLE
    5   HOW TO SEARCH BY A COMBINATION OF SUBJECT, AUTHOR, TITLE
    6   TO GET FULL BIBLIOGRAPHIC INFORMATION (PUBLISHER, DATE, ETC.)
    7   HOW TO USE FAST SCAN
    8   LOCATION CODES
    PLEASE TYPE IN THE DIGIT FOR THE HELP YOU NEED :1

The TLS help facility is menu-driven, thus the user obtains access to the specific help displays by first retrieving the help options menu and then entering the line number of the desired explanation in response to the specific help prompt. The above request (line number 1) produced this display:

EACH OF THE PROGRAM FUNCTIONS WILL REQUEST SEARCH INFORMATION
FROM YOU. SEE "HELP" TEXT FOR PROPER FORMAT OF AUTHOR/EDITOR,
AUTHOR/TITLE, AND CALL NUMBER SEARCHES.

ONCE YOUR SEARCH HAS BEEN ENTERED, THE PROGRAM WILL BEGIN TO
DISPLAY RECORDS AT THAT POINT (OR, IF AN EXACT MATCH IS NOT
FOUND, IT WILL BE THE NEXT ALPHABETICAL CHARACTER IN LINE).
THESE WILL BE SHOWN TO YOU ONE AT A TIME. PRESS THE SPACE BAR
TO SEE NEXT ENTRY. USE "FAST SCAN" TO DISPLAY GROUPS OF 12 BRIEF
RECORDS EACH.
*** PRESS "/" (SLASH) TO STOP THE SEARCH MODE IN PROGRESS***
     PRESS "@" KEY TO SEE THE FULL BIBLIOGRAPHIC INFORMATION
     PRESS "J" FOLLOWED BY ONE NUMERAL TO JUMP FORWARD IN THE FILE
          BY 1 TO 9 ENTRIES.
     PRESS "K" FOLLOWED BY ONE NUMERAL TO JUMP BACKWARD IN THE FILE
          BY 1 TO 9 ENTRIES
     PRESS "C" TO DISPLAY CIRCULATION DATA ABOUT THE ENTRY DISPLAYED
               ABOVE.
     PRESS CONTROL AND "H" KEY TO BACK UP TO CORRECT TYPING ERRORS
* AT LEAST 3 CHARACTERS MUST BE SUPPLIED FOR AUTHOR, TITLE, OR
SUBJECT SEARCHES.
* ALWAYS SUPPLY THE LONGEST CORRECT KEY THAT YOU KNOW. FOR INSTANCE,
IF YOU KNOW THE AUTHOR NAME TO BE KURT VONNEGUT, SUPPLY
"VONNEGUT, KURT" INSTEAD OF "VO".

The selection of line number 3 from the help menu would have retrieved the
following help display which explains how to conduct an author search and
suggests an additional search formulation which may restrict the results to a
topical area of interest:

SEARCHING AUTHOR'S NAME: ENTER AS FEW AS "3" OR MANY CHARACTERS OF
NAME AS DESIRED. USE SPACES, COMMAS, ETC. ONLY IF PRESENT IN RECORD.
FORMAT: LAST NAME, COMMA, SPACE, FIRST NAME, SPACE, MIDDLE NAME
AUTHOR= HARPER, JOHN L
ENTER: HAR (OR) HARPER (OR) HARPER, J (OR) HARPER, JOHN L (ETC)

** AUTHOR NAME COUPLED WITH A SUBJECT HEADING **
TO FIND AN AUTHOR NAME COUPLED WITH THE USE OF A SUBJECT HEADING,
USE THE 'E' SEARCH. KEYWORD PHRASES (ONE OR MORE WORDS) ARE LIMITED
TO 32 CHARACTERS.

A fuller explanation of the E search ("Boolean") mentioned here may be
obtained by selecting item number 5 from the help menu. However, the help
menu must be retrieved first, then the line number 5 may be entered to
retrieve an explanation of "HOW TO SEARCH BY A COMBINATION OF SUBJECT, AUTHOR,
TITLE."

OCLC and The Ohio State University

The OCLC and the LCS online catalog search systems do not currently have help facilities as that concept is defined in this report. Neither system provides capabilities for the user to retrieve separate help displays, nor automatically supplies unrequested help when a user experiences difficulty in the search process.

The LCS staff at Ohio State are currently developing a help facility for their OPAC which will be installed by the summer of 1982. Larry Besant, Assistant Director for Public Services at the OSU libraries, reports that the new help facility will include several user-retrievable help displays. The entry of the command, HELP, will retrieve an introductory display which will guide the user to specific help displays. These displays will provide basic "how to" guidance for the use of the major search commands (e.g., HELP, TITLE), or offer a structured series of "lessons" for training in the fullest use of the system (e.g., HELP,1, HELP,2, etc.).

MELVYL, MSUS/PALS, and LCS: System Components and File Structure

11.1 Uncommon Beginnings, Common Aims

The online public access catalog systems at The University of California, The Mankato State University, and The Ohio State University represent three different design philosophies and development efforts to produce powerful computer systems capable of managing large files of data and providing fast access to that data through multiple access points. In terms of search power and flexibility, these three OPACs are among the most sophisticated online catalogs available to library users today. Each system was developed independently of the others (LCS in the late 60s, and the other two in the late 70s) to solve locally defined problems of access and file maintenance, and each presents a different interface to the user, as described in the preceding chapters.

In this chapter we present a brief history of the development of these systems, a set of tables which identifies their hardware and software components, and end with a discussion of the file design and maintenance methods employed by each to support online access to catalog records.

11.1.1 The University of California's Online Public Access Catalog (MELVYL)

In 1977, The University of California Libraries: A Plan for Development 1978-1988* outlined the need for increased access to all UC library resources through a union catalog and projected an automated catalog for online access to those union records. Since 1977, the planning and development for these projects has been carried out. Retrospective conversion of catalog records to machine-readable form began in April 1979. The first microfiche production union catalog appeared in spring 1980 and included 1976 and later imprints along with additional records from the retrospective conversions on each campus. In spring 1981, the UC Union Catalog was produced with 600,000 union records. These records consolidated 1.2 million monographic records from all nine UC campuses and Hastings College of Law. Retrospective conversion projects are ongoing and are currently being supported on five UC campuses.

---

*University of California, Office of the Executive Director of University-wide Library Planning, The University of California Libraries: A Plan for Development, 1978-1988 (Berkeley: University of California, 1977).

After an initial pretest period, in July 1981 the Union Catalog entered the test phase as a prototype online catalog with more than 700,000 monographic records. Based on test results and data analysis regarding use of the prototype, a production version of the online catalog will become operational in 1982 with an expanded database projected at 2 million records and 1,600 terminals.

The University of California's MELVYL OPAC system is currently operational in prototype with 100 CRTs available to library users on UC campuses. The two Magnuson M 80/4 CPUs are dedicated to the OPAC. The system is up for 168 hours per week with 99% uptime. The bibliographic database currently contains 733,000 records. New records for the Union Catalog are primarily processed through OCLC and RLIN.

Monograph records in the online catalog are accessible by author, title, subject, series, uniform title, and keyword. Full online name authority control is employed, and the replacement of variant forms of names with the authoritative forms takes place automatically. The user may browse the name authority file to view both the authoritative form and the variant forms. MELVYL's designers devoted particular attention to creating a friendly man-machine interface by using several techniques: (1) three dialogue modes, (2) extensive help/error facilities, (3) different levels of printed materials, (4) feedback mechanisms for evaluating system performance, (5) minor modifications to dedicated patron terminals. Two dialogue modes are functional in the prototype catalog: LOOKUP mode (menus and prompts) for the user with no prior experience with the MELVYL system, and COMMAND mode for the experienced user. The tutorial mode, designed to instruct use of the command mode, has not yet been implemented and will be examined in view of the prototype evaluation.

The microfiche edition of the UC Union Catalog will serve as a backup to the online system, or its substitute where terminals are not available. The card catalogs on each campus serve as backups for local holdings. In the future when all retrospective conversion is complete, all machine-readable records regardless of date or type of material will be incorporated into the catalog.

11.1.2 Mankato State University's Online Public Access Catalog (MSUS/PALS)

Planning for the MSUS/PALS (Minnesota State University System's Project for Automation of Library Systems) began in 1977 on two concurrent fronts. At Mankato State University, the OCLC Implication Task Force was organized to recommend how best to utilize its new machine-readable records produced as a result of joining OCLC. In March 1978, the OCLC Task Force recommended a State University System online catalog with COM support as the most economically feasible way for Mankato to proceed.

On the larger front, during the 1977-78 academic year, the State University Advisory Committee on Libraries/Media Services was established to perform a comprehensive study to advise on the future growth and development of information services in the libraries. The resulting report of May 1978 had two important parts: (1) a statement of MSUS goals and objectives, and (2) fourteen recommendations for the System's direction. The recommendations emphasized high service levels and cost avoidance in light of current and projected programs. The foundation of the report was based on four

recommendations for automation. In July 1979, the decision was made to
proceed with a cooperative computer-based bibliographic system. In August,
key personnel were appointed for the State University System project for
library automation. Nine institutions chose to participate in the project:
six from the State University System, plus three other institutions, including
MINITEX.

Part 1 of the project called for "indexing access" to the bibliographic
database, i.e., an online catalog. By May 1980, the online catalog system's
capabilities were demonstrated in prototype. During the summer of 1980, a
limited database of 23,000 records and two terminals were used for staff
training. By September, the full database was up for use on three public
service terminals; and by October, the number of terminals had increased to
nineteen. In spring 1981, a total of thirty-one terminals in the other six
state universities were operational.

The MSUS/PALS online catalog has 22 CRTs available to library users at Mankato
State and 120 CRTs throughout the Minnesota State University System. The OPAC
uses only 8% of the capacity of the Univac 1100 model 80A, the mainframe it
shares with all other academic applications. The system is up for 105 hours
per week with 98% uptime. The bibliographic database contains approximately
1,760,000 records (July 1981). The system backup is COM microfiche. The
online catalog has five basic search strategies: author, title, combination
of author and title, subject, and descriptive term (keyword). A mnemonic
command language is required for search and retrieval.

The Minnesota State University System Project for Automation of Library
Systems continues with plans for acquisitions, serials control, and
circulation. The initial timetable projected four years, July 1979–June 1983
for achieving the totally integrated system.

11.1.3 The Ohio State University's Online Public Access Catalog (LCS)

In the late 1960s, the OSU Libraries investigated four problem areas for
computer applications: cataloging, acquisitions, serials/periodicals, and
circulation. To aid in cataloging, OSU became an OCLC user in August 1971.
Since OCLC had planned to offer both acquisitions and serials systems in
1974-5, OSU decided to automate book circulation.

In 1970, OSU contracted with IBM to develop software for its circulation
system. LCS (Library Control System) became operational in 1971 with limited
author/title online access. All of the more than 1.7 million titles in LCS
are represented by these brief bibliographic records. Public access terminals
became available in January 1975. Faced with the problems of maintaining a
massive, growing card catalog and the impending conversion to AACR2, in the
late 70s OSU began planning for the expansion of LCS into a full online
catalog for titles received after January 1974. Capabilities needed to expand
the circulation functions into an online catalog were identified. In June
1978, for titles cataloged after April 1978 through OCLC, three of the
capabilities were added: full bibliographic records, subject access through
LCSH, and joint author access.

The State Library of Ohio and OSU have maintained close ties through
reciprocal borrowing privileges, interlibrary loan, and daily courier service.

In May 1974, the State Library received an LCS terminal with access to OSU
materials and the capacity for remote borrowing of OSU books. An OCLC
retrospective conversion project at the State Library provided full
bibliographic records for its 142,000 monographs. The State Library
administration expressed interest in LCS as a means to close its catalog and
increase utilization of the collection. Negotiations took place in 1977 and a
contract was finalized in March 1978. In December 1978, the State Library's
bibliographic records were added to LCS and patron access terminals were
brought up at the State Library in March 1979.

The OSU Library Control System has 115 CRTs available to library users in the
OSU libraries, two terminals located in academic departments, and dial-access
capabilities. There are eight terminals at the State Library of Ohio. The
OPAC uses 11% of the Amdahl V7 mainframe it shares with other academic
applications. The system is up for 103 hours per week with 98.5% uptime. The
bibliographic database contains approximately 1,700,000 records (July 1981).
Updates are loaded from OCLC tapes, OCR input, ERIC RIE tapes and new
acquisitions tapes provided by vendors.

LCS currently functions as an automated circulation control system and an
online catalog. The online catalog is searchable by author, title,
combination of author and title, call number and subject. A three-letter
command is used to identify the type of search followed by a combination of
letters or numbers whose formula is determined by the search type. In
December 1981, a new version of the system, LCS III, was implemented. It
provides two additional features: (1) headings control for author, subject,
series, uniform title, including a universal updating capability, and (2) a
syndetic structure of "see" and "see also" references which displays on the
CRT to the user.

Currently, the card catalog and online catalog are maintained as 100% parallel
files. In the summer of 1982, the card catalog will be frozen and nothing
else will be filed into it. The online catalog will replace it for all new
materials.

11.2 System Hardware and Software

Before describing how each of these three OPACs organizes data files and
working files to facilitate the processing of search and retrieval (and other)
commands, Tables 14-16 are presented to permit identification and comparison
of the fundamental components and characteristics of each system's host
processor hardware, telecommunications hardware, and system software.
Depictions of each system's file structure and message/command processing
paths are included in section 11.3 Files and Indexes.

Table 14. Host Processor Hardware*

HOST PROCESSOR SYSTEM	California, University of	Mankato State University	Ohio State University
System's mainframe computer	Magnuson M 80/43	Univac 1100 model 80A	Amdahl V7
Number of CPU's used by mainframe	3	1	1
Core memory currently available	24 Mbytes	4 Mbytes	8 Mbytes
Is mainframe shared or dedicated?	dedicated	shared[a]	shared[b]
Disk drives currently available to OPAC	14 CDC 33502 8 CDC 33302	6 Univac 84/34	8 IBM 3330-11 and equivalents
Total online mass storage available to OPAC	11,000 Mbytes[e]	1,200 Mbytes[c]	1,600 Mbytes[d]
Type of mass storage used to duplicate OPAC database	microfiche, magnetic tape	microfiche, magnetic tape	magnetic tape
Quantity and types of I/O processors used	18 channels (15 block, 3 byte multiplexors)	1 I/O driver; 4 channels (1 block, 2 word, 1 byte multiplexors)	12 channels (10 block, 2 byte multiplexors)
Total system hours per week	168 hours	105 hours	103 hours
Percent up-time	99%	98%	98.5%

* As reported July, 1981

NOTES: a. Host processor is used for all academic applications; OPAC uses only 6% of host's capacity.
         b. Host processor is used for all academic applications; OPAC uses only 11% of host's capacity.
         c. Only 900 Mbytes currently used, leaving 300 Mbytes for growth and retrospective conversion.
         d. Online mass storage capacity allows 8 years of growth at current rate of updating.
         e. Only 7000 Mbytes currently used, leaving 4000 Mbytes for growth.

Table 15.   Telecommunications Hardware*

TELECOMMUNICATIONS	California, University of	Mankato State University	Ohio State University
Front-end processor(s)	1 Computer Communications C80	2 Univac V77200	1 Memorex 1270
Total number of ports	100	120	100
Total number of multiplexed ports[a]	75	2[b]	6
Total number of dial-up ports[a]	8	3	2
Total number of communication lines	33	32	100
Total number of terminals the system can support simultaneously with current hardware configuration	100	120	200
Baud rates of communication lines	300, 1200, and 9600 baud	300 and 1200 baud	300, 1200, and 9600 baud
Type of transmission	half duplex	half duplex	half duplex
Type of network	point to point	point to point	multipoint, and point to point
Type of line protocol supported	asynchronous	asynchronous	synchronous, and asynchronous
Access via a commercial network (e.g., Telenet)	not allowed	not allowed	not allowed
Number of hardcopy terminals available to library users	none	none[f]	2
Number of CRT's (video terminals) available to library users	100	22[c]	115
Number of CRT's with attached printers available to library users	none	none[f]	2
Number of hardcopy terminals available to staff only	none	1[f]	35[d]
Number of CRT's available to staff only	none	1[f]	100[d]
Number of CRT's with attached printers available to staff only	none	none[f]	10[d]
Number of offline printers available	none	1[f,g]	none

Table 15. Telecommunications Hardware (cont.)*

TELECOMMUNICATIONS	California, University of	Mankato State University	Ohio State University
Estimated maximum number of online terminals system can support without modifying current version of software	1000	250	more than 300[h]
Online terminals available to system's users	Perkin-Elmer Bantams; 1200 baud Televideo 920; 1200 baud Microterm ACT 5A; 1200 baud	ADS 20; 300 and 1200 baud	IBM 3278; 9600 baud IBM 3101; 1200 baud Beehive Minibee; 1200 baud Beehive Microbee; 1200 baud
Character code used by system	ASCII	ASCII	ASCII and EBCDIC[e]

* As reported July, 1981.

NOTES: a. This number is included in the total number of ports.
        b. The 2 Univac V77200 allow up to 8 multiplexed ports, only 2 are currently used.
        c. The figure for the entire Minnesota State University System is 105 CRT's.
        d. Estimated figure
        e. Data are stored in EBCDIC by system, but both ASCII and EBCDIC terminals may be used when searching database.
        f. For Mankato State University only, not applicable to the entire Minnesota State University System
        g. Mankato State University has several offline printers, but only 1 is currently in use.
        h. Disk space allocated to the display file called Detail Page File allows only up to 316 terminals, but, according to system staff, this can be modified easily to accommodate more terminals.

Table 16.   System Software*

SYSTEM SOFTWARE	California, University of	Mankato State University	Ohio State University
Operating system	OS/360 MVT 21-8F	Univac 1100 OS 36.R2D	IBM MVS 3.8
Environment	real memory, multiprogramming, multiprocessing	virtual memory, multibanking, multiprogramming; multiprocessing capability	virtual memory, multiprogramming
Database online users lost during system's crashes?	yes	no, 98% recovery rate	yes
Origin of applications software	developed locally	developed locally	developed on site by IBM
Applications software computer language(s)	PL/I and Assembler	ASCII Standard Cobol	PL/I and Assembler
Software under current development?	yes[d]	yes[b]	yes[c]
Number of programmers currently involved in maintaining software	12	1	4
Software currently being "run" at other sites?	no	no	yes[a]
Commercially supplied database manager used?	yes, ADABAS	yes, DMS 1100	no[e]

* As reported July, 1981

NOTES: a. At the University of Illinois and the State University of New York at Albany
         b. Authority management
         c. Title, series, and author headings control
         d. Incremental update of database, support of other MARC formats (system currently supports monographs only)
         e. Database manager developed in-house by system staff.

11.3 Files and Indexes

Comprehensive descriptions of online system file structure, maintenance, and access procedures require an advanced knowledge of current computing equipment, operating systems, and database management concepts. This knowledge would include a familiarity with the specialized terminology used by the various vendors of computer hardware, and operating and database management systems, to describe their products and explain their use. In this section a brief outline is presented for the general reader which illustrates three different design approaches to organizing large amounts of machine-readable data for the purpose of facilitating online access and retrieval.

The bibliographic database of an online catalog is typically made up of two groups of files. One group, the data files, contains the stored bibliographic and location data. The other group, the work files, supports search and retrieval operations performed on the data files. The organization and contents of the data files determine the ways in which the online catalog can be searched (e.g., by author, by title, by subject, by keyword within a field, etc.), as well as what data can be retrieved from such searches (e.g., call number, truncated records, brief records, full MARC records with tags, etc.).

Data files are of two types: bibliographic files and access point (index) files. Each of these files usually consists of a set of variable length logical records*1. In the bibliographic file, each bibliographic record contains descriptive data representing a bibliographic item (e.g., a monograph, a sound recording, etc.) owned by a member library of the OPAC system. In the access point file (also known as the index file), each record has two main parts: a character string called the index key, and a set of pointers. The index key is derived from one or more fields called access points (see Project Glossary) in the bibliographic record, and the pointers are addresses*2 of these records in the bibliographic file. Thus, by linking an index key to all bibliographic records associated with that key, each access point file is an index of the bibliographic file.

Work files play mainly a supportive role in the online catalog. They support access operations which range from a simple and straightforward inverted index lookup to a complex search using Boolean intersection which may require multiple sort/merge operations on the bibliographic record pointers stored in the index records. They also support retrieval operations such as displaying search results at an online terminal or printing these results offline. Work files also differ from data files from the perspective of data maintenance. Data files require periodic maintenance which includes updating, adding, and deleting records, but usually the bulk of the data stored in these files remains unchanged. In contrast, the contents of work files are much more volatile; data are added to and deleted from the work files at a rapid rate during system hours.

---

*Refer to corresponding numbered note at end of chapter.

11.3.1 The University of California's Online Public Access Catalog (MELVYL)*[3]

The current version of MELVYL (first half of 1982) is a prototype developed by the Division of Library Automation of the University of California. Future versions of MELVYL will include expanded versions of this prototype's database which, at the current stage, is not updatable and supports the searching of monograph records only.

The MELVYL prototype is made up of four main data files: the Bibliographic File, the Index Control and Short Display File, the Heading File, and the Location File*[4].

11.3.1.1 The Bibliographic File

The Bibliographic File contains about 733,000 bibliographic records of monographs owned by the University of California campus libraries. Each stored record includes bibliographic data from all of the locally cataloged records of a monograph. These data are merged together to produce one comprehensive union record in the Bibliographic File. Variant entries that are not eliminated by the consolidation process are retained in the master record. The size of the bibliographic records varies from an average of 1,000 bytes to a maximum of 15,000 bytes. Access to the Bibliographic File is through the Index Control and Short Display File, and the Heading File (see Figure 16).

11.3.1.2 The Index and Short Display File

The Index Control and Short Display File contains the same number of records as the Bibliographic File, i.e., about 733,000 records. Each Index Control and Short Display record includes the main entry (fields 1XX), the title (field 245), the call number (field 090), the edition statement (field 250), and the imprint statement (field 260) of a monograph. These elements are used to develop brief displays of search results.

The Index Control and Short Display record also includes the LC card number, the ISBN, the ISSN, the RLIN control number, and the OCLC control number to allow the retrieval of bibliographic records by these fixed length access points. The language code (field 041), the geographic code (field 043), and the chronological code (field 045) are used in combination with fields 250 and 260 to provide limiting parameters for search results.

11.3.1.3 The Heading File

The Heading File includes six types of heading records:

_   --   Personal author (534,758 records averaging 81 bytes in length)

_   --   Corporate author (100,698 records averaging 155 bytes in length)

_   --   Title (1,120,689 records averaging 145 bytes in length)

_ --   Uniform title (28,120 records averaging 92 bytes in length)

_ --   Series (317,220 records averaging 175 bytes in length)

_ --   Subject (464,118 records averaging 129 bytes in length)

Basically, each heading record includes one access point of one of the six
types above to the records in the Bibliographic File. Table 17 lists the MARC
fields indexed for each type of heading.

Table 17. MARC Fields Included in MELVYL's
Primary Search Indexes**

Index Name	Accessible Fields
Personal Author (PA)	100, 400, 700, 800
Corporate/Conference Author (CA)	110, 111, 410, 411, 710 711, 810, 811
Title (TI)	100, 110, 111, 130, 240, 241, 242, 243, 245, 400, 410, 411, 440, 490, 700, 710, 711, 730 740, 800, 810, 811, 830, 840
Uniform Title (UT)	130, 240, 243, 730, 830
Series (SE)	400, 410, 411, 440, 490, 800, 810, 811, 830, 840
Subject (SU)	600, 610, 611, 630, 650, 651 660, 670, 690, 691

**Currently the database contains records for monographs only.

11.3.1.4 The Location File

The Location File currently contains sixteen records corresponding to sixteen
campus locations. Each location record includes several bit strings, each
preceded by a campus code and a sequence number. Each bit in the string
corresponds to an Index Control and Short Display record, and represents a
monograph cataloged by a University of California library. "On" bits
(bits= 1) denote ownership of the monographs by the location in question.

11.3.1.5 Summary

Figure 16 captures the essence of the MELVYL prototype OPAC which is built on
top of the ADABAS database management system. The principal OPAC activity is
the resolution of users' search requests leading to the display of search
results. This activity is shown as a series of four processes.

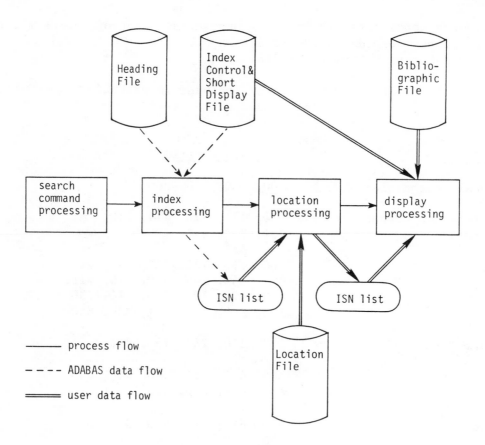

Figure 16. University of California's File Design for the
            Prototype Online Public Access Catalog

The system starts with the search command processing which involves
interpreting the input of a user at an online terminal. For example, the user
may enter a personal author's name either surname first, or first name
followed by the surname. The system identifies the surname in either case for
lookup in the Heading File. The next step is index processing which,
depending on the user-entered command/argument, may involve fixed length
access points (LC card number, ISBN, ISSN, RLIN control number, and OCLC
control number) from the Index Control and Short Display File, or variable
length access points (personal author, corporate author, title, uniform title,
series, and subject) from the Heading File. The result of the index
processing is a set of pointers called the ISN (Internal Sequence Number) list
which leads to the records in the Bibliographic File directly associated with
the access points processed*[5].

The location processing which follows the index processing entails limiting the search results (represented by the ISN list) to a particular location. This step usually results in a smaller ISN list, as the ISN list obtained in the index processing is system-wide in scope.

The last step is the display processing which fetches brief displays of search results from the Index Control and Short Display File, or longer displays from the Bibliographic File.

11.3.2 The Mankato State University's Online Public Access Catalog (MSUS/PALS)*[6]

Mankato State University's OPAC is supported by twelve files:

-- The Bibliographic File contains bibliographic records for items of all formats (monographs, serials, recordings, filmstrips, etc.) in the Minnesota State University System's libraries

-- The Author Index File, Title Index File, Author/Title Index File, Subject Index File, Term Index File, and ID Index File are indexes which provide access to the Bibliographic File

-- The Language Index File allows the use of foreign languages as search limiting parameters

-- The Help File holds all help-related information that can be displayed online

-- The Work Area/Sets File, Screen Displays File, and Offline Print File are work files used respectively for searching, displaying search results or help information online, and printing search results offline.

Once every month the MSUS/PALS OPAC is updated from OCLC archive tapes. Close to 20,000 bibliographic records are added to the Bibliographic File. (This figure also includes records of the ongoing retrospective conversion encompassing all libraries currently represented in the database.) Corresponding index records are updated, or created and merged into the existing index files in the same monthly update operation which is always run in batch mode during system off hours.

11.3.2.1 The Bibliographic File

The Bibliographic File contains two types of logical records referred to respectively as "base" records and "correction" records in the OPAC system documentation.

When the archive tapes are read during the monthly database update operation, the first occurrence of an OCLC number not found in the OPAC database causes the corresponding OCLC record to be incorporated in the Bibliographic File in the following way: local data (i.e., data in MARC fields 040, 049, 590, 910, and 949 pertinent only to the institution in the Minnesota State University System which has used this particular OCLC union record) are put in a correction record, the remaining data from the OCLC record are stored in a base record. Each subsequent occurrence of the same OCLC number on the archive tapes (indicating the use of the OCLC record for the cataloging of the same bibliographic item by another MSUS institution) causes one more correction record to be created. The result of the updating process is that for every bibliographic item owned by the system, there shall be a single base record in the Bibliographic File, plus one correction record for every institution that holds a copy of this item.

When the holdings of an institution are searched by an online catalog user, the system applications software provides the user with unique institution records by merging data in the base records with local data in the pertinent correction records. In the Bibliographic File, each base record is followed by, but does not include, all related correction records with the latter being sorted by institution. Either type of record may be retrieved individually. As of July 1981, the Bibliographic File included 606,776 base records and 1,159,279 correction records. These records are variable in length. The average length is 620 bytes for a base record, and 90 bytes for a correction record. The maximum length allocated to either type is 5,024 bytes.

11.3.2.2 The Index Files

The MSUS/PALS OPAC's index files (Author, Title, Author/Title, Subject, Term, ID, and Language) are all similarly structured. Each file is made up of variable length records that comprise two main parts: a fixed length index key, and a number of fixed length pointers that link this key with records in the Bibliographic File.

The keys in the Author Index File, Title Index File, Author/Title Index File, and Subject Index File are character strings derived from the corresponding access points using truncation algorithms. These truncation algorithms are needed to reduce storage required by lengthy multiword access points. The keys in the Term Index File, ID Index File, and Language Index File come from single-word access points, and for that reason require no truncation algorithm.

Pointers are assigned to an index key in multiples of 400, and theoretically, there is no limit to the number of pointers a key can have (i.e., a key is permitted to "point" to an unlimited number of bibliographic records). Each pointer is sixteen bytes in length and includes:

--   A four-byte sort key which comes from the first four characters of the first title word not an article

--   One byte for the record type (this subfield will be used later to distinguish items "on order" from items already owned)

--   Three bytes for the OCLC number which is stored in binary

--   A three-byte institution symbol

--   One byte for the term type (needed to differentiate corporate author terms, title terms, and subject terms)

--   Two bytes for the publication date which is stored in binary

--   One byte for the serial flag (to indicate whether an item is a serial or not)

--   One byte for the material format (to indicate the physical format of the item)

The OCLC number links the index key associated with the pointer to a base record in the Bibliographic File while the institution symbol links it to the appropriate correction record. The subfields in the pointer reserved for the publication date, the serial flag, and the material format are used in restricting search results.

In each index file the records are sorted successively by institution symbol, index key, sort key, and OCLC number.

Six of the index files, (Author, Title, Author/Title, Subject, Term, and ID) are access point files and are directly searchable. The only index file not directly searchable is the Language Index File which is used solely in restricting search results by foreign language.

The Author Index File includes 755,510 records with an average length of fifty-seven bytes. 1,539,522 pointers have been assigned. The index keys are derived from MARC fields 100, 110, 111, 700, 705, 710, 711, and 715 using the truncation algorithm 8,5,1: the first eight characters of the author's last name plus the first five characters of the first name and the middle initial are stored in the sixteen-byte index key. Index key storage is allocated in groups of four bytes (8,12,16, etc.), thus two bytes of the index key are not used at this time.

The Title Index File includes 1,254,642 records with an average length of forty-five bytes. 1,614,504 pointers have been assigned. The index keys are derived from MARC fields 130, 212, 240, 241, 242, 243, 244, 245, 246, 247, 400, 410, 411, 440, 730, 740, 800, 810, 811, 830, and 840 using the truncation algorithm 6,3,3,2: omitting any initial article, the first six characters of the first title word, plus the first three characters of the second title word, plus the first three characters of the third title word, and the first two characters of the fourth title word are stored in the sixteen-byte index key.

The Author/Title Index File contains 1,371,377 records with an average length
of forty-three bytes. 1,597,960 pointers have been assigned. The index keys
are derived from MARC fields 100, 110, 111, 700, 705, 710, 711, and 715 for
the author part, and from MARC fields 245 and 740 for the title part. The
truncation algorithm 6,6 is used: the first six characters of the author's
last name plus the first six characters of the first title word (omitting any
initial article) are stored in the sixteen-byte index key.

The Subject Index File includes 497,275 records with an average length of
eighty-four bytes. 1,856,483 pointers have been assigned. The index keys are
derived from MARC fields 6XX using the truncation algorithm 8,3,3,2: the
specified number of characters from the first four words of the subject
heading are stored in the sixteen-byte index key.

The Term Index File includes 497,275 records with an average length of 310
bytes. 10,246,760 pointers have been assigned. The index keys are derived
from MARC fields 110, 111, 710, 711 and 715 for the corporate author terms;
from MARC fields 130, 212, 240, 242, 243, 245, 246, 247, 400, 411, 440, 730,
740, 800, 810, 811, 830, and 840 for the title terms; and from MARC fields 6XX
for the subject terms.

Unlike the keys of the previous index files which are made up of truncated
parts of several words, each Term Index Key comes from a single word pulled
out of one of the MARC fields just enumerated using free text indexing. A
short stopword list of about fifty words is used to eliminate nonsignificant
words. Sixteen bytes of storage are allocated to each Term Index Key which
will hold the first sixteen characters of the term word, or the entire term
word plus blanks if the term word is shorter than sixteen characters.

The Language Index File includes 312 records with an average length of 1,720
bytes. 32,986 pointers have been assigned. The index keys are derived from
the fixed field 'Lang' of the MARC records and are allocated three bytes of
storage each. For example, FRE is the index key for French language records.
A pointer is assigned to each unique language index key for each stored
bibliographic record of a work in that language. This accounts for the rather
large average length of language index records.

The ID Index Files include sixteen-byte index keys consisting of ISBN, ISSN,
or LCCN standard identification numbers

11.3.2.3 The Help File

This rather special file which is neither a data file nor a work file
(according to the distinction we have made in the introduction of section
11.3) is used by the MSUS/PALS OPAC to hold all "Help" information available
online. As of July, 1981, the file was twenty-nine pages in length, and
included a one-page directory and twenty-eight pages of displayable data*7.
Each page provides help information on a topic designated by a two-character
code. These two-character codes are stored in the directory which serves as a
table of contents to the file.

11.2.3.4 The Work Files

The Work Area/Sets File is used by the system mainly as a temporary storage
for index records retrieved by successful searches during a search session at
the terminal*[8]. For every terminal serviced by the online catalog, the file
provides ten storage areas, each capable of holding a maximum of 8,000 index
pointers. (A search yielding more than 8,000 pointers will have its results
truncated by the system at the 8,000 "hits" cutoff point.) One of these ten
storage areas holds the result (i.e., index keys and accompanying pointers) of
the latest successful search, and is the theater of all Boolean operations
(AND, OR and NOT) on the index keys. It is called the "work area." The other
nine areas may be used by the online searcher to preserve (SAVE) results of
previous searches. They are called "sets." The searcher preserves the result
of a search by copying the contents of the work area onto a set, and recalls a
saved search by copying the contents of the pertinent set onto the work area.
As previously mentioned, this file only keeps data temporarily. The contents
of the work area and the sets are lost after the searcher has keyed in the
command "END" that marks the end of a search session. The Work Area/Sets File
can accommodate 120 terminals, allocating 100 pages of storage to each
terminal.

The Screen Displays File makes possible the display at a terminal of online
help information and search-generated bibliographic records. The file is
configured to handle 120 terminals, allocating two pages of storage to each
terminal with each page capable of holding data for three VDU terminal
screens*[9]. When displaying bibliographic records, the system uses the first
page for individual record displays and the second page for multiple record
displays, with both types of displays coming from the search result in the
work area of the Work Area/Sets File. When online help is requested, the
directory of the Help File is scanned for the help topic that matches the
two-character help code keyed in by the searcher, and the appropriate help
information is copied onto the first page reserved to that particular terminal
by the Screen Displays File.

The Offline Print File allows offline printing of search results. The file
consists of a one-page directory serving as a table of contents, and a print
queue made up of copies of work areas from the Work Area/Sets File. Every
time a user requests offline printing, he is assigned a print ID number, and
the contents of his working area (i.e., the result of his most current
successful search, or the contents of a given set he has just copied onto the
work area) get copied onto the print queue of the Offline Print File. The
print ID number and the name of the institution where the print request takes
place are entered in the directory. The system processes these print requests
at night, during system off hours, by going through the directory and printing
out the jobs in the queue sequentially. After all printing has been done, the
system reinitializes the file for use in the next day by clearing the
directory.

The size of the Offline Print File depends on the number of daily print
request; but on the average, the file seldom needs more than twenty-five pages
of storage.

11.2.3.5 Summary

Figure 17 graphically captures the database architecture of the MSUS/PALS OPAC; there are twelve files, two input paths, and two output paths. The input is either an online search-related command or a "Help" request entered by the OPAC user at a terminal. The two input paths mark the logical flow of the input from the terminal to the Work Area/Sets File and the Help File where the input is processed.

The output consists of the search results or help information displayed at an OPAC terminal, or the search results printed at a line printer during system off hours. The two output paths mark the logical flow of output from the Screen Displays File to an OPAC terminal, and from the Offline Print File to a line printer. The lines linking the files summarize the position of each file in the database vis-a-vis the other files.

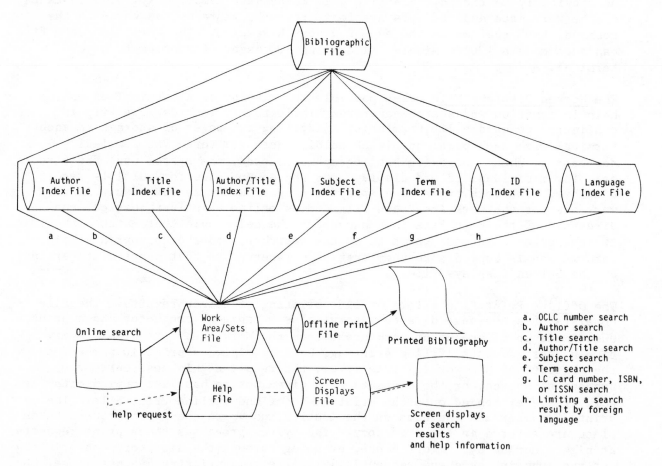

Figure 17. Mankato State University's Online Public Access Catalog File Structure

Table 18 links some notable command capabilities of MSUS/PALS OPAC with their respective supporting files.

Table 18. Supporting Files for Command Capabilities: MSUS/PALS

Command Capabilities	Supporting Files
Select collection location	Index files
Save or purge search results	Work Area/Sets file

Use of access points
    Author
    Title
    Author/Title
    Subject
    ISBN, ISSN, LCCN
	
	Author Index file
	Title Index file
	Author/Title Index file
	Subject Index file
	ID Index file

Search free text	Term Index file
Restrict search results	Language and other index files
Use Boolean operators	Work Area/Sets file
Display forward and backward	Screen Displays file
Request offline print	Offline Print file
Get news or help online	Help file

11.3.3 The Ohio State University's Online Public Access Catalog (LCS)*[10]

At The Ohio State University, the Online Public Access Catalog is integrated
in a dual function system called the Library Control System (LCS) that
supports both circulation and catalog search functions. LCS includes more
than forty tape and disk files of which the following disk files play a major
role in bibliographic searching:

1. The Master File, Circulation and Save File, Serial Holdings File, and
    Bibliographic Record File contain bibliographic data, location and
    circulation status of bibliographic items (print and nonprint) owned
    by the State Library of Ohio and The Ohio State University Libraries;

2. The Call Number File, Call Number Cross Reference File, Title Number
    File, Search Code File, Search Code Cross Reference File, and
    Bibliographic Index File are indexes that make access to the Master
    File possible;

3. The Subject File and its two indexes, the Subject Code File and the
    Subject Cross Reference File, are used for subject heading authority
    control;

4. The General Page File, Detailed Page File, and Subject Page File are
    work files used to develop screen displays for all search results.

File maintenance is done during a weekly batch run that updates all files
supporting the online search function of the Library Control System, with the
exception of the Serial Holdings File, the Circulation and Save File, and the
name records of the Master File whose maintenance is done partially or
entirely online by staff members during system hours.

About 2,000 bibliographic records from the system machine-readable archive
tapes are added to the online catalog every week. Data from these records are
stored in the Master File, Bibliographic Record File, and Subject File. The
indexes to the Master File and Subject File are updated accordingly to make
the newly added bibliographic data retrievable by online searches.

11.3.3.1 The Bibliographic Files

Bibliographic data on each cataloged item in LCS are spread over four files:
the Master File, the Serial Holdings File, the Subject File, and the
Bibliographic Record File.

The Master File contains two types of logical records: short bibliographic
records and name records. The file has a short bibliographic record for every
bibliographic item cataloged and currently owned by the system. Data in this
record include the LC card number, the LC or local call number, the main entry
(MARC fields 100, 110, 111, and 130), the main title (MARC field 245, subfield
a), and holdings information if the item is a monograph (holdings information
for items classified as serials or monographic sets is in the Serial Holdings
File).

Name records are used to store data on library patrons and library technical
processing divisions. They can be retrieved at staff reserved terminals but
not at public access terminals. They belong to the circulation subsystem of
LCS, but are not a component of the public access catalog.

The Master File is organized randomly, i.e., its records are not sorted in any
way. The relative position of each record within the file is determined by a
hashing technique*[11] using either the call number (for the short bibliographic
records) or the ID number (for the name records). As of July 1981, the file
had 103,643 name records and 1,782,433 short bibliographic records. These are
variable length records with an average length of 103 bytes.

The Serial Holdings File contains holdings information for all items
classified as serials or monographic sets. The file is basically organized by
title number (a unique positive integer assigned to a Master record when it is
created). A recent check by the system staff (about July 1981) revealed
722,056 Serial Holdings records with an average length of 636 bytes.

The Subject File contains all subject headings currently used in LCS. The
main purpose of the file is to provide subject heading authority control. The
OPAC user must start a subject search with an SUB/ (subject headings index
search) command whose argument is a subject heading provided by the user. The
system then goes to the Subject File via the Subject Cross Reference File to
find the closest match for the first seventeen characters of the search
argument. Thirty subject headings will be retrieved along with the number of
Master records associated with each one of them: in addition to the subject
heading word or phrase entered by the user, there will be fourteen headings

that precede it and fifteen that follow it alphabetically in the file. At
this point, the user may retrieve the bibliographic records cataloged under
any of the thirty retrieved subject headings by doing a TBL/ (Titles By Line)
search, followed by a DSL/ search (retrieves a short record with circulation
data), or an FBL/ search (retrieves the full bibliographic record).

Each record in the Subject File includes a three-byte subject code (a unique
positive integer assigned to a subject heading when it is added to the Subject
File), the number of short bibliographic records in the Master File associated
with this subject code, and the variable length subject heading derived from
MARC fields 600, 610, 611, 630, 650, 651, 690, 691, 100, 110, 111, and 130
(the 1XX fields are used when the main entry is treated as the subject).   As
of July, 1981, the Subject File had about 115,000 records alphabetically
sorted by subject heading, with an average length of fifty bytes.

The 115,000 subject headings in the Subject File are not all the headings
needed by the system for its 1,782,433 short bibliographic records in the
Master File. Quite a few Master records have yet to be assigned a subject
heading simply because the Master File was created much earlier than the
Subject File, but a system-wide retrospective conversion is taking care of
this problem.

The Bibliographic Record File contains all bibliographic data available for an
item in the online catalog which are not already in the other bibliographic
files. When a bibliographic record is added from the archive tapes to the
database, this record, which is in MARC format, will have some of its data
stored in a Master record, some data go to a Serial Holdings record, data in
the 6XX fields go to a Subject record, and whatever remains goes to a record
in the Bibliographic Record File. The file is organized randomly. The
relative position of each record in the file is determined by a hashing
technique using the title number. As of July, 1981, the file had 422,832
variable length records with an average length of 500 bytes.

11.3.3.2 The Index Files

Index Files Providing Access to the Master File

The system allows access to the Master File by title number through the Title
Number File, by call number through the Call Number Cross Reference File and
the Call Number File, by subject through the Bibliographic Index File, and by
search code through the Search Code Cross Reference File and the Search Code
File.

The Title Number File included 2,815,310 three-byte records as of July,1981.
The only thing stored in the record is the pointer, i.e., the relative address
of the Master Record which has been assigned this title number. The title
number is not physically stored, but is given implicitly by the position of
the record in the Title Number File, e.g., the fifth record in the file is for
title number "5."

There are currently more Title Number records than Master records because over
the years a number of Master records have been deleted (lost books, departed
patrons, etc.), but once a title number has been assigned, it will not be
reused by the system.

The Call Number Cross Reference File and the Call Number File form a two-level
index to the Master File. The Call Number Cross Reference File has a short
(fourteen bytes) fixed length record for every block of 379 logical records in
the Call Number File. Each record in the Call Number File is seventeen bytes
in length and consists of two main parts: an index key constituted by the
call number, and the relative address of the Master record associated with
this call number. As of July 1981, the Call Number File had 1,793,374 records
sorted by call number.

When a call number search is done online, the system goes to the Call Number
Cross Reference File to get the address of the block of records in the Call
Number File where a match for the call number entered as the search argument
may be found. The matching Call Number record has the address of the searched
for Master record. This Master record is then retrieved individually, in the
case of a DSC (Detailed Search by Call number) or FBC (Full Bibliographic
search by Call number) search*[12]. But if an SPS (Shelflist Position Search)
command has been used instead, thirty-three items on the shelf list (with the
match at the sixteenth position) will be retrieved.

The Bibliographic Index File permits the retrieval of each record in the
Master File having a designated subject code. Each record in the index file
consists of two main parts: the subject code and a variable number of
pointers. The pointer is eleven bytes in length and includes the title number
of the Master record associated with the subject code. The file is organized
randomly by subject code using a hashing technique. File size and record size
statistics are not available at the time of this writing.

The Search Code Cross Reference File and the Search Code File form a two-level
index to the Master File. The Search Code Cross Reference File has a short
(twelve bytes) fixed length record for every block of 402 logical records in
the Search Code File. Each record in the Search Code File is sixteen bytes
long and consists of two main parts: the first part is made up of a nine-byte
search code and a one-byte code indicator, the second part is the address of
the Master record associated with the search code. The code indicator is used
to indicate whether the search code is an author, title, or author/title code,
and whether the code is for a serial or a monograph. The author code is made
up of the first six characters of the author's last name and the first three
characters of the first name, with the name being derived from MARC fields
100, 110, 111, 130, 400, 410, 411, 700, 710, 711, 800, 810, and 811. The
title code is made up of the first four characters of the first significant
title word (a stoplist is used) and the first five characters of the second
significant title word, with the title being derived from MARC fields 130,
222, 240, 245, 246, 400, 410, 411, 440, 700, 710, 711, 730, 740, 800, 810,
811, 830, and 840. The author/title code consists of the first four
characters of the author's last name and the first five characters of the
first significant title word.

When an author, title, or author/title search is done online, the system goes
to the Search Code Cross Reference File to get the address of the block of
records in the Search Code File where matches for the search argument (the
nine-character string entered by the OPAC user after an author, title, or
author/title search command) may be found. As each record in the Search Code
File contains the search code and the address of one Master record, and as
Search Code records are sorted by search code, searching the area of the

Search Code File indicated by the Search Code Cross Reference record will retrieve all Master records associated with the search code matching the user's search argument.

Even though the size of the Search Code File is not known precisely at the time of this writing, one can expect it to be much larger than the Master File in terms of number of records because, on the average, there are three Search Code records (one for the author code, one for the title code, and one for the author/title code) for every Master record.

Index Files Providing Access to the Subject File

The Subject Code File links subject codes with their corresponding subject headings. This file has roughly the same number of records as the Subject File. Each Subject Code record is three bytes long and contains only the relative address of a Subject record. The subject code is not stored physically but is given implicitly by the position of a record in the Subject Code File, e.g., the third record in the Subject Code File has "3" as its subject code.

The Subject Cross Reference File is an index to the Subject File whose main purpose is the support of subject searches. Each Subject Cross Reference record consists of the address of a block of records in the Subject File, and the first seventeen characters of the first subject heading in that block. Subject Cross Reference records are sorted by this truncated subject heading.

When an SUB/ command is used online, the system scans the Subject Cross Reference File for the closest match to the search argument entered, and gets the address of a block of records in the Subject File. Thirty records will be retrieved from that area of the Subject File.

11.3.3.3 The Circulation and Save File

The Circulation and Save File contains the current status of all bibliographic items in circulation as well as save requests for these items. This rather special file, which seems to belong more to the circulation subsystem than to the bibliographic search subsystem, is described here because the information it provides can be retrieved by LCS users.

The file is organized according to an addressing algorithm using the title number. The contents of the file are fairly volatile, as all record additions and deletions are done online.

Circulation and Save records are of fixed length, and a recent check (about July, 1981) revealed 149,583 records in the file.

11.3.3.4 The Work Files

The General Page File develops screen displays for a successful general search*[13] or a shelf list position search. The file allocates three 1055-byte records (equivalent to three screens) to each LCS terminal, and can handle up to 348 terminals. Data for both the general search result displays and the shelf list position displays come from the Master File.

The Detailed Page File develops screen displays for a detailed search*[14] or a full bibliographic search*[15] . The file allocates three 1171-byte records to each LCS terminal, and is big enough to handle 316 terminals. Data for the detailed search result displays come from the Master File, Serial Holdings File, and Circulation and Save File. Data for the full bibliographic search result displays come from the Master File, the Bibliographic Record File, and the Subject File.

The Subject Page File develops screen displays for a subject index search (done with the SUB/ command.) The file allocates three 1055-byte records to each LCS terminal, and is configured to handle up to 348 terminals. Data for the subject index displays come from the Subject File.

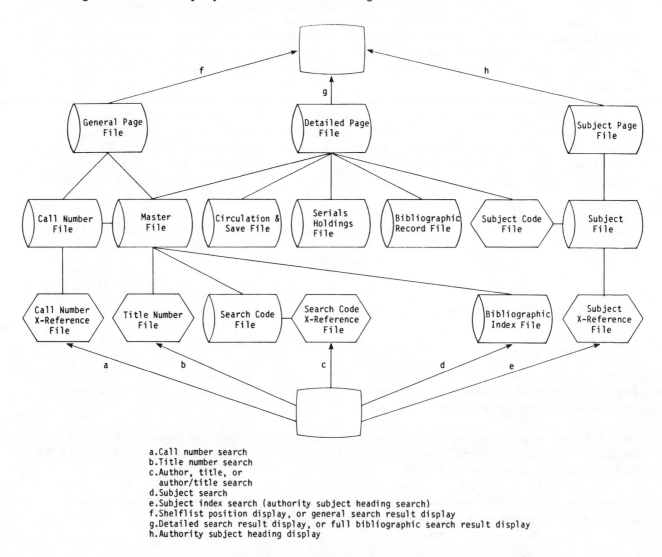

a.Call number search
b.Title number search
c.Author, title, or
   author/title search
d.Subject search
e.Subject index search (authority subject heading search)
f.Shelflist position display, or general search result display
g.Detailed search result display, or full bibliographic search result display
h.Authority subject heading display

Figure 18.   Ohio State University's Online Public Access
              Catalog File Structure

11.3.3.5 Summary

Figure 18 graphically captures the database architecture of the LCS system, depicting its sixteen files, five input paths, and three output paths.

The input consists entirely of search-related commands. The five input paths mark the logical flow of the input from the terminal to the files. The output is the shelf list position, general search results, detailed search results, full bibliographic search results, or the authority subject headings displayed at an LCS terminal. The three output paths mark the logical flow of output from the files to the terminal.

In the same manner as Figure 17, the lines linking the files summarize the position of the files in the database vis-a-vis one another. Files which are indexes to other indexes, and whose function is mainly to speed up the access time to these indexes, are represented in Figure 18 by hexagons instead of the more conventional cylindrical figures because these files would not be needed in a system using a commercial database manager*[16]. The LCS system, which does not use a commercial database manager to support its software, has five such files: Call Number Cross Reference, Title Number, Search Code Cross Reference, Subject Code Cross Reference, and Subject Code.

Table 19 links some notable LCS command capabilities with their supporting files.

Table 19. Supporting Files for Command Capabilities: LCS

Command capabilities	Supporting files
Use of access points	
Author, Title, Author/Title	Search Code X-Reference and Search Code files
Title number	Title Number file
Call number	Call Number X-Reference and Call Number files
Subject	Subject X-Reference, Subject, and Bibliographic Index files
Restrict search results	Search Code and Serial Holdings files
Display forward and backward	General Page, Detailed Page, and Subject Page files
Show subject index terms	Subject file
Indicate item location/availability	Master, Circulation & Save, and Serial Holdings files
Browse thru shelflist	Call Number file

Notes

1. A logical record is a data cluster perceived and treated as a logical entity. The MARC record is an example of a logical record. A logical record should be differentiated from a physical record (better known to programmers as a "block") which is a collection of bits physically recorded on a storage medium and which may be read or written with one machine input/output instruction.

2. These addresses are usually symbolic addresses (i.e., numbers or character strings that uniquely identify the records) or relative addresses (i.e., relative positions of the records in the file) that can be converted into actual physical addresses of the record on the storage medium.

3. This section is based primarily on "Prototype On-line Union Catalog System," a report by David Lee, Division of Library Automation, University of California.

4. These four files are discussed in detail in David Lee's report. Additional files of the prototype OPAC (e.g., the work files, ADABAS indexes, etc.) are not covered here because documentation was not obtained.

5. What actually happens is more complex than depicted here. Index processing involves the ADABAS associator indexes which are not explained here for the sake of brevity.

6. This section is based on conversations with Michael Barnett, MSUS/PALS software manager at Mankato State University.

7. The page size is set at 1792 words or 7168 bytes of storage (the length of each word on the Univac equipment is four nine-bit bytes).

8. A search is termed successful if the system can find at least one match when comparing the search key entered by the user at the terminal with the keys stored in the index file being searched.

9. This explains why the MSUS/PALS OPAC has the commands S1, S2, and S3 for showing, respectively, screen 1, screen 2, and screen 3, but does not need display commands like S4 or S5.

10. This section is based on conversations and documentation provided by Susan Miller, Coordinator of Automated Library Systems, The Ohio State University Libraries, and Conchita Beaton, LCS staff member.

11. This is an address calculation technique which converts a data entity (e.g., the call number or the ID number, in the case of the OPAC's Master File) into a near random number that determines where the logical record must be stored in the file.

12. The LCS OPAC has three search commands that use the call number as argument: DSC (Detailed Search by Call number), FBC (Full Bibliographic search by Call number), and SPS (Shelflist Position Search).

13. LCS OPAC system documentation refers to searches that retrieve brief
    one-line bibliographic entries (each with the author, the partial title,
    and the publication date of a bibliographic item) as "general searches."
    OPAC users are allowed three types of general searches: the author search
    (AUT), the title search (TLS), and the author/title search (ATS).

14. An LCS OPAC "detailed search" retrieves a display of up to three screens
    of information on a bibliographic item. The display includes the call
    number, the full author, the title, the publication date, the location and
    the circulation status of the item.

15. An LCS OPAC "full bibliographic search" retrieves a catalog card-like
    format display of a bibliographic item.

16. Building the database on top of a commercially available database manager
    appears to be the current trend in database design. For example, The
    University of California uses ADABAS and The Mankato State University uses
    DMS 1100. The use of a commercial database manager, which optimizes the
    storage and retrieval of records in the database, relieves the OPAC
    systems programmer of some aspects of access processing and redundancy
    control. Because a commercial database manager is not geared toward the
    specific needs of any particular system (it is rather aimed at a host of
    systems on the market), it may pose certain constraints that create
    additional problems for the database designer, e.g., about 1% of the
    records in the MELVYL OPAC Bibliographic File exceed the size of an ADABAS
    block, forcing the segmentation of these records into smaller pieces.

Project Bibliography

Allen, Bryce. PHOENIX I: Development of an on-line catalogue system. Canadian Library Journal. 39(1): 7-8; 1982 February.

American National Standards Institute Standards Committee on Standardization in the Field of Library Work, Documentation and Related Publishing Practices, Z39. A Compilation of Terms and Definitions Appearing in Z39 Standards. New York: The Committee; 1977.

Baker, Christine A.; Eason, Kenneth D. An observational study of man-computer interaction using an online bibliographic information retrieval system. Online Review. 5(2): 121-132; 1981.

Barnard, P.J. [and others]. Consistency and compatibility in human-computer dialogue. International Journal of Man-Machine Studies. 15:87-134; 1981.

Bates, Marcia J. Search techniques. Annual Review of Information Science and Technology. Knowledge Industry Publications, Inc. (for ASIS); 16: 139-169; 1981.

Bausser, Jaye. Authority files and the online catalog. RTSD Newsletter. 6(6): 65-68: 1981 November/December. (a)

Bausser, Jaye. Online catalogs. RTSD Newsletter, 6(4): 43-44; 1981 July/August. (b)

Beech, David. What is a command language? In: Beech, David, ed. Command Language Directions. North-Holland Publishing Co. 7-27; 1980.

Bennett, John L. The user interface in interactive systems. Annual Review of Information Science and Technology. 7: 159-196; 1972.

Berman, Sanford. Cataloging for public libraries. In: Freedman, Maurice J.; Malinconico, S. Michael, eds. The Nature and Future of the Catalog. The Oryx Press: 225-238; 1979.

Borgman, Christine L. Theoretical approaches to the study of interaction with computers. Prepublication draft of winner of ASIS Student Paper Award, 1981.

Boss, Richard W.; Marcum, Deanna B. The library catalog: COM and on-line options. Library Technology Reports. 16(5): 443-556; 1980 September-October.

Boyle, Stephen O.; Miller, A. Patricia. Feature comparison of an in-house information retrieval system with a commercial search service. Journal of the American Society for Information Science. 31(5): 309-317; 1980 September.

Brenner, Lisa P. [and others]. User-computer interface designs for information systems: a review. Library Research. 2: 63-73; 1980-81.

Cakir, A.; Hart, D.J.; Stewart, T.F.M. Visual Display Terminals: A Manual Covering Ergonomics, Workplace Design, Health and Safety, Task Organization. New York: John Wiley and Sons; 1980.

CHANNEL 2000: Description and Findings of a Viewdata Test Conducted by OCLC in Columbus, Ohio, October-December 1980. Research Department, OCLC Online Computer Library Center, Inc.; 1981 April; ED 206312.

Cochrane, Pauline Atherton; Kirtland, Monika. Critical views of LCSH--the Library of Congress subject headings; a bibliographic and bibliometric essay and an analysis of vocabulary control in the Library of Congress list of subject headings (LCSH). Syracuse, NY: 1981; ED208900.

Cochrane, Pauline A. Where do we go from here? Online. 30-41; 1981 July.

Cochrane, Pauline A. Subject access in the online catalog. Research Libraries in OCLC: A Quarterly. 5: 1-7; 1982 January.

Conger, Lucinda D. Online Command Chart. Weston, CT: Online, Inc.; 1980.

Croft, W. Bruce. Incorporating different search models into one document retrieval system. Proceedings of the Fourth International Conference on Information and Retrieval, May 31-June 2, 1981, Oakland, CA. Sponsored by the Association for Computing Machinery, Special Interest Group on Information Retrieval. 40-45; 1981.

Dataflow Systems. A Glossary for Library Networking. Washington D C.: Library of Congress; 1978.

Davis, Charles H.; Rush, James E. Guide to Information Science. Westport, CT: Greenwood Press; 1979.

Dillon, Martin; Knight, C.; Lospinuso, Margaret F.; Ulmschneider, John. The use of automatic indexing for authority control. Journal of Library Automation. 14(4): 268-277; 1981 December.

Doszkocs, T.E.; Rapp, B.A. Searching MEDLINE in English: a prototype user interface with natural language query, ranked output, and relevance feedback. Proceedings of the ASIS Annual Meeting, 1979. 16: 131-139; 1979.

Dwyer, Barry. A user-friendly algorithm. Communications of the ACM. 24(9): 556-561; 1981 September.

Dwyer, Jim. Libraries, funding, and technological change: dinosaurs face a new ice age. Technicalities. 1(1): 10-11; 1980 December.

Earl, Lois L. Experiments in automatic extracting and indexing. Information Storage and Retrieval. 6: 313-334; 1970.

Eason, K.D. Understanding the naive computer user. Computer Journal. 19(1): 3-7; 1976.

Ehrenreich, S.L. Query languages: design recommendations derived from the human factors literature. Human Factors. 23(6): 709-725; 1981 December.

Fenichel, Carol Hansen. The process of searching online bibliographic databases: a review of research. Library Research. 2: 107-127; 1980-81.

Fitter, M. Towards more "natural" interactive systems. International Journal of Man-Machine Studies. 11: 339-350; 1979.

Fryser, Benjamin Scott. The Effects of Spatial Arrangement, Upper-Lower Case Combinations, and Reverse Video on Patron Response to CRT Displayed Catalog Records. Research paper submitted to the School of Library and Information Sciences, Brigham Young University. Provo, UT. 1981 August.

Furlong, Elizabeth J. Index access to on-line records: an operational view. Journal of Library Automation. 11(3): 223-238; 1978 September.

Gaines, Brian R. The technology of interaction--dialogue programming rules. International Journal of Man-Machine Studies. 14: 133-150; 1981.

Gebhardt, Friedrich; Stellmacher, Imant. Opinion paper: design criteria for documentation retrieval languages. Journal of the American Society for Information Science. 29(4): 191-199; 1978 July.

Goldstein, Charles M.; Ford, William H. The user-cordial interface. Online Review. 2(3): 269-275; 1978.

Gorman, Michael. Cataloging and the new technologies. In: Freedman, Maurice J.; Malinconico, S. Michael, eds. The Nature and Future of the Catalog. The Oryx Press: 127-152; 1979.

Hansen, Wilfred J. User engineering principles for interactive systems. Proceedings of the AFIPS Fall Joint Computer Conference. 523-532; 1971.

Hawkins, Donald T. Online information retrieval systems. Annual Review of Information Science and Technology. 16: 171-208; 1981.

Hawkins, Donald T.; Wagers, Robert. Online bibliographic search strategy development. Online. 6(3): 12-19; 1982 May.

Hayes, Philip J.; Ball, J. Eugene; Reddy, Raj. Breaking the man-machine communication barrier. Computer. 14(3): 19-30; 1981 March.

Hebditch, D. Design of dialogues for interactive commercial applications. Man Computer Communication: Invited Papers, vol. 2, Infotech state of the art report, Infotech International Ltd. Maidenhead, England. 171-192; 1979.

Helander, G.A. Improving system usability for business professionals. IBM Systems Journal. 20(3): 294-305; 1981.

Hildreth, Charles R. The concept and mechanics of browsing in an online library catalog. Proceedings of the Third National Online Meeting, New York. Medford, NJ: Learned Information Inc. 181-196; 1982 March 30 - April 1.

Hildreth, Charles R. Optimal Response Times in an Online Interactive Computing Environment: Considerations and Guidelines for System Design. Columbus OH: Online Computer Library Center, Inc., OCLC technical report: 1981; OCLC/DD/TR-81/3; ED208898.

Huckle, Barbara. The Man-Machine Interface: Guidelines for the Design of the End-User/System Conversation. Savant Institute, Savant Research Studies: 1981.

Kaske, Neal K.; Sanders, Nancy P. On-line subject access: the human side of the problem. RQ. 52-58; 1980 Fall.

Krichmar, Albert. Command language ease of use: a comparison of Dialog and Orbit. Online Review. 5(3): 227-240; 1981.

Lancaster, F. Wilfrid. Information Retrieval Systems: Characteristics, Testing and Evaluation. New York: Wiley; 1979.

Larson, Ray R. Evaluating Public Access On-Line Catalogs, Phase I, Development and Testing of Data Collection and Analysis Tools. Final Report to the Council on Library Resources; Division of Library Automation, University of California: 1981 July.

Lawrence, Barbara; Prewitt, Barbara G. Online Commands: A User's Quick Guide for Bibliographic Retrieval Systems. Philadelphia, PA: National Federation of Abstracting and Indexing Services; 1977.

Ledgard, Henry; Whiteside, John A; Singer, Andrew; Seymour, William. The natural language of interactive systems. Communications of the ACM. 23(10): 556-563; 1980 October.

Mandel, Carol A. Subject Access in the Online Catalog: a Report Prepared for the Council on Library Resources, Bibliographic Service Development Program. Washington D.C.: 1981 August.

Mann, William C. Man-Machine Communication Research: Final Report. Advanced Research Projects Agency, Marina del Ray, CA: USC/Information Sciences Institute; 1977 February. ARPA Report No. ISI/RR-77-57. Available from NTIS, Arlington, VA. AD-A037108.

Marcus, Aaron. Designing the face of an interface. IEEE Computer Graphics and Applications. 2(1): 23-29; 1982 January.

Marcus, Milton J. Concerning the nature of information processing end use. In: Granda, Richard E.; Finkelman, Jay M., eds. The Role of Human Factors in Computers. Human Factors Society, New York Metropolitan Chapter. 23-26; 1977.

Marcus, Richard S.; Reintjes, J. Francis. Experiments and Analysis on a Computer Interface to an Information-Retrieval Network. Report to the National Science Foundation; Division of Information Science and Technology: NSF IST-76-82117.

215

Marcus, Richard S.; Reintjes, J. Francis. The Networking of Interactive Bibliographic Retrieval Systems. 1976 March; MIT Report ESL-R-656; NTIS PB252407.

Markey, Karen; Atherton, Pauline; Newton, Claudia. An analysis of controlled vocabulary and free text search statements in online searches. Online Review. 4(3): 225-236; 1980.

Markey, Karen. Analytical Review of Catalog Use Studies. Dublin OH: Online Computer Library Center Inc. OCLC research report: 1980 February; OCLC/OPR/RR-80/2; ED 186041.

Martin, James. Design of Man-Computer Dialogues. Engelwood Cliffs, NJ: Prentice-Hall, Inc.; 1973.

Martin, Thomas H. A Feature Analysis of Interactive Retrieval Systems. Prepared for The National Science Foundation; Institute for Communication Research: 1974 September; NTIS PB-235 952.

Matthews, Joseph R. Requirements for an online catalog. Technicalities. 1(11): 11-13 1981; October.

Meadow, Charles T.; Cochrane, Pauline Atherton. Basics of Online Searching. New York: John Wiley and Sons; 1981.

Meadow, Charles T. The computer as a search intermediary. Online. 3(3): 54-59; 1979 July.

Meadow, Charles T. Matching users and user languages in information retrieval. Online Review. 5(4): 313-322; 1981.

Miller, Lance A.; Thomas, Jr., John C. Behavioral issues in the use of interactive systems. International Journal of Man-Machine Studies. 9: 509-536; 1977.

Mischo, William H. Expanded subject access to library collections using computer-assisted indexing techniques. Proceedings of 43rd ASIS Annual Meeting. 7: 155-157; 1980.

Mischo, William H. A Subject Retrieval Function for the Online Union Catalog. Dublin OH: Online Computer Library Center Inc. OCLC technical report: 1981; OCLC/DD/TR-81/4; ED 212263.

Mischo, William. Library of Congress subject headings: a review of the problems, and prospects for improved subject access. Cataloging & Classification Quarterly. 1(2/3): 105-124; 1982.

Moran, Thomas P. An applied psychology of the user. ACM Computing Surveys. 13(1): 1-11; 1981 March. (a)

Moran, Thomas P. The command language grammar: a representation for the user interface of interactive computer system. International Journal of Man-Machine Studies. 15(1): 3-50; 1981 July. (b)

Negus, A.E. EURONET Guideline: Standard Commands for Retrieval Systems.
London: The Institution of Electrical Engineers: 1977 December.

Negus, A.E. Development of the EURONET-Diane common command language.
Proceedings of the Third International Online Information Meeting. London:
1979 December. New York, NY: Learned Information, Inc.; 95-98; 1979.

Neumann, A.J. A Guide to Networking Terminology. Washington D.C.: U.S.
Government Printing Office; 1974.

Neville, H.H. Computers and the language of bibliographic descriptions.
Information Processing & Management. 17: 137-148; 1981.

Newman, I.A. Personalized user interfaces to computer systems. Eurocomp 78.
473-486; 1978.

Ng, Henry H.; Puchkoff, Steven J. Touch sensitive screens ensure a user
friendly interface. Computer Design. 135-137; 1981 August.

Nickerson, Raymond S.; Elkind, Jerome I.; Carbonell, Jaime R. Human factors
and the design of time sharing computer systems. Human Factors. 10(2):
127-134, 1968.

Nievergelt, J.; Weydert, J. Sites, modes, and trails: telling the user of an
interactive system where he is, what he can do, and how to get places.
Methodology of Interaction. North-Holland Publishing Company: 327-338; 1980.

O'Neill, Edward T.; Aluri, Rao. Subject Heading Patterns in OCLC Monographic
Records. Columbus, OH: OCLC research report: 1979; OCLC/RDD/RR-79/1; ED183167.

Penniman, W.D.; Dominick W.D. Monitoring and evaluation of on-line information
system usage. Information Processing & Management. 16(1): 17-35; 1980.

Penniman, W. David. Modeling and Evaluation of Online User Behavior. Final
Report to the National Library of Medicine; OCLC, Inc. 1981 September; NLM/EMP
(1R01 LM 03444-01).

Pritchard, Sarah M. SCORPIO: A Study of Public Users of the Library of
Congress Information System. Unpublished report. Library of Congress. 1981
January.

Quinn, Karen Takle. STAIRS search strategy: ideas and opinions. Online Review.
4(2): 163-168; 1980.

Ramsey, H.R.; Atwood, M.E. Human Factors in Computer Systems: a Review of the
Literature. U.S. Department of Commerce, Springfield, VA; 1979; NTIS Report
AD/A-075 679.

Rayner, David. Designing user interfaces for friendliness. In: Beech, D. ed.
Command Language Directions. Amsterdam: North-Holland Publishing Co.; 233-243;
1980.

Reisman, Sorel. What is "interactive video"? E-ITV. 13(6): 29; 1981 June.

Reisner, Phyllis. Human factors studies of database query languages: a survey and assessment. ACM Computing Surveys. 13(1): 13-31; 1981 March.

Relles, Nathan; Sondheimer, Norman K. Recent advances in user assistance. Paper presented at: Joint Conference on Easier and More Productive Use of Computing Systems. Ann Arbor Michigan: 1981 May.

Reynolds, Linda. The Presentation of Bibliographic Information on Prestel. Graphic Information Research Unit, Royal College of Art. London: 1980; British Library Research and Development Report No. 5536.

Rush, James E. Development and operation of a database machine for online access and update of a large database. Online Review. 4(3): 237-261; 1980.

Schilling, D.E. Coping with the casual user. Man/Computer Communication: Invited Papers, vol. 2, Infotech state of the art report, Infotech International Ltd. Maidenhead, England. 289-297; 1979.

Scilken, Marvin H. The catalog as a public service tool. In: Freedman, Maurice J.; Malinconico, S. Michael, eds. The Nature and Future of the Catalog. The Oryx Press; 89-101; 1979.

Shackel, B. Dialogues and language--can computer ergonomics help? Ergonomics. 23(9): 857-880; 1980.

Shinebourne, J. User needs, the new technology and traditional approaches to library services. Journal of Information Science. 2: 135-140; 1980.

Shneiderman, Ben. A note on human factors issues of natural language interaction with database systems. Information Systems. 6(2): 125-129; 1981.

Shneiderman, Ben. Hardware options, evaluation metrics, and a design sequence for interactive information systems. Information & Management. 3(1): 3-18; 1980 February.

Shneiderman, Ben. Software Psychology: Human Factors in Computer and Information Systems. Cambridge, MA: Winthrop; 1980.

Shneiderman, Ben. System message design: guidelines and experimental results. Unpublished draft to appear in Badre, Al; Shneiderman, Ben, eds. Directions in Human-Computer Interaction. Norwood, NJ: Ablex Publishing Corp.; 1982.

Sippl, Charles J. Data Communications Dictionary. New York: Van Nostrand Reinhold; 1976.

Sippl, Charles J.; Sippl, Roger J. Computer Dictionary and Handbook. 3d ed. Indianapolis, IN: Howard W. Sams and Co., Inc.; 1980.

Smith, Linda C. Implications of artificial intelligence for end user use of online systems. Online Review. 4(4): 383-391; 1980.

Stewart, Tom. Communicating with dialogues. Ergonomics. 23(9): 909-919; 1980.

Stibic, V. A few practical remarks on the user-friendliness of online systems. Journal of Information Science. 2: 277-283; 1980.

Thimbleby, Harold. Dialogue determination. International Journal of Man-Machine Studies. 13: 295-304; 1980.

Thompson, Elizabeth H. A.L.A. Glossary of Library Terms: With a Selection of Terms in Related Fields. Chicago, IL: American Library Association; 1971.

Tullis, Thomas S. An evaluation of alphanumeric, graphic, and color information displays. Human Factors. 23(5): 541-550; 1981 October.

Walker, Donald E., ed. Interactive Bibliographic Search: The User/Computer Interface. Montvale, NJ: AFIPS Press; 1971.

Weik, Martin H. Standard Dictionary of Computers and Information Processing. Rochelle Park, NJ: Hayden Book Company; 1977.

Wessel, Andrew E. Computer-Aided Information Retrieval. Los Angeles: Melville Publishing Co.; 1975.

Willers, Jean Marie. A survey of retrospective conversion of existing catalogues. Program. 15(2): 91-99; 1981 April.

Appendixes

Project Glossary

Access points
(1) Any and every data element of the bibliographic record which may be used to search for the item it represents. (2) Designated components of a bibliographic record, usually fields or subfields (including preassigned content descriptors), whereby the record can be retrieved by the user. In common practice, a certain number of fields or subfields are chosen to reference a record by inclusion in an index or thesaurus. These index and thesaurus terms then constitute the access points or entries to the records themselves. Access paths usually lead from an entry in an index or thesaurus to the stored record itself. If one considers all indexable components of a record, including controlled vocabulary terms assigned to represent an item's content, cross references, and various sophisticated techniques of searching an online database (e.g., the use of Boolean operators, truncation, word proximity), the number of access points to a record is almost unlimited. (3) Main and added entries in the card catalog.
See also: Entry, Heading, Main entry.

Acoustic coupler
A modem that enables a remote terminal to be connected with the central processor using the handset of a conventional telephone receiver and by dialing over a public or leased telephone line.
See also: Dial access.

Adjacency
See: Proximity operators.

Algorithm
A set of well-defined rules to solve a problem, or a set of instructions to carry out a procedure, in a finite sequence of steps.

Alphanumeric
Pertaining to a character set or string that contains both letters and numerals.

Argument, search
  The search term or keyword, often preceded by a command word or symbol,
  entered by the user of an online information retrieval system to retrieve
  all records which match the search argument.
  See also: Character string, Keyword, Term.

ASCII
  American Standard Code for Information Interchange; a widely used 7-bit
  character code which can represent up to 128 characters. ASCII is the USA
  standard data code.

Authority control
  The methods by which the authoritative form of a name or term is applied and
  maintained uniformly in records across the database. Includes files of
  records containing the authoritative form with appropriate cross-references,
  and the mechanism whereby all records can be updated automatically to
  maintain consistency with the authority files.

Authority file
  A set of records that identifies the established or authoritative forms for
  headings or access points for a set of bibliographic records. Authority
  files include cross-references from variants to the preferred forms of
  headings, and links from earlier to later forms and between broader and
  narrower terms and related terms.

Auxiliary keyset
  A separate pad or block of keys, usually numeric, in addition to the main
  alphanumeric keyset on the terminal keyboard. Usually, but not necessarily,
  an integral part of the main keyboard.
  See also: Keyboard.

Availability status
  Information indicating the status of one or more copies of a bibliographic
  item pertinent to the patron's desire to obtain and/or use the item. Typical
  statuses are "on loan" (often with due date), "on reserve,"
  "non-circulating," "on hold," "on shelf," "in process," "missing," and
  "lost."
  See also: Location data.

Backup
  See: Display backward.

Baud
  A measure of the transmission speed capability of a communications line or
  system. In a sequence of binary signals, 1 Baud = 1 Bit/sec.

Bibliographic database
  A file or files of document descriptions consisting of records that one can
  use for deciding whether to search for the document itself. The documents
  may be journal articles, reports, patents, books, or the like. The
  descriptive information in these records contains such information as title,
  author, publisher and date, and subject information, which may include
  subject classification terms or key words and may also include an abstract.
  See also: Catalog, File, Online public access catalog, Record.

Bibliographic item
   A unique document or set of documents in any physical form considered a
   single entity, and which is capable of description within a single
   bibliographic record.
   See also: Bibliographic record, Catalog, Record.

Bibliographic record
   A collection of bibliographic data fields treated as one logical entity that
   describes a specific bibliographic item.
   See also: Catalog, Record.

Bit, Binary digit
   The smallest unit of information and storage capacity in a computer system.
   A bit, in the binary system, may be either a '0' or a '1'. Combinations of
   bits can be used to represent letters or numbers.

Boolean logic operators
   Named for the logician and mathematician, George Boole, these operators
   include the linguistic entities "AND," "OR," and "NOT." In formulating a
   search, "OR" is usually used to combine related terms to broaden a search,
   "AND" is used to intersect terms with distinct meanings, and "NOT" is used
   for term exclusion. The latter two operators are used to narrow a search.
   See also: Boolean searching.

Boolean searching
   Searching an online information retrieval system with search terms or sets
   connected by Boolean operators. Combining terms or sets with "OR" broadens
   the search to include the results of both (or all) terms or sets.
   Intersecting terms or sets with "AND" narrows the search to include only the
   results which are common to both (or all) terms or sets.
   See also: Boolean logic operators.

Break
   See: Interrupt results.

Browse index list
   See: Show index listing.

Byte
   A group of adjacent bits (usually 8) which can be used to represent a single
   character in machine-readable code (e.g., EBCDIC).

Call number
   The notation used to identify and locate a particular item in a collection;
   it may also be used when truncated to identify a subject area where more
   than one desired item may be found. This notation is usually derived from a
   classification schedule like the Library of Congress or the Dewey Decimal
   Classifications.

Cancel offline print
   A command which enables the user to cancel a previously entered request for
   the offline printing (hard copy) of information acquired online (e.g., a
   bibliography or abstract).

Catalog
  A list of records, arranged systematically, which describes materials (e.g.,
  books, maps, recordings, serials) that comprise a collection.
  See also: Bibliographic database, Bibliographic record, Online Public
  Access Catalog.

Cathode ray tube, CRT
  An electronic vacuum tube in which an electron beam is generated and used to
  energize a phosphor screen which thereby emits visible light. Often used as
  synonymous with "visual display unit."
  See also: VDU.

Central processor
  See: CPU.

Character
  The actual or coded representation of a digit, letter or special symbol.
  See also: Byte.

Character string
  A continuous sequence of alphanumeric and/or other symbols which may
  constitute part or all of a word, phrase, or sentence. For purposes of
  searching, the character string to be scanned and identified in an index or
  document text is usually indicated by the search term or argument entered by
  the user.
  See also: Alphanumeric, Argument, Keyword, Term.

CODEN
  A mnemonic, alphabetic code assigned to a periodical which functions as a
  unique and unambiguous permanent identifier for a specific title. The CODEN
  is used in place of full or abbreviated titles of publications in processing
  and storing bibliographic data in many computer-based information handling
  systems. For example, BUWEA is the CODEN for "Business Week."

Command
  (1) A user-entered request at the terminal for the execution by the computer
  of a specific operation (e.g., search the database, display a portion of an
  index, print search results, etc.). Commands may be entered by typing a
  predefined character string (usually followed by a term or "search
  argument"), depressing a special function key, or responding to a question
  or option list ('menu') displayed on the screen. (2) An electronic pulse,
  signal or set of signals to start, stop or continue some computer operation.
  See also: Dialogue modes, Menu.

Command mode
  See: Dialogue modes.

Connect time
  The amount of time that elapses while the user of a remote terminal is
  connected to the system. Connect time is usually measured by the duration
  between sign-on (logon) and sign-off (logoff).

Control character
  A character whose occurrence in a particular context initiates, modifies, or
  stops a function. There are 32 such characters in the ASCII data code.

Control number
  A sequential number or an alphanumeric symbol uniquely associated with a
  bibliographic record and assigned by the system creating this record (e.g.,
  the OCLC or RLIN control number).

Controlled term indexing
  Indexing in which the terms or symbols chosen to represent a document or
  record, for the purposes of identification and retrieval, are assigned to
  that document or record from a controlled vocabulary or syndetic structure
  which exists independently of any document or record to be indexed. Such
  terms or symbols may coincidentally appear in the text of the document or
  record, but they are selected from a pre-established and controlled (by
  rules of inclusion and syndetic structure) list of terms or symbols
  specifically organized to improve indexing and access to documents or
  records. Examples of such controlled lists or syndetic structures are the
  LC Subject Headings, formal classification schemes, and various subject
  thesauri and name authority lists.
  See also: Free text term indexing, Indexing, Syndetic structure.

Controlled term searching
  Searching a file (or "catalog" or "database") using assigned terms.
  See also: Controlled vocabulary terms.

Controlled vocabulary terms
  Terms included in a thesaurus or an authority list used to represent a
  document's intellectual content. A search done with controlled vocabulary
  terms will only retrieve bibliographic records that have these terms in
  certain searchable fields, or which have been assigned these terms in the
  indexing process (usually to denote the subject content of the bibliographic
  item). For example, a controlled vocabulary term search in ERIC will only
  retrieve the records that contain these terms in the major & minor
  descriptor and/or identifier fields.
  See also: Controlled term searching, Descriptor.

Conversational mode
  See: Interactive.

Cost
  The cost of a search as charged by the system. It is interesting to note
  that the charge levied by the majority of database vendors is based on
  connect time, not CPU time.

CPU
  Central Processing Unit. The central processor of a computer system where
  instructions are interpreted and executed.

CPU time
  The actual computational time necessary for a computer to process a set of
  instructions.

CRT
  See: Cathode ray tube.

Cursor
  A symbol or sign which acts as a flag to identify one and only one of the
  character spaces on the display screen of a visual display unit (VDU) that
  will be affected by a command or action.

Cursor control keys
  Those keys which specifically control the movement of the cursor on the
  screen of a visual display unit; necessary for editing operations and for
  rapid access to any part of the display screen.

Data base
  See: Database.

Data element
  A defined unit of information. Constitutes part or all of a field in a
  record.

Database
  (1) A structured collection of data developed according to uniform
  standards.   (2) A collection of related files treated as an entity and
  available to a computer system.
  See also: File.

Default
  A predetermined alternative value or option automatically assumed by the
  system when none has been supplied by the system's user. In some systems,
  certain default values may be set by the user prior to normal interaction
  with the system.

Delete
  The ability to remove surplus material from text, simultaneously eliminating
  the gaps which would otherwise be formed.

Delimiter
  A symbol that groups or separates items of data. Delimiters are used in
  bibliographic record fields to indicate subfields, and may also be required
  in a specific command language to indicate different types of data items in
  a command/argument string.

Derived search key
  A predetermined format or code (number of characters and/or punctuation)
  applicable to designated fields or combinations of fields to be followed
  when constructing and entering a search in an online information retrieval
  system. The components of the coded search key are compared with data from
  one or more fields of a record for the purposes of identification when
  conducting a search. Examples of derived search keys are the abbreviated
  search keys used by OCLC or Ohio State University's LCS.
  See also: Key, Keyword, Search.

Descriptor
  A special term used to describe a document's subject content, and assigned
  to the document by an indexer.

Dial access

    The use of a dial or pushbutton telephone to initiate a telephone call.
    This action may be taken to establish a data transmission circuit between a
    terminal and another communications device or computer system over a
    switched (non-dedicated) line.
    See also: Dial-up terminal.

Dial-up

    See: Dial access.

Dial-up terminal

    A terminal on a switched (non-dedicated, non-leased) line.
    See also: Dial access.

Dialogue

    Human-computer dialogue consists of information conveying interaction in
    real time applications which is analogous to human to human conversation.
    Like human conversation, computer dialogue has two dimensions, time and
    socio-space. The conversation must take place at a certain pace, usually
    measured in seconds, and requires meaningful interchange based on the
    interpretation of exchanged messages within a purposive or intentions-shaped
    context. Dialogue with a computer usually involves paired-sets of
    interchanges of information and control, some human originated, some
    computer originated. The information may be couched in terms of a command
    or question, or conveyed by a message response to a command or question.
    See also: Dialogue modes, Online, Query, Search, System message.

Dialogue modes

    Online interaction between the user and the computer may consist of
    computer-inititated/guided dialogue or user-initiated/guided dialogue. In
    computer-initiated dialogue, the computer originates the transactional
    interchange and leads the user step by step through a sequence of
    operations; the user enters commands or parameter values in response to some
    form of directive prompting by the computer. Menu selection,
    question/answer, and form filling are common computer-initiated dialogue
    techniques. In user-initiated dialogue, no directive prompting or
    preimposed structure or sequence is present; the user enters commands at his
    discretion in a self-determined sequence. Examples range from a simple
    query where only an item number is entered, to the input of a mnemonic or
    natural language command word, qualified by a field identifier, and followed
    by one or more search arguments. In some systems these dialogue modes are
    integrated, and in others, the user may select the preferred mode.
    See also: Command, Dialogue, Interactive, Menu, Prompts.

Direct Use

    Unmediated use of an information retrieval system by an end user at a
    terminal. Direct use requires the user to engage in a dialogue with the
    computer system to retrieve the desired information, without the assistance
    of a human intermediary.
    See also: Dialogue, Dialogue modes, End user, Intermediary.

Directory Key

    See: Key.

Display
  While online, to display on the screen (when using a visual display unit
  such as a CRT), or to print on paper (when using a hard copy terminal) the
  results of a search, the search history or strategy, or other information
  requested by the user such as help screens or a portion of an index.
  See also: Display backward, Display forward, Page, Scroll.

Display backward
  The provision for the user to select a previously displayed screen (some
  systems limit this to the immediately preceding screen), or to select from a
  numbered series of screens or records an undisplayed screen or record that
  numerically precedes the currently displayed screen or record.
  See also: Display, Display forward, Page.

Display forward
  The provision for the user to select the next screen in a retrieved set of
  screens, or to select from a numbered series of screens or records a screen
  or record that numerically follows the currently displayed screen or record.
  See also: Display, Display backward, Page.

Display memory
  The internal storage capacity of a visual display unit to permit a greater
  character display capacity than the screen is able to accommodate. The
  display memory is accessed by means of a scrolling facility.

Document number
  A number assigned by a particular agency to a government publication which
  uniquely identifies that document. More than one number may be assigned to
  the same document by different agencies.

Down time
  The period of time when the system is not functioning as designed to serve
  the user.

EBCDIC
  Extended Binary Coded Decimal Interchange Code; an 8-bit character code
  which can represent 256 characters and which is used primarily in IBM
  equipment.

Echo
  The return of a message or command, entered by the user, to inform the user
  of the manner in which the system understands the message or command.

Edit input
  The capability to erase or modify commands or messages to be sent to the
  system.

End user
  The person who ultimately desires, receives, and uses the information and
  related services provided through the use of an interactive retrieval
  system. The information provided may be acquired directly or indirectly by
  the end user. Unmediated utilization of the system by the end user at a
  terminal, the point where the information is requested and ultimately
  provided. A direct end user engages in an interactive dialogue with the
  system to retrieve the desired information for himself.
  See also: Direct use, Intermediary.

Entry
  (1) A bibliographic record in the catalog. If the catalog is a
  machine-readable database the record which uniquely identifies and describes
  the bibliographic item need only be entered and stored once, thereby
  obviating the need for a "main entry" and its "added entries." (2) The
  access point to a record, for retrieval purposes. Authors, titles,
  subjects, call numbers can be entry points.
  See also: Access points, Heading, Main entry, Record.

Entry point
  See: Access point.

Explain system messages
  A command/inquiry feature which enables the user to view an explanation of a
  coded (or otherwise unclear) message supplied by the system.
  See also: System message.

Field
  One or more data elements that form a logical unit. Fields are the
  constituent parts of a record. In a bibliographic record, for example, the
  subject heading constitutes one field, the author name another one, etc.

File
  A collection of logically related records, usually, but not necessarily,
  arranged in sequence according to a directory key contained in each record
  (e.g., all monographs in a bibliographic database).
  See also: Record.

Fixed data
  Data that is written on the display screen of a visual display unit but
  which cannot be altered by the operator.

Formatting
  The structuring of the display screen into protected and accessible areas
  within which various actions can be performed in fields.

Form filling
  The entering of information into pre-defined areas or fields in the display
  screen.

Free text term indexing
  Indexing in which the terms or symbols chosen to represent a document or
  record, for the purposes of identification and retrieval, are derived from
  the text of the document or record itself. Such terms or symbols are
  extracted from their natural (pre-indexed) occurrence in the document or
  record, although certain rules or conventions--word or punctuation
  stoplists, maximum character lengths, and key construction algorithms--may
  be applied in the selection process. The terms chosen in this method of
  indexing are often referred to as "keywords," or when a construction
  algorithm is applied, as "derived search keys."
  See also: Controlled term indexing, Indexing, Key, Syndetic structure.

Free text term searching
  Searching a field or entire record in a file or database using keywords
  selected as significant for the field in which they occur, words which
  usually are not included in a controlled vocabulary.
  See also: Free text terms.

Free text terms
  Every significant word in a record not previously controlled by inclusion in
  thesauri or authority files. A search done with free text terms will
  retrieve all bibliographic records that have these terms in any of their
  searchable and user specified fields. Compare: Controlled vocabulary terms.
  See also: Free text term searching.

Function (functional)
  Refers to the desired ends or uses of an action (operation, transaction,
  command) or related set of actions which may be operational from the user's
  point of view in interactive search and retrieval activities. To say of an
  operation or capability that it is functional is to place particular
  emphasis on its purpose or intended use to produce a specific result. This
  usage allows for there being operations and commands that are not
  functional, and also covers the case where more than one operation or
  command may, in fact, perform (accomplish, achieve, fulfill) the same
  function. For one function there may be multiple operations, and for one
  operation there may be multiple commands. Some high level functions are,
  generally speaking, cataloging, book ordering/receiving, and bibliographic
  searching and retrieval for item verification or circulation status.
  See also: Operation, Process, Transaction.

Function keyset
  A collection of keys, each of which is associated with a specific command.
  See also: Command, Function.

General search command
  A single command used uniformly throughout a dialogue to initiate a search.
  The command may be qualified by a field parameter, and is accompanied by a
  search value such as a word, phrase, line, or set number.
  See also: Query, Search.

Hard copy
  A record on paper of machine output, usually in human-readable form.

Hardware
  Physical equipment such as mechanical or electronic devices. Computer
  hardware consists of tangible objects (integrated circuits, printed circuit
  boards, cables, power supplies, memories, card readers, line printers,
  terminals, etc.) rather than abstract ideas or instructions.
  See also: Software.

Heading
  (1) The form of a name, subject, uniform title, series, etc., used as an
  access point to a bibliographic record or authority record. (2) Derived
  from the traditional library practice of placing a name, word, or phrase at
  the top of the catalog card, and by which the card is filed in the catalog.
  In a card catalog, each assigned heading represents a separate entry of the
  record in the file.
  See also: Access points, Entry, Main Entry, Subject heading.

Help
   A user assistance feature which may provide a description/explanation of the
   system's features, options, dialogue characteristics, displays and record
   formats, and assist the user on how to proceed. Help screens answer specific
   questions for the user. The information available may range from an
   introductory overview to an entire online user's manual.

Host computer
   A computer system in a network that performs actual processing operations
   against a database, and with which other network nodes communicate.

Identification
   (1) The process of providing personal, equipment, or organizational
   characteristics or codes to gain access to a computer system. (2) The
   process of determining personal, equipment, or organizational
   characteristics or codes to permit access to a computer system.
   See also: Logon.

Identify offline assistance
   See: Offline assistance.

Index
   An ordered reference list of the contents of a file, record, or document,
   which includes keys or reference notations as pointers for identifying and
   accessing those contents.
   See also: Inverted index.

Index list
   See: Show index listing.

Indexing
   The process of selecting terms or symbols to represent part or all of a
   document or record in order to facilitate the identification and retrieval
   of that document or record. The terms or symbols chosen provide a reference
   guide to the document or record through the use of some linking factor which
   identifies and/or points to the document or record in question. The terms
   or symbols which constitute an index may be derived from the document or
   record itself, or assigned to the document or record from a list of
   controlled vocabulary terms, or assigned arbitrarily in a random or
   sequential manner to provide control numbers or codes.
   See also: Controlled term indexing, Free text term indexing, Index,
   Thesaurus.

Input prompt
   The visible signal, to the user, that the system expects some input
   (normally defined) before further processing can occur.
   See also: Prompts.

Inquiry
   An information requirement formulated into a search.
   See also: Dialogue, Query, Search.

Intelligent terminal
   A terminal which incorporates a microprocessor capable of performing
   processing functions independently of the central processor.

Interactive
   A mode of interaction between a user and a computer wherein communication is
   effected through online terminals. Unlike the batch mode of operation, users
   interact with the computer continuously on a transaction-oriented basis.
   Information transmitted from the terminal is processed immediately (i.e., in
   seconds or fractions of seconds) and a response is transmitted to the user.
   Because of the fast pace, continuity, and interchange characteristics of
   this mode, it is often referred to as "conversational" or "dialogue."
   See also: Dialogue modes, Interactive system, Online, System message.

Interactive system
   A system which performs processing or problem-solving tasks by carrying on a
   dialogue with the user. The basic task/work unit of such systems is a
   transaction which consists of at least one paired message set
   (command/query-response).
   See also: Interactive.

Interface
   The point or process which joins two or more system components. (1) A
   shared boundary, defined by common physical, signal, and logical
   characteristics, across which data travel. (2) A device that facilitates
   interoperation of two systems, as between data communications equipment and
   data processing equiptment or terminal installations. Interfaces between
   computers and communication systems may be divided into various classes of
   functions, e.g., physical, electrical, logical and procedural.

Intermediary
   A trained information specialist who assists the system's user in
   formulating a search and/or performs searches for the user. Also referred
   to as search specialist, information specialist, or data systems librarian.
   See also: Direct use.

Interrupt online output
   See: Interrupt results.

Interrupt results
   Interruption of continuing output resulting from a search or request.

Interrupt scroll
   The provision for the user to interrupt (stop) the scroll.
   See also: Scroll.

Inverted index
   A sequentially arranged (e.g., alphabetically) list of terms or symbols
   which have been extracted from designated fields of the documents or records
   being indexed. Associated with each of these terms or symbols is a set of
   reference codes or location pointers which link the index term or symbol to
   all the documents, records, or fields in which it occurs.
   See also: Index, Indexing.

ISBN
  International Standard Book Number.
  See also: Standard number.

ISSN
  International Standard Serial Number.
  See also: Standard number.

Key
  The components of a record by which it can be indexed and accessed in the
  search process. Some keys may be of fixed character length, such as the
  ISBN and the LC card number. Others may be of variable character length
  (authors, titles, call numbers and subjects). Keys may also consist of
  several words as stored in a field or a record, or be constructed
  according to an algorithm to produce "derived search keys."
  See also: Derived search key, Keyword.

Keyboard
  A set or panel usually accompanying a video display or printer terminal, and
  consisting of an array of keys resembling, typically, the keyboard of a
  typewriter. Depressing a key causes the generation of a specific character
  or symbol in electrical, printed or other form. The keyboard permits the
  generation of coded symbols for interpretation by or storage in a computer.

Keyword
  Generally, any search term chosen such as a name, controlled vocabulary
  term, "free text" (natural language) term, or special code or number. In
  some systems, its use is restricted to one of these types.
  See also: Argument, Free text term searching, Term.

Limit
  See: Restrict search results.

List commands
  A request for a display of all system commands available to the user.

List files
  A request by the user for a display of accessible files or databases.

List searchable fields
  A request by the user for a display of all fields accessible through the
  system's search methods.
  See also: Field, Search field control.

Location data
  The identification of the institution(s) or site(s) holding one or more
  copies of a bibliographic item. This identification may be achieved through
  the presearch selection of a particular institution's or site's collection
  (file), or by a display of the institution(s) branch or department library
  which holds the item. The call number (shelf location identifier) is
  frequently included in such a display.
  See also: Availability status.

Logoff
  The procedure by which the user exits from a system. Sy. sign-off, logout.

Logon
  A user access procedure to a system involving identification and access
  control. [Sometimes referred to as] "login," or "sign-on."
  See also: Identification.

Machine-readable data
  Data coded in such a way that it can be interpreted directly by the internal
  circuitry of the computer. Such data is usually stored on magnetic tape or
  disk.

Main entry
  In traditional cataloging practices, the fullest description of a work to be
  entered in the card catalog. The main entry point is usually the author, and
  this entry (card) includes all the other headings under which the work is
  entered in the catalog. Obsolete in online bibliographic database searching
  where many equal access or entry points are provided for one record.
  See also: Access points, Entry, Heading.

MARC
  Machine readable cataloging.

MARC format
  A format used to facilitate the communication and exchange of
  machine-readable records.

Menu
  A list of options--files, records, functions, etc., that are available at a
  given time to the system's user as the result of previous processing. The
  menu is displayed to the user and the user selects the next operation from
  among those featured in the menu. The menu display is typical of the
  computer-initiated dialogue mode.
  See also: Command, Dialogue modes.

Merge results
  Combining records resulting from a search on different files, or more than
  one search on the same or different files. For example, combine for output
  all monographs and serials having the same title or keyword in the title.

Mode
  One of several alternative patterns of communicating with a computer system.
  See also: Dialogue modes, Interactive.

Modem
  A contraction of the term "modulator-demodulator." A device used to convert
  serial digital data from a transmitting terminal to a signal that is
  suitable for analog transmission over a telephone channel, and to reconvert
  the signal to serial digital data for acceptance by a receiving terminal.

Network
  In a telecommunications environment, the configuration of nodes and
  telecommunication paths or links throughout which information is processed,
  shared, or exchanged.
  See also: Host computer, Node, Protocol, Terminal.

News
> Information usually given at the beginning of a terminal session (search session) by the system to its users concerning latest changes in procedures, database contents, etc. Sy. broadcast messages.

Node
> A point in a communications network where information is received, processed, or transmitted. In a computer-based network, the node will include a terminal or communications processor, or both, to support the activities of information processing and exchange.
> See also: Host computer, Network, Protocol, Terminal.

Offline
> Pertaining to equipment or services not under control of the central processing unit (CPU). This may include hard copy printing services, staff assistance, and instructional manuals.
> See also: Online.

Offline assistance
> Telephone number(s) or address(es), or other identification of staff displayed by the system for the user when assistance is needed.

Offline system
> A system configuration in which the input/output devices (e.g., data entry terminals and printers) are not in direct communication with the central processor.

Online
> (1) Pertaining to equipment or devices under control of the central processing unit. (2) Pertaining to a user's ability to interact with a computer. The online use of the computer means that the user has at his/her disposal a terminal device (i.e., a CRT, a teletype, etc.) by which he/she can converse with an operating computer program during the course of its operation. At his/her terminal, he/she can insert data, instructions or commands before, during, and at the completion of the program's operation.
> See also: Dialogue, Interactive, Offline.

Online public access catalog
> A computer-based and supported library catalog (bibliographic database) designed to be accessed via a terminal so that library patrons may directly and effectively search for and retrieve bibliographic information without the assistance of an intermediary such as a specially trained member of the library staff.
> See also: Bibliographic database, Catalog, Direct use.

Online system
> A system configuration in which the input/output devices, e.g., the terminals, are in direct communication with, or controlled by, the central processor.

OPAC
  See: Online public access catalog.

Operation
  (1) A defined action or set of actions specified by an instruction or rule.
  (2) The practical application of principles or rules in processes.
  See also: Function, Process, Transaction.

Page
  The action of a terminal in displaying information by successive discrete
  pages (hard copy terminal) or screens (CRT). Most systems allow only one
  page (screen) to be displayed at a time. To move to the next page or the
  previous page, the user has to enter a command.
  See also: Display, Display backward, Display forward.

Password
  A word, code, or other message used to identify the operator of a terminal
  which permits access to otherwise restricted functions of a computer system.

Polling
  The interrogation of each terminal in a network by the computer to determine
  whether it is ready to receive or transmit data. This is necessary if data
  transmission can only be initiated by the computer.

Precision
  As a measure of the results of information retrieval, precision is the ratio
  of the number of relevant items retrieved to the total number of items
  retrieved in a search of a database(s). Precision equals the number of
  relevant documents retrieved divided by the total number of documents
  retrieved.
  See also: Recall.

Print offline
  The provision for the user to request that the system produce a hardcopy
  print of his search results at some later time, after the search session.

Printer
  A peripheral (to the CPU) output device that produces hard copy of
  information stored in machine-readable code.

Procedure
  The step-by-step process for the solution of a problem.

Process
  A sequence or series of continuous actions or events occurring during a time
  period which brings about change in an initial state according to a plan or
  predetermined design. The intermediary actions or events may consist of
  operations, transactions, or tasks.
  See also: Operation, Task, Transaction.

Produce online hardcopy print
  Provision for user to obtain hardcopy print during the search session, by
  means of a printer terminal or printer attached to a CRT terminal.

Program
  A sequence of instructions describing (to the computer) how to perform a
  certain task.

Prompt mode
  See: Dialogue modes, Prompts.

Prompts
  System cues or messages which indicate to the user that the system is ready
  for input, direct the user to the next required action or choice, suggest a
  course or alternative courses of action, or ask the user what system action
  should be executed next. There are two distinct classes of system prompts,
  (1) directive and (2) suggestive.

  (1)   Directive prompts belong to the general category of dialogue mode
        that is computer guided and controlled. This type of dialogue is
        based on a preestablished course of action, and consists of messages
        which direct the user to a required action or forced choice. Examples
        are:

        (a)   ENTER AUTHOR'S LAST NAME:
        (b)   DO YOU WISH TO ADD TO YOUR SEARCH? (YES_NO_)
        (c)   LINE NUMBER?
        (d)   TYPE CALL NUMBER IN THIS FORMAT (Format shown)
        (e)   21 RECORDS RESULT FROM YOUR SEARCH REQUEST. DO YOU WISH TO
              DISPLAY ALL RECORDS? (YES_NO_)

  (2)   Suggestive prompts inform the user of possible action(s) which may
        or may not be taken. The user is free to pursue the suggested course
        of action, select from among a specific set of choices offered, or
        pursue an unstated course of action in a self-directed manner.
        Guidance on how to proceed frequently accompanies these suggestions
        for further action. Examples are:

        (a)   PRESS RETURN (OR TYPE NS) TO SEE THE NEXT SCREEN
        (b)   FOR A REVIEW OF COMMANDS TYPE "HELP" OR "?"
        (c)   YOUR SEARCH RESULTS EXCEED THE MAXIMUM FOR RETRIEVAL. LIMIT
              YOUR RESULTS BY ADDING A DATE OR FORMAT QUALIFIER TO YOUR SEARCH
              STATEMENT.
        (d)   ENTER "BIB" TO SEE A DISPLAY OF THE FULL RECORD

  Suggestive prompts are usually found in a user guided dialogue mode,
  but may appear at some points in a dialogue that is predominately
  computer guided. The tone or format of a prompt may not be sufficient
  to distinguish the directive from the suggestive. However, the
  system's response, in the form of an error message, a reiteration of
  the prompt, or command execution, will indicate whether a user action
  taken following a prompt has been permitted.
  See also: Dialogue modes.

Protect(ed)
  Information displayed to the user may be either "protected" or "not
  protected." When information in a display is protected, the user is not
  able to change the information. The user can change information that is not
  protected.

Protected field
   A designated field on a display screen within which changes cannot be made
   through keyboard-initiated actions.

Protocol
   (1) A set of rules governing the flow of information within a system. (2)
   The conventions used in communicating between nodes and levels in a network,
   specifically a formal set of conventions governing the format and relative
   sequencing of message exchanges.

Proximity operators
   Symbols which allow the user formulating a free text term search to specify
   the position, within fields, of certain terms vis-a-vis one another. On some
   systems the user can even specify how many words may separate two terms. An
   example of proximity operators is the ADJ used by BRS. Term-1 ADJ term-2,
   means term-1 must be adjacent to term-2 in that specific order with nothing
   but blank(s) and/or stopword(s) between them.

Purge search statements
   Delete search statements (and their results) which are no longer needed in
   the formulation of a query.

Query
   A unitary message or developed set of messages input by the user of an
   online information retrieval system in a manner specifically intended to
   elicit a response. The intent is usually to access one or more records in a
   file or catalog to ascertain if some desired informational attribute is
   represented by that record (or records), and to have the system respond
   accordingly.
   See also: Dialogue, General search command, Search.

Query language
   A formal language (consisting of a controlled vocabulary governed in use by
   rules of grammar and syntax) specifically designed or chosen for
   constructing queries to retrieve information from a database stored in a
   computer system. Query languages range from highly artificial, procedural,
   and rigid programming languages, to artificial but natural language-like
   languages, or even to subsets of natural language itself. The use of the
   latter is currently confined, for the most part, to experimental
   applications.
   See also: Dialogue, Query, Search

Recall
   As a measure of the results of information retrieval, recall is the ratio of
   the number of relevant items retrieved to the total number of relevant items
   in the database(s) being searched. Recall equals the number of relevant
   documents retrieved divided by the number of relevant documents in the
   database.
   See also: Precision.

Record
   A named collection of data items (fields) treated as a unit, and stored in a
   computer. A data item is the smallest unit of named data. The data items
   (fields) in a record all share a particular attribute or attributes; that

is, they all pertain to a particular entity. An employee record contains a
number of data items (e.g., name, age) related to an employee; a
bibliographic record contains a number of data items (e.g., title,
pagination) related to a bibliographic document.
See also: Bibliographic database, Bibliographic record, Entry.

Refine
    See: Restrict search results.

Relational operators
    Symbols for greater than, less than, equal, and combinations of these.
    Usually used with numeric fields (e.g., date) as part of a restrict search
    command.

Request offline hardcopy print
    See: Print offline.

Response time
    The time period extending from the last keystroke made by the user in the
    input operation (this usually involves depressing some message-terminating
    key, e.g., the carriage return, at the terminal) to the instant the first
    character of the system response is or typed at the user's terminal. With
    terminals employing a keyboard lock feature, it has been suggested that the
    response time period extend to the unlocking of the keyboard.

Restrict (limit, refine) search results
    The use of parameters such as language, type of publication, publication
    date, etc. to reduce the results of a search to a specific range. These
    parameters are normally not available as primary search indexes, but are
    used in conjunction with search field control of primary indexes.

Sample searches
    Prestored examples of searches which show the user the acceptable language,
    syntax, and structure for entering a search command and its accompanying
    argument(s). Explanatory comments are usually displayed along with the
    example.

Save search
    A command which enables the user to have one or more search statements
    retained by the system to be executed in another file or at another time. A
    saved search may be temporary (for same session or same day use) or
    permanent. Permanently saved searches may perform as standing searches to
    which the system automatically posts new listings.

Screen
    See: Display, Page.

Scroll
    The action of a terminal in displaying information line by line,
    successively, until the end of the information, or until some system default
    value is reached.   There are two distinct types of scroll: pan and roll.

    (1)   Pan (soft) scrolling is a variation of roll scrolling in which the
           movement of the lines of data up and down the screen is smoother,
           i.e.,less jerky, than the conventional roll scroll and more similar to
           the smooth panning of the credits following a TV program.

(2)   Roll Scrolling occurs as each line of text is recalled. All existing
       lines on the display screen move up or down by one line to make room
       for the new line. The movement of the lines of data is discontinuous
       and similar to the line feed movement of paper in a line printer.

Search (bibliographic)
(1)   To look for a record or set of records in a bibliographic file to
       ascertain if the record (or records) has a desired informational
       property (or properties) such as author(s), title, subject(s), date of
       publication, location, etc.
(2)   To identify records for the purpose of retrieval.
See also: Derived search key, Dialogue, General search command, Query.

Search argument
   See: Argument, Derived search key, Keyword, Query, Search, Term.

Search default mode
   The state of the system ready for searching by the user, requiring no
   preliminary action by the user prior to proceeding with a search.

Search field control
   Selection of a particular field or fields from among those accessible, using
   search methods permitted by the system. e.g., author, subject,
   author/title, etc.
   See also: List searchable fields.

Search formulation
   The statement or series of statements which express an information need or
   query in the language and format acceptable to a specific information
   retrieval system. The construction, use, and development of search
   statements are largely dependent on the search and operational (command)
   mechanics provided by a specific information retrieval system.
   See also: Search mechanics, Search Strategy.

Search history
   See: Show search history.

Search mechanics
   The means provided in a specific information retrieval system to access,
   search, and display/print the results of a search within that system.
   Search mechanics are the command capabilities and operations provided in the
   design of a system to enable the functional use of the system. Common
   operations such as truncation or Boolean intersection may vary in their
   actual implementation in different retrieval systems.
   See also: Search formulation, Search strategy.

Search mode
   See: Search, Search default mode.

Search strategy
   A plan for part or all of a search which guides the selection of search
   statements in the formulation of the search. Search strategies incorporate
   logical approaches to information retrieval which are independent of
   specific retrieval systems and their databases. However, the vocabulary and
   search mechanics of a specific retrieval system must be utilized when

formulating a search according to one strategy or another. Examples of
search strategies are the "building blocks" approach and "citation pearl
growing."
See also: Search formulation, Search mechanics.

Select dialogue mode
   The provision for the user to choose the desired dialogue mode or technique
   (computer-guided, user-guided, menu-selection, command-language, etc.)
   See also: Dialogue modes.

Select display format
   Display bibliographic records under different formats as requested by the
   user.

Select display from predefined formats
   See: Select display format.

Select field(s)
   Specify the field(s) of the bibliographic record(s) to be displayed. Sy.
   online formatting.
   See also: Field.

Select files
   Select the databases upon which the search is to be carried out.

Select function
   The provision for user selection of a function (search, interlibrary loan,
   circulation) in a multi-function system.

Select record(s)
   The provision for the user to choose specific records among those retrieved
   in a search, and have them displayed.

Select specific field(s) for display
   See: Select field(s).

Select specific record(s) for display
   See: Select record(s).

Set
   A group of objects (records, documents) that share some common
   characteristic(s). Subset or superset are relative terms. A subset (or
   subsets) of a set is a set whose members, in addition to sharing the
   characteristics that define membership in the set, also share
   characteristics that distinguish them from other members of the set. A
   superset of a set is a set whose members bear the same relation to the
   superset as do subset members to a set.

Set default values
   See: Default.

Set system message length
   The provision for the user to choose the length of system messages, such as
   "terse" or "verbose."

Show index listing

A request by the user to have a portion of the specified index or thesaurus
displayed. This may include a display of an alphabetical segment of an
index, or a grouping of related terms as assigned by the indexer.

Show news

See: News.

Show search history

A request by the user to review a description of how the user's search
formulation led to the results displayed. If more than one search statement
was included, the sequence and logic of the search formulation is displayed.
Sy. search logic tracing.

Show time

See: Time.

Software

Algorithms (detailed instructions telling how to do something) and their
computer representations, namely programs. Programs can be represented on
punched cards, magnetic tape, photographic film, and other media, but the
essence of software is the set of instructions that make up the programs,
not the physical media on which they are recorded.
See also: Hardware.

Sort results

The provision for the user to arrange and organize bibliographic records
(retrieved in an online search) according to the values of one or more
designated fields for display or print. This feature allows search results
to be sorted, for example, alphabetically by author, or title, or subject,
or in ascending order by date of publication, at the user's discretion.

Stack commands

Multiple command input with one message-ending keyboard operation such as
the depression of the return key.

Standard number

Assigned control numbers like the International Standard Number(ISN),
International Standard Book Number(ISBN), International Standard Serial
Number(ISSN), or any other internationally agreed upon number, that uniquely
identifies an item.

Subject heading

A word or a group of words indicating a subject under which all material
dealing with the same theme is entered in a catalog or a bibliography, or is
arranged in a file.
See also: Access points, Entry, Heading.

Syndetic structure

A systematically organized scheme of relationships holding among concepts in
a body of knowledge, or among terms in a conventional universe of discourse.
The scheme is used to indicate logical relationships between concepts
("equivalent to," "deduced from"), or to indicate semantic relationships
between terms ("synonymous with," "broader term," "narrower term"). The
mechanisms frequently used to express these various relationships include

numbered classification tables or schedules, cross references like "see also" and "see from" and scope notes. Syndetic structures provide guidelines for selecting terms to describe and index documents, and aid in the selection of terms for formulating a search. Examples of syndetic structures are subject heading lists, subject classification schemes, and subject thesauri.
See also: Controlled term indexing, Free text term indexing.

System
For the purpose of this project, system invariably means an online computer catalog with the minimal functions of search, retrieval and display. Also the hardware, software, and database(s) which support the online catalog are implicitly included in this definition.

System file default
In a multi-file system, the file automatically accessed by the system when none has been named (chosen) by the user.

System function default
In a multi-function system, the function assumed by the system when none has been chosen by the user.

System message
In interactive dialogue with a computer system, many kinds of messages are exchanged between the user and the system. System messages are displayed or printed at a terminal output device and include the following types:

   (1) acknowledgement of data entry or query acceptance,
   (2) announcement of the completion of a requested transaction or
       function,
   (3) confirmation of a correct user response,
   (4) indication of a user error,
   (5) instructions or suggestions for what to do next,
   (6) explanations of system-related problems,
   (7) guidance or training in the operation of the system or functional
       activity to be undertaken.
Some systems permit the user to select in advance either the nature or the length of the messages conveyed by the computer system during interactive dialogue.
See also: Dialogue, Explain system messages, Interactive, Set system message length.

Tag
   (1) An alphanumeric code which identifies a field in a record.
   (2) In MARC a three character number which identifies the content of a field in the bibliographic record (e.g., "245" = title field).

Task
   (1) A unit or assigned piece of work to be completed within a certain time.
   (2) A routine, identifiable activity which is required to complete an operation, or attain some desired result. An operation may consist of one or more tasks, to be completed either by the user, or by the system.
See also: Process.

Telecommunications
   The transmission of data over long distances by electric, electronic, or
   electromagnetic means such as telegraph, radio, television, telephone,
   microwave, or satellite.

Term
   Often used as synonymous with "word," in database searching a "term" may be
   a word, word stem or otherwise incomplete word, or a sequence of words
   constituting a phrase (sometimes called a compound term or a multiple-term
   concept). The search argument in a query of a database may consist of a term
   or a combination of terms.
   See also: Argument, Keyword.

Terminal
   (1) A device for entering data into or receiving data from a computer system
   or computer network.
   (2) The point at which the user interfaces with the computer system and its
   database(s).
   See also: Interface.

Time
   The elapsed connect time. For most systems, it is the time interval between
   logging on and logging off.
   See also: Connect time.

Tracing
   In traditional library practice, data included in the bibliographic record
   which indicate additional headings under which a bibliographic item is filed
   in the catalog, or data which indicate references to a name or to the title
   of a bibliographic item represented in the catalog.
   See also: Acess points, Entry, Heading.

Training, embedded
   The use of an interactive system to train its own users, employing an
   explicit tutorial package, in the operations of the system and terminal,
   and/or how to use the system's features to accomplish the task at hand.
   See also: Tutorials.

Transaction
   An operation or process in an interactive system consisting of a structured
   sequence of information and control exchanges between the user at a terminal
   and the system (or some system process) to perform a particular functional
   objective. A transaction consists of a logical set of component tasks to be
   executed by the user and the system involving some interchange of
   information and control. A transaction may include user-system interaction
   which takes place in a conversational, dialogue mode.
   See also: Function, Operation, Process.

Truncation
   The shortening of a search term (word or phrase) by cutting off or omitting
   certain characters or words of the term. This may be done by entering a
   special character in place of the omitted characters, or by simply entering
   the shortened term followed by one or more blanks. When the suffix of a word
   is omitted, this is referred to as "root" searching. Truncated term
   searching indicates to the system that all terms in the designated index(es)

or searchable fields beginning with the character string entered are to be included in the search statement.

Tutorials
A structured series of instructional lessons provided by the system concerning terminal and typing procedures, the command repertoire, characteristics of the data base and hints for good searching, etc. The purpose of a tutorial is to teach the user, interactively, how to use the system in an effective way.
See also: Training, embedded.

Unit record
See: Bibliographic record.

Unprotected field
Any part of a visual display, the structure or contents of which may be altered on command from the terminal operator.

User-system interaction
In interactive systems, a function is performed (that is, a purpose is fulfilled or a desired end is attained) through the execution of a well-defined operation or operations which include both user and system tasks and transactions. These operations may be initiated and/or driven by user input in the form of commands and arguments, responses to system-generated prompts, or selections from a displayed "menu" of choices.

Variable data
Data on a display screen that may be modified, e.g., added to or deleted, by the terminal operator.

VDU
Visual Display Unit; a terminal which usually includes a keyboard for data input and a display screen for output and indication of the input. Other input techniques include the use of light pens and touch-sensitive screens.
See also: Cathode ray tube.

Window
A portion of a video display unit screen. A window defines a relative portion of a screen in which the display elements share some common characteristics. For example, the area of the screen in which institutional identification information (such as name, location, etc.) is displayed in one window on the screen.

Word adjacency
See: Proximity operators.

Command Capabilities of the Library of Congress Online Public Access Catalogs (SCORPIO and MUMS)

Functional Area I. Operational Control

COMMAND CAPABILITIES (available to, or under the control of the user)	MUMS	SCORPIO
Logon (begin session protocol)	Yes	Yes
Select function desired	No	No
System has default for function	Yes	Yes
Select file desired	Yes	Yes
System has default for file	No	No
Set default values for session	No	Yes
Set system message length	No	Yes
Select dialogue mode	No	No
Edit input (erase/modify)	Yes	Yes
Interrupt online output	No	No
Stack commands	No	No
Save search statements	No	No
Purge search statements	No	No
Logoff (end session protocol)	No	Yes

Functional Area II. Search Formulation Control

COMMAND CAPABILITIES (available to, or under the control of the user)	MUMS	SCORPIO
Search is default function	Yes	Yes
General search command is used	Yes	Yes
Derived search keys are required	Yes	No
Controlled term searching	No	Yes
Free-text term searching:		
entire record	No	No
selected field(s)	Yes	Yes
Restrict/limit search results	Yes	Yes
Boolean operators, explicit use	Yes	Yes
Relational operators, explicit use	No	Yes
Truncation, explicit use	No	No
Proximity operators, explicit use	Yes	No
ACCESS POINTS		
Personal author	Yes	Yes
Corporate author	Yes	Yes
Author/title	Yes	No
Title	Yes	Yes
Subject	Yes	Yes
Call number	No	Yes
LC card number	Yes	Yes
ISBN	Yes	No
ISSN	Yes	No
Government document number	No	No
Other control number	No	No
Additional access points	Yes	No

Command Capabilities of the Library of Congress Online Public Access
Catalogs (SCORPIO and MUMS)

Functional Area III. Output Control

COMMAND CAPABILITIES (available to, or under the control of the user)	MUMS	SCORPIO
General command to display results	Yes	Yes
Select display from predefined formats	Yes	Yes
Select specific record(s) for display	Yes	Yes
Select specific field(s) for display	No	No
Sort results for display	No	No
Merge results for display	No	Yes
Display forward (records or screens)	Yes	Yes
Display backward (records or screens)	Yes	Yes
Scroll	Yes	No
Interrupt scroll	No	No
Request offline hardcopy print	No	No
Produce online hardcopy print	Yes	Yes
Cancel offline print request	No	No

Functional Area IV. User Assistance:
Information and Instruction

COMMAND CAPABILITIES (available to, or under the control of the user)	MUMS	SCORPIO
List files for review	No	Yes
List searchable fields for review	No	No
List commands for review	No	Yes
Show index or thesaurus terms	No	Yes
Show search history	No	Yes
Show time elapsed or cost	No	Yes
Show news or special messages	No	Yes
Explain system messages	No	No
Identify offline assistance	Yes	Yes
Indicate item location	No	No
Indicate item availability	No	No
Prompts or guidance comments	No	Yes
Help displays retrievable	No	Yes
Online tutorial(s)	No	No

Bibliographic Display Formats
of the Participating OPACs

UNIVERSITY OF CALIFORNIA ONLINE PUBLIC ACCESS CATALOG

Bibliographic Display Formats (Review, Brief, and Long)

Review

```
Search request: FIND PA LIONEL TIGER
Search result:  8 records at UC libraries

1. FEMALE HIERARCHIES / edited by Lionel Tiger and Heather T. Fowler.  1978
2. FEMALE HIERARCHIES / edited by Lionel Tiger and Heather T. Fowler.  1978
3. Tiger, Lionel, 1937-  THE IMPERIAL ANIMAL BY LIONEL TIGER & ROBIN FOX.  1971
4. Tiger, Lionel, 1937-  MEN IN GROUPS.  1969
5. Tiger, Lionel, 1937-  MEN IN GROUPS.  1969
6. Tiger, Lionel, 1937-  OPTIMISM : THE BIOLOGY OF HOPE / by Lionel... 1979
7. Tiger, Lionel, 1937-  WOMEN IN THE KIBBUTZ / Lionel Tiger and Joseph... 1975
8. Tiger, Lionel, 1937-  WOMEN IN THE KIBBUTZ / Lionel Tiger and Joseph... 1976
```

Brief

```
Search request: FIND PA LIONEL TIGER
Search result:  8 records at UC libraries

3. Tiger, Lionel, 1937-
      The imperial animal by Lionel Tiger & Robin Fox. 1st ed.
      New York, Holt, Rinehart and Winston 1971
         UCI  Main Lib  HM107 .T5
         UCSD Central   HM107 .T5
         UCSD Cluster   HM107 .T5
```

Long

```
Search request: FIND PA LIONEL TIGER
Search result:  8 records at UC libraries

3.
Author:       Tiger, Lionel, 1937-
Title:        The imperial animal [by] Lionel Tiger & Robin Fox. [1st ed.]
                 New York, Holt, Rinehart and Winston [1971]
              xi, 308 p. 24 cm.

Notes:        Bibliography: p. 255-296.

Subjects:     Civilization, Modern -- 20th century.
              Psychobiology.

Other entries: Fox, Robin, 1934-, joint author.

Call numbers:  UCI  Main Lib  HM107 .T5   (CU-I)
               UCSD Central   HM107 .T5   (CU-SCu)
               UCSD Cluster   HM107 .T5   (CU-SCL)
```

CLAREMONT COLLEGES ONLINE PUBLIC ACCESS CATALOG

Bibliographic Display Formats (Short and Full)

```
ENTER CODE LETTER;D FOR CODE LIST;H FOR HELP:S
ENTER SUBJECT (3 CHARACTERS OR MORE OF THE ENTRY) :
------------------------------------------------------------
WOMEN IN LITERATURE
****INQ:  S       WOMEN IN LITERATURE
WOMEN IN MATHEMATICS -- CONGRESSES
        MATHEM.     QA  27.5  H95 1976
HYMAN BLUMBERG SYMPOSIUM ON RESE
WOMEN AND THE MATHEMATICAL MYSTIQUE :   PROCEEDINGS OF TH
```

Short

```
@
HYMAN BLUMBERG SYMPOSIUM ON RESEARCH IN EARLY CHILDHOOD EDUCATION/WOME
N AND THE MATHEMATICAL MYSTIQUE :   PROCEEDINGS OF THE EIGHTH  ANNUAL H
YMAN BLUMBERG SYMPOSIUM ON RESEARCH IN EARLY CHILDHOOD EDUCATION /    E
DITED BY LYNN H. FOX, LINDA BRODY, AND DIANNE TOBIN. /BALTIMORE :   JOH
NS HOPKINS UNIVERSITY PRESS, C1980. /VIII, 211 P. :   ILL. ;   24 CM. /
(STUDIES OF INTELLECTUAL PRECOCITY ;  8 )/# WOMEN IN MATHEMATICS - CON
GRESSES. /# WOMEN MATHEMATICIANS - CONGRESSES. /# SEX DIFFERENCES IN E
DUCATION - CONGRESSES. /# MATHEMATICS - STUDY AND TEACHING - CONGRESSE
S. /& FOX, LYNN H., 1944-  CN /& BRODY, LINDA.  CN /& TOBIN, DIANNE.
 CN /& AMERICAN ASSOCIATION FOR THE ADVANCEMENT OF SCIENCE.  CN /( 111
)/MAN BLUMBERG SYMPOSIUM ON RESEARCH IN EARLY  CHILDHOOD EDUCATION,  8
TH,  JOHNS HOPKINS UNIVERSITY, 1976.   /
```

Full

DARTMOUTH COLLEGE ONLINE PUBLIC ACCESS CATALOG

Bibliographic Display Formats (Title and Full)

```
      1
LO DRBB.
   GN365-9-T53.
TI Optimism: the biology of hope / by Lionel Tiger.

R0601 * END OF DOCUMENTS IN LIST
```

Title

```
      1
LO DRBB.
   GN365-9-T53.
ME Tiger, Lionel, 1937-.
TI Optimism: the biology of hope / by Lionel Tiger.
IM New York: Simon and Schuster, c1979.
CO 318 p.; 23 cm.
SU Optimism.
NT Includes index.  Bibliography: p. 285-300.
NU LC: GN365-9-T53. DDC: 301-2.
   LCCN: 78031328.  ISBN: 0671229346.
FF PD: 1978.  CP: nyu.  LG: eng.
AN ocl74549447.

R0601 * END OF DOCUMENTS IN LIST
```

Full

MANKATO STATE UNIVERSITY ONLINE PUBLIC ACCESS CATALOG

Bibliographic Display Formats (Index, Long, and Total)

Index

```
Screen 001 of 001
NMBR DATE --------------------------TITLE-------------------- -------AUTHOR-------
0001 1978  Female hierarchies /                              Tiger, Lionel,
0002 1971  The imperial animal                               Tiger, Lionel,
0003 1969  Men in groups.                                    Tiger, Lionel,
0004 1979  Optimism :  the biology of hope /                 Tiger, Lionel,
----Type DI NMBR(s) to display specific records
>
```

Long

```
 DI 2 LONG
 Screen 001 of 001    Record 0002 of 0004 MSU
 LOCTN: HM107 .T5
 AUTHR: Tiger, Lionel, 1937-
 TITLE: The imperial animal [by] Lionel Tiger & Robin Fox.
 EDITN: [1st ed.]
 PUBLR: New York, Holt, Rinehart and Winston [1971]
 DESCR: xi, 308 p. 24 cm.
 NOTES: Bibliography: p. 255-296.
 SUBJT: Psychobiology.
 SUBJT: Civilization, Modern--20th century.
 AAUTH: Fox, Robin, 1934- joint author.
 OCLC# 00216250
 >
```

Total

```
 DI 2 TOTAL
 Screen 001 of 001    Record 0002 of 0004 MSU
 IDL 00216250 MNM 810724 MST 0577
 LDR      00577cam 2200133    45 0
 001      ocl70216250
 008      711214s1971    nyu       b     00110 eng
 010         78155535
 020      0030865824
 040      DLC #c DLC #d MNM
 049      MNMA
 050   0  HM107 #b .T5
 082      301.2
 100   10 Tiger, Lionel, #d 1937-
 245   14 The imperial animal #c [by] Lionel Tiger & Robin Fox.
 250      [1st ed.]
 260   0  New York, #b Holt, Rinehart and Winston #c [1971]
 300      xi, 308 p. #c 24 cm.
 350      $6.95
 504      Bibliography: p. 255-296.
 650   0  Psychobiology.
 650   0  Civilization, Modern #y 20th century.
 700   10 Fox, Robin, #d 1934- #e joint author.
 >
```

MISSION COLLEGE ONLINE PUBLIC ACCESS CATALOG

Bibliographic Display Formats (Review and Full)

```
HH?A=TIGER, LIONEL
HJH?                                                      A=TIGER, LIONEL
Line# Call #          Author            Title

1     HM 107 .T5      Tiger, Lionel, 1937 The imperial animal / by Lionel Tiger &
2     HQ1067 .T53     Tiger, Lionel, 1937 Men in groups
3     GN365.9 .T53    Tiger, Lionel, 1937 Optimism : the biology of hope
4     HQ1781.P2 T5    Tiger, Lionel, 1937 Women in the kibbutz




7mTo determine the location and availability of a specific title, type ST=
followed by the line number. EXAMPLE:  ST=2 and RETURN0m
For more detailed information on a specific title, type  BI= followed by the
line number. EXAMPLE:  BI=5 and RETURN
H?
```

Review

```
  BI=1
HJH?                                                  BI=1
HM       Tiger, Lionel, 1937-
 107
 .T5     The imperial animal / by Lionel Tiger & Robin Fox. 1st ed.

         New York : Holt, Rinehart and Winston, 1971

         xi, 308 p. ; 24 cm.

         Bibliography: p. 255-296

         1. Civilization, Modern--20th century
         2. Psychobiology
         I.  Fox, Robin, 1934-
         ISBN/ISSN  0030865824      L.C.CARD NUMBER  78--155535



To repeat previous screen type PS and RETURN
7mTo determine the location and availability of a specific title, type ST=
followed by the line number. EXAMPLE:  ST=2 and RETURN0m
```

Full

NORTHWESTERN UNIVERSITY ONLINE PUBLIC ACCESS CATALOG

Basic Bibliographic Display Format

```
LUIS SEARCH REQUEST:  S=ENERGY POLICY -UNITED

BASIC BIBLIOGRAPHIC RECORD -- NO. 89 OF 148 ENTRIES FOUND

Commoner, Barry, 1917-

    The poverty of power : energy and the economic crisis / Barry Commoner. -- 1st

ed. -- New York : Knopf : distributed by Random House, 1976

    HOLDINGS IN NORTHWESTERN UNIVERSITY LIBRARY

LOCATION:  main

CALL NUMBER:  333.7;C734p

LOCATION:  core (copy 2)

CALL NUMBER:  333.7;C734p

LOCATION:  main (copy 3)

CALL NUMBER:  333.7;C734p

TYPE m FOR NEXT RECORD, d FOR CIRCULATION STATUS (FIRST WRITE DOWN CALL NO.)

TYPE i TO RETURN TO INDEX, g TO RETURN TO GUIDE, e TO START OVER, h FOR HELP.

TYPE COMMAND AND PRESS ENTER
```

OCLC ONLINE PUBLIC ACCESS CATALOG

Bibliographic Display Formats (Truncated Entry and Full Record)

```
Screen 1 of 2
¬ 1  Tiger, Lionel,   Advances in the behavioral sciences.    1972   [Spoken
recording]
  ¬ 2  Tiger, Lionel,   Birds of a feather.   1975  [Spoken recording]
  ¬ 3  Tiger, Lionel   Faces of violence.   1973  [Spoken recording]
  ¬ 4  Tiger, Lionel,   Female hierarchies /   Chicago :    1978
  ¬ 5  Tiger, Lionel,   The imperial animal   New York,    1971  DLC
  ¬ 6  Tiger, Lionel,   The imperial animal.   [New York,    1971
  ¬ 7  Tiger, Lionel,   The imperial animal   Toronto,    1971  DLC
  ¬ 8  Tiger, Lionel,   The imperial animal   [New York]   1972
  ¬ 9  Tiger, Lionel,   The imperial animal   [New York,    1974
  ¬10  Tiger, Lionel,   Men in groups.   New York,    1969
  ¬11  Tiger, Lionel,   Men in groups.   London,    1969  DLC
  ¬12  Tiger, Lionel,   Men in groups.   New York,    1969  DLC
  ¬13  Tiger, Lionel,   Men in groups /   New York :    1970
  ¬14  Tiger, Lionel,   Optimism : the biology of hope /   New York :    1979
DLC
```

Truncated Entry

```
¬NO HOLDINGS IN OCC -  FOR HOLDINGS ENTER dh DEPRESS  DISPLAY RECD SEND
 OCLC: 216250        Rec stat: c Entrd: 711214         Used: 820514
¬Type: a Bib lvl: m Govt pub:    Lang:  eng Source:    Illus:
 Repr:    Enc lvl:    Conf pub: 0 Ctry:   nyu Dat tp: s M/F/B: 10
 Indx: 1 Mod rec:    Festschr: 0 Cont: b
 Desc:    Int lvl:    Dates: 1971,
 ¬ 1 010      78-155535
 ¬ 2 040      DLC c DLC d m.c.
 ¬ 3 019      256001
 ¬ 4 020      0030865824
 ¬ 5 050 0    HM107 b .T5
 ¬ 6 082      301.2
 ¬ 7 049      OCCL
 ¬ 8 100 10   Tiger, Lionel, d 1937- w cn
 ¬ 9 245 14   The imperial animal c [by] Lionel Tiger & Robin Fox.
 ¬10 250      [1st ed.]
 ¬11 260 0    New York, b Holt, Rinehart and Winston c [1971]
 ¬12 300      xi, 308 p. c 24 cm.
 ¬13 350      $6.95
 ¬14 504      Bibliography: p. 255-296.
 ¬15 650 0    Civilization, Modern y 20th century.
 ¬16 650 0    Psychobiology.
 ¬17 700 10   Fox, Robin, d 1934- e joint author. w cn
```

Full Record

OHIO STATE UNIVERSITY ONLINE PUBLIC ACCESS CATALOG

Bibliographic Display Formats (Index, Review, and Full)

Index

```
AUT/TIGER

   11      1 Tift, Thomas Nelson, 1951-
   12      1 TIFTICKJIAN, DAVID SARKIS
   13      2 Tigar, Michael E , 1941-
   14      1 Tigay, Alan M .
  "15        TIGER
   16      1 TIGER, GEORGIANNA
   17      1 TIGER HUNT
   18      2 Tiger, Lionel, ed.
   19      7 Tiger, Lionel, 1937-
   20      1 Tiger, Peggy, 1943-
PAGE 2 OF 3   FOR PRECEDING PAGE, ENTER PS1; FOR FOLLOWING PAGE, ENTER PS3
ENTER TBL/ AND LINE NO. FOR TITLESTBL/19
```

Review

```
   Tiger, Lionel, 1937-                                          (7 TITLES)
 01*                        The imperial animal                  1971 FBR
 02                         THE IMPERIAL ANIMAL $1ST ED          1971
 03*                        Men in groups.                       1969 FBR
 04                         Men in groups.                       1970 FBR
 05                         Men in groups.                       1969 FBR
 06                         Optimism :                           1979 FBR
 07                         Women in the kibbutz /               1975 FBR
PAGE 1   END    FOR AVAILABILITY ENTER DSL/ AND LINE NO.
```

Full

```
 FBL/1

 S.301.2T448I
 Tiger, Lionel, 1937-
   The imperial animal (by) Lionel Tiger & Robin Fox.  :1st ed.:  New York,
 Holt, Rinehart and Winston  (1971)  xi, 308 p.  24 cm.
   Bibliography: p. 255-296.
 SUB: 1. PSYCHOBIOLOGY  2. CIVILIZATION, MODERN--20TH CENTURY
 AE : 1. Fox, Robin, 1934- joint author.
 LC CARD #:78-155535   TITLE #:2416890  OCLC #:0216250     &ZZ760005
 PAGE 1  END
```

PIKES PEAK LIBRARY DISTRICT ONLINE PUBLIC ACCESS CATALOG

Bibliographic Display Formats (Short and Expanded)

```
Call Number     Author / Title     LCCN:78-155535
                TIGER,LION
301.2           IMPERIAL ANIMAL BY LIONEL TIGER & ROBIN FOX
T566I           BC:101355642        Penrose (Main)
Subjects: Psychobiology.
          Civilization, Modern - 20th century.
```

Short

```
PPL> E/

010       78-155535
020       0030865824
050   1   HM107.T5
082       301.2
099       301.2 T566I
100   10  Tiger, Lionel, @d 1937-
245   10  The imperial animal @c [by] Lionel Tiger & Robin Fox.
250       [1st ed.]
260   0   New York, @b Holt, Rinehart and Winston @c [1971]
300       xi, 308 p. @c 24 cm.
504       Bibliography: p. 255-296.
650   0   Civilization, Modern @y 20th century.  Psychobiology.
700   10  Fox, Robin, @d 1934-  @e joint author.
PPL>
```

Expanded

RLIN ONLINE PUBLIC ACCESS CATALOG

Bibliographic Display Formats (Multiple and Primary)

```
:MUL? MUL

Result: 14 clusters

1) Commoner, Barry, 1917- THE POVERTY OF POWER : (New York : Knopf :
     distributed by Random House, 1976.)
NYPG (c-1665 NN)    CGGL (c-9610 CSfGG-L)    CLCG (c-9610 CLCo)
CMSL (c-9610 CSM)    CNBG (c-9610 CStrNB)    CSCG (c-9660 CSjCL)
CSFX (c-9610 CSf)    CSUG (c-9610 CSt)    CSUU (c-9660 CSt)    CUBG-1 (c-9610 CU)
CUBG-2 (c-9610 CU)    CUDL (c-9610 CU-AL)    DCLC (c-9110 DLC)
IAUL (c-9610 IaU-L)    NYCG (c-9617 NNC)

2) THE SOCIAL COSTS OF POWER PRODUCTION : (New York : Macmillan Information,
     c1975.)
CSUB (c-9110 CST-B)    CSUG (c-9660 CSt)    CUBG (c-9660 CU)
CUDL (c-9120 CU-AL)    DCLC (c-9110 DLC)    TXSC (c-9660 TxHSOF)
:+?
```

Multiple

```
    PRI

Cluster 1 of 1

Commoner, Barry, 1917-
  The poverty of power : energy and the economic crisis / Barry Commoner. 1st
ed. New York : Knopf : distributed by Random House, 1976.
  314 p. ; 22 cm.

  ISBN 0394403711 : $10.00
  LCCN: 7536798
  050: HD9502.A2 C643 1976
  ID: NYPG764414909-B              CC: 1665       DCF:
- - - - - - - - - - - - - - - - - - - - - - - - - - - - - - - - - - -
NYPG (c-1665 NN)    CGGL (c-9610 CSfGG-L)    CLCG (c-9610 CLCo)
CMSL (c-9610 CSM)    CNBG (c-9610 CStrNB)    CSCG (c-9660 CSjCL)
CSFX (c-9610 CSf)    CSUG (c-9610 CSt)    CSUU (c-9660 CSt)    CUBG-1 (c-9610 CU)
CUBG-2 (c-9610 CU)    CUDL (c-9610 CU-AL)    DCLC (c-9110 DLC)
IAUL (c-9610 IaU-L)    NYCG (c-9617 NNC)
:?
```

Primary

Author Index

General Index